IMAGES
of America

HENRY COUNTY

I0805886

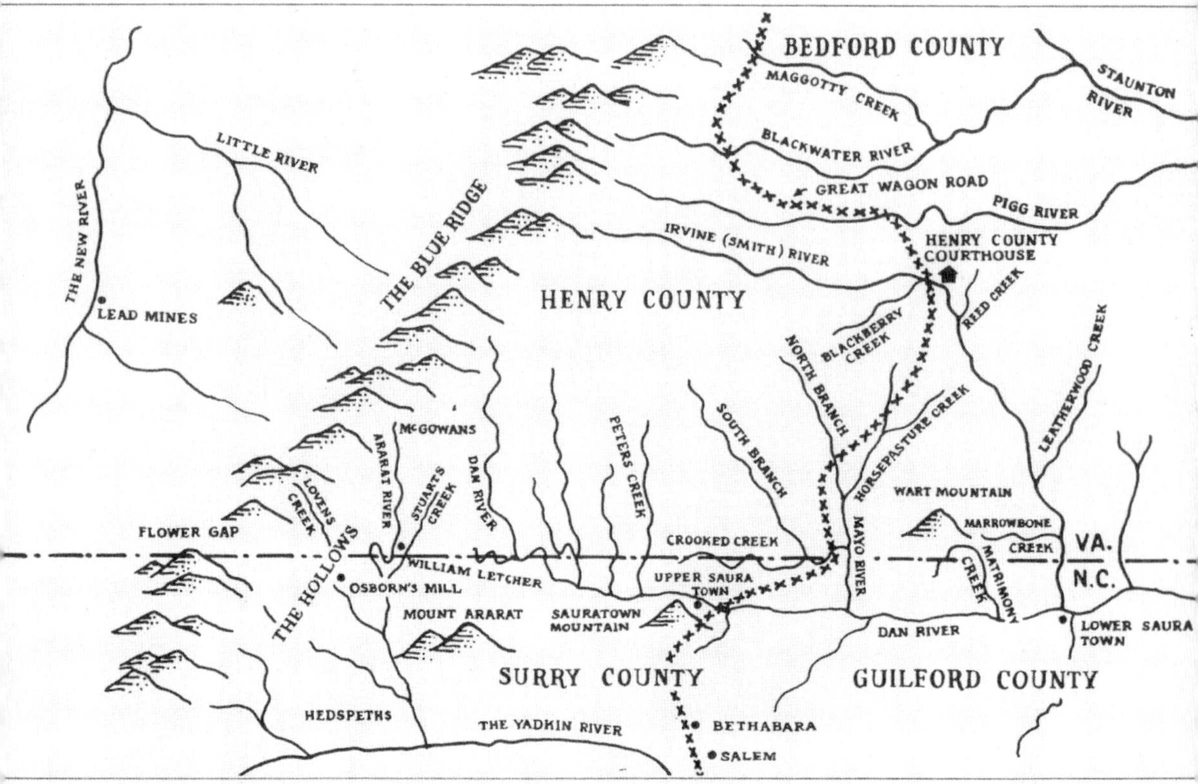

Henry County, formed in 1777, once contained parts of modern Carroll, Franklin, and Patrick Counties extending west along the North Carolina–Virginia border, which was surveyed by groups including William Byrd and Peter Jefferson to the Appalachian Mountains. The Great Wagon Road traversed the county from north to south, starting in Philadelphia, Pennsylvania, and ending in Augusta, Georgia. (Courtesy of Douglas G. Belcher.)

ON THE COVER: The John D. Bassett High School varsity cheerleaders are pictured in the 1970 Bassett Christmas Parade. From left to right are (first row) captain Myra Terry '71 (partially blocked), Lynne Joyce '71, Pam Akers '71, and Carol Anthony '72; (second row) Clarke Stanley '72, Cindy Filcher '71 (sitting behind Clarke), co-captain Vickie Price '72, Betsy White '72, and Genett Hite '72. (Courtesy of the Bassett Historical Center.)

IMAGES
of America

HENRY COUNTY

Thomas D. Perry

ARCADIA
PUBLISHING

ISBN 978-0-7385-6704-4

Published by Arcadia Publishing
Charleston, South Carolina

Printed in the United States of America

Library of Congress Catalog Card Number: 2008931386

For all general information contact Arcadia Publishing at:
Telephone 843-853-2070
Fax 843-853-0044
E-mail sales@arcadiapublishing.com
For customer service and orders:
Toll-Free 1-888-313-2665

Visit us on the Internet at www.arcadiapublishing.com

For my friends at the Bassett Historical Center,

> *"Many of the children born today really have no reference point. You really don't know yourself until you know something of your history. For the most part, we are concerned about our future generations. If a child knows about where he came from and how important he is, that is going to do a lot for his values, his destiny in life. It will give him the vision he needs to make it through all the various obstacles in life today."*
>
> *—Beverly R. Millner*

Contents

ACKNOWLEDGMENTS

Thanks to Marie Ashworth, Douglas Belcher, Dr. John Bing, David Bowles, Jerry Brock, Marvin Bryson, Joel Cannaday, Barnie Carter, Galilee Clark, Posie Collins, Teddy Compton, Anne Copeland, Claudia Deans, David Dyer, Rebecca Dyer, Sam Eanes, Carolyn Eggleston, Jane Eggleston, Jesse and Joan Frith, Ross Gale, Cynthia Headen, Deborah Hodges, Pamela Hollandsworth, Darlene Isom, Bernard Joyce, Kenney Kirkman, Rachel Koontz, Beverly Millner, David Minter, Ronnie Payne, Elizabeth Price, Paul and Patricia Ross, Jean Shorter, Harold Smith, Lisa Smith, C. M. Stafford, Douglas Stegall, Glenda Stone, Julia Terry, Avis Turner, Vickie Helmstutler, Juanita Wells, Betsy Whitlow, Linda Willard, Beverly Yeager, and Bill Young for contributing photographs and text to this project. A special thanks to the staff of the Bassett Historical Center—Anne Copeland, Sam Eanes, Cynthia Headen, and Director Patricia Ross—for their assistance on this project. Collections used from the center include those of Martha Wells Clark, Virginia Stone Windle, and O. E. Pilson. Thanks for the patience that Brooksi Hudson, my editor on this book, showed in not giving up on this project.

INTRODUCTION

As 13 colonies declared their independence from Great Britain, a movement was underway to form Henry County, Virginia, from its neighbor to the east, Pittsylvania County. In January 1777, Henry County was formed and named for the first non-British governor of Virginia, Patrick Henry, who lived in the county from 1779 until 1784. Over a decade later, land from Henry County became Patrick County, forever allowing map-readers to remember the name of the man who stated, "As for me, give me liberty or give me death!"

Located along the border with North Carolina first surveyed by William Byrd in 1728, the county was once home to the famous antebellum Hairston family. In the 20th century, textiles, furniture, and the chemical manufacturer DuPont made up the large industrial base of the county. With the recent outsourcing of jobs, the county is turning to other economic sources such as tourism with the Martinsville Speedway, Virginia Museum of Natural History, and the Bassett Historical Center, which provided many of the photographs in this book.

History is a strong part of life in the county. The land that is today Henry County was Charles City County a quarter-century after the founding of Jamestown. Native peoples roamed this land long before the English first arrived in Virginia. Evidence of their life abounds in Henry County, researched in the last century by Richard Gravely and today by the Virginia Museum of Natural History in Martinsville. The county is known as a place to research genealogy, and the Bassett Historical Center of the Blue Ridge Regional Library is known worldwide (and by this author) as the "Best Little Library in Virginia," as people come from all 50 states and overseas to research the collection.

Henry County was part of Prince George and Brunswick Counties when William Byrd and a group of surveyors mapped the line with North Carolina in 1728. It was later part of Lunenburg, Halifax, and Pittsylvania Counties. The area today is famous for racing, as the Martinsville Speedway hosts two NASCAR races each year.

Before the American Revolution, George Washington visited Fort Trial along the Smith River, which flows into the Dan River, which meanders back and forth across the state line until eventually reaching Albemarle Sound in North Carolina. Henry County is flat land and the rolling hills of the Piedmont. It suffered terrible floods until the Philpott Reservoir tamed the Smith River, creating opportunities for boating, swimming, and fishing. Many of the photographs in this book document the flooding, especially the deluge of 1937.

During the antebellum period, Henry County was a place for growing tobacco and of large plantations such as that of the Martins, who gave their name to the county seat, Martinsville. The Hairston family, who had homes in Virginia, North Carolina, and Mississippi, dominated the county so much that tradition holds one could walk the entire east-to-west length of the county without leaving their land. The evidence of the Hairstons still exists in the county—many of their plantation homes still stand, such as Beaver Creek and Marrowbone, and names such as Magna Vista and Chatmoss recall homes no longer standing. Thoughts of romance entered the mind of a young visitor to Henry County in the 1850s, when James Ewell Brown "Jeb" Stuart courted young Elizabeth "Bettie" Hairston in 1852 and again two years later at Beaver Creek north of Martinsville. Tradition holds she rebuffed the future Civil War general and married her cousin J. T. W. "Watt" Hairston, literally keeping the money in the family. One can still see the grandeur of their lives built on the back of slave labor, but almost everyone today with the name Hairston is of African descent, taking the name of their former owners.

Henry County contributed to the Southern effort in the War Between the States with many men. The only significant visit by Union forces came under the command of William Jackson

Palmer, a brigade commander under George Stoneman, in one of the war's last raids. Palmer, a Quaker from Delaware, grew up in Philadelphia and was a railroad man before the war. He left Martinsville on April 9, 1865, the day R. E. Lee surrendered at Appomattox Court House, after fighting Confederate cavalry under the command of Col. James T. Wheeler the day before.

Railroads and industry dominated Henry County in the 20th century. The Danville and Western Railway—"The Dick and Willie"—came from east to west through the county before terminating in Patrick County. The Norfolk and Western Railway, now the Norfolk Southern, came from Winston-Salem, North Carolina, on the way to Roanoke, Virginia, north of the county. Henry County became a crossroads of steel tracks that brought people and industry.

The furniture industry in the county made Bassett, Stanley, American, and Hooker Furniture household names. Companies such as Bassett-Walker, Fieldcrest, Tultex, and Pannill—named for the family of J. E. B. Stuart's uncle William Letcher Pannill—made the county a hub for textiles in the 20th century. DuPont came to Martinsville, producing fibers that changed the world along the banks of the Smith River. Sadly almost all of this industry left late in the century, forcing the county to rethink its direction.

Tourism via racing, history, and recreation at the Philpottt Reservoir today make up a large part of the county's economic impact. The Philpott Dam, built along the Smith River, created the largest man-made lake east of the Mississippi River. The Virginia Museum of Natural History came to Martinsville, and the new state-of-the-art facility now attracts visitors. Nearby Piedmont Arts offers a vibrant cultural setting, and the New College Institute and Patrick Henry Community College provide education for a population in the process of change.

This book reflects this history. Half of the images presented are from the collection of the Bassett Historical Center; the author will donate his proceeds from the sale of this book to assist the expansion underway there. Most of the images in this work came from people who brought their photographs to the library for the author to scan, and those who shared drive the scope of the book. Many people and events will not make the 200 images presented here, but it is important to the author to preserve the history of those willing to share, and the library will preserve the history for future generations. Please visit www.freestateofpatrick.com to learn more about the history surrounding our county.

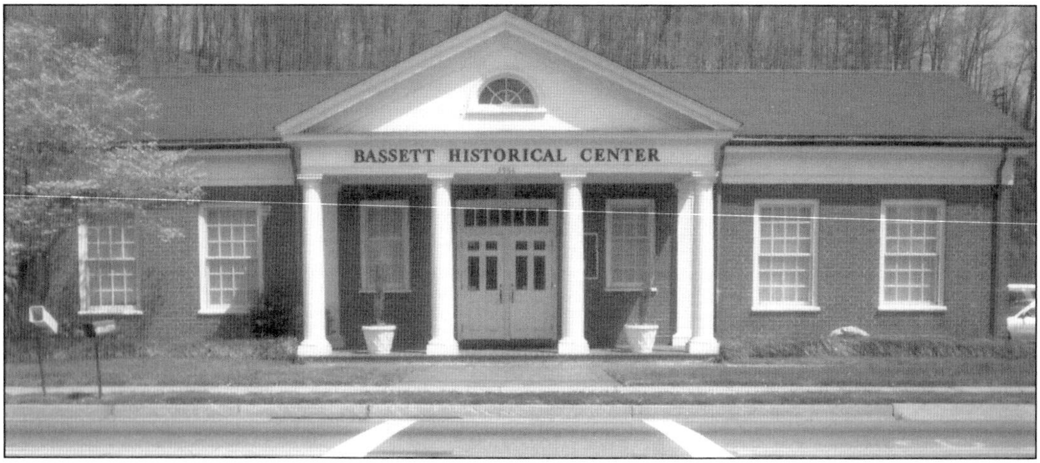

The author's proceeds from the sale of this book go to the building fund of the Bassett Historical Center of the Blue Ridge Regional Library. (Courtesy of the Bassett Historical Center.)

One

Bassett

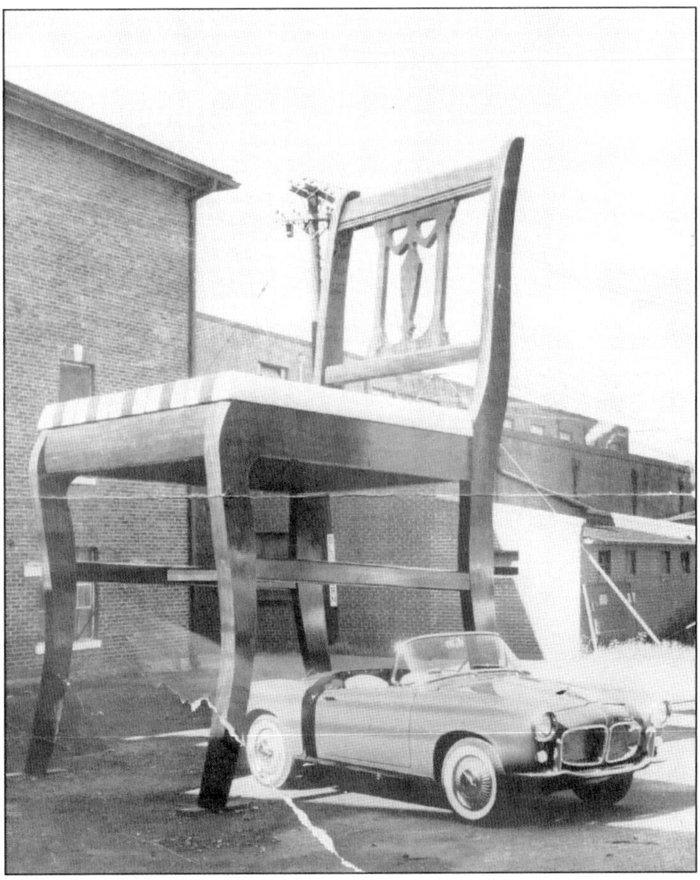

Built by Bassett Furniture Company of mahogany from the Congo for Curtis Brothers Furniture, the "World's Largest Chair" sat at 2041 Nichols Avenue in Washington, D.C. Weighing 4,600 pounds, the chair was 19 feet high, 9 feet wide, and 12 feet deep and represented the furniture industry that was a vital part of the economy of Henry County. (Courtesy of Rachel Koontz.)

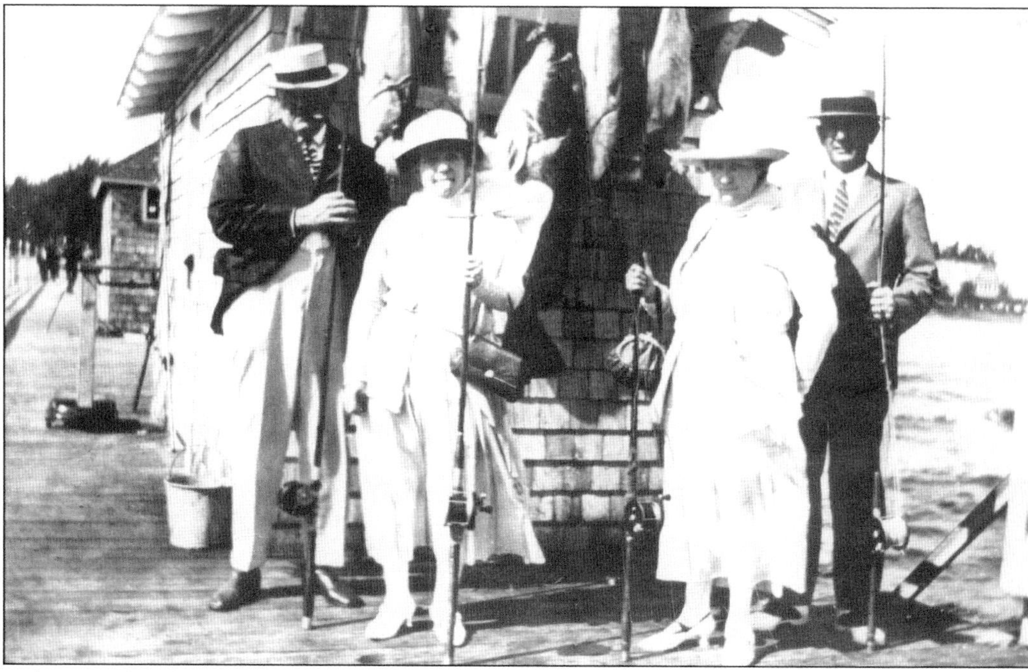

Fishing in the Florida Keys during the 1920s are, from left to right, John D. Bassett Sr.; his wife, Pocahontas; Charles C. Bassett; and his wife, Roxie. The Hundley sisters married the Bassett brothers. The brothers started Bassett Furniture Company with Reed L. Stone; the company has over 130 stores in North America today. (Courtesy of the Bassett Historical Center.)

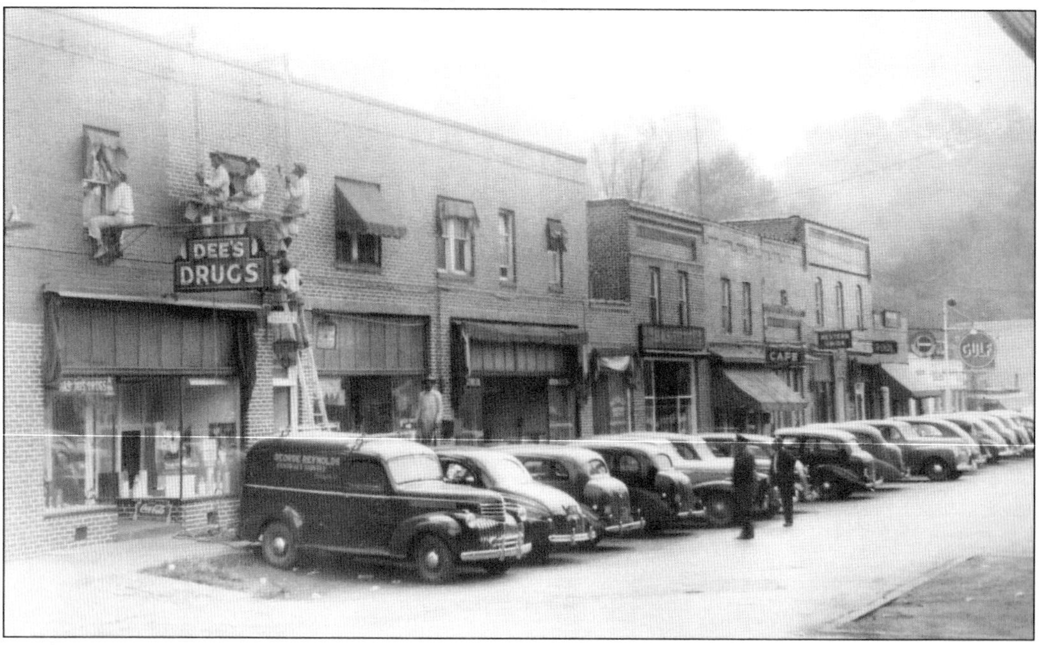

Workers repair the Reed Stone Block's brick facing and clean windows while a police officer and people watch after World War II. Stone and the Bassett brothers started the furniture company across the main street of the town. Today they are the only original stores still standing in this block. (Courtesy of the Bassett Historical Center.)

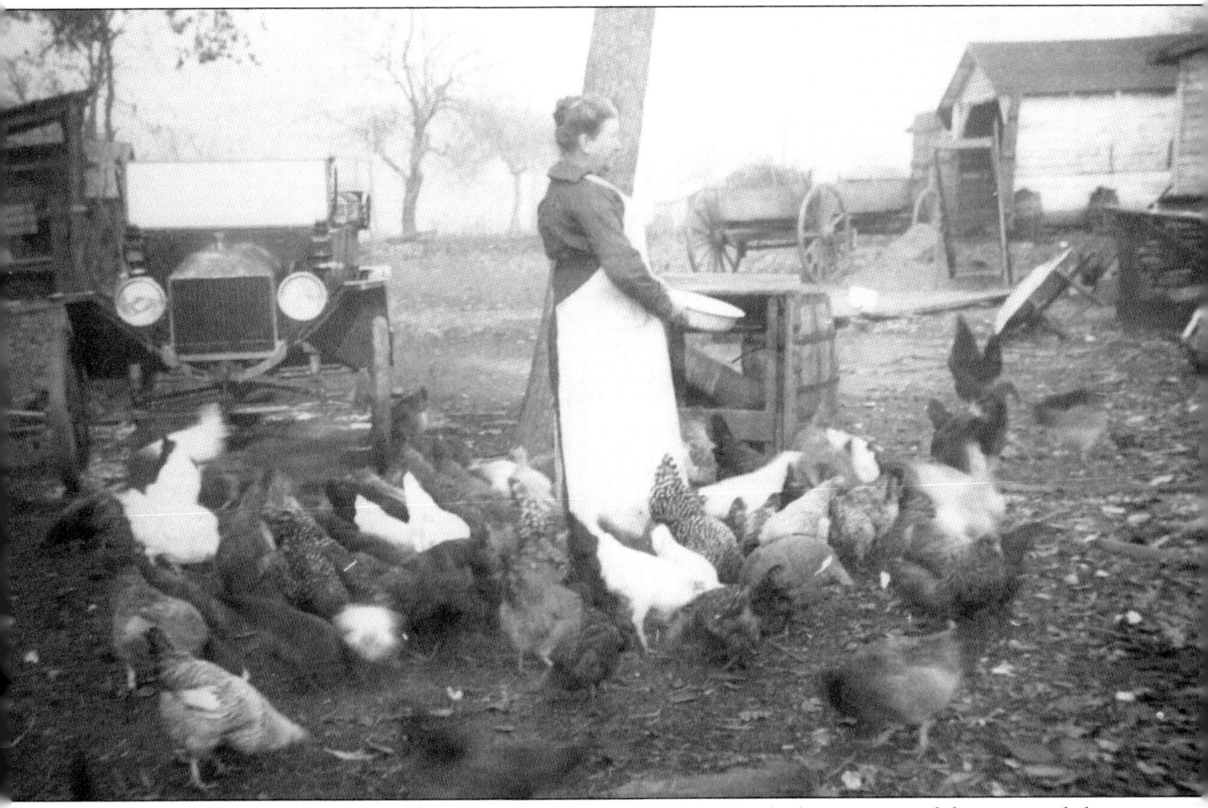

In this photograph, contrasting the changes in transportation with the coming of the automobile versus the farm wagon, is Mary Druscilla "Grandma Sissie" Bassett Ramsey (1862–1950). The wife of John W. Ramsey and the daughter of John Henry and Nancy Jane Spencer Bassett is doing her daily chores, including feeding chickens. (Courtesy of the Martha Jane Clark Collection of the Bassett Historical Center.)

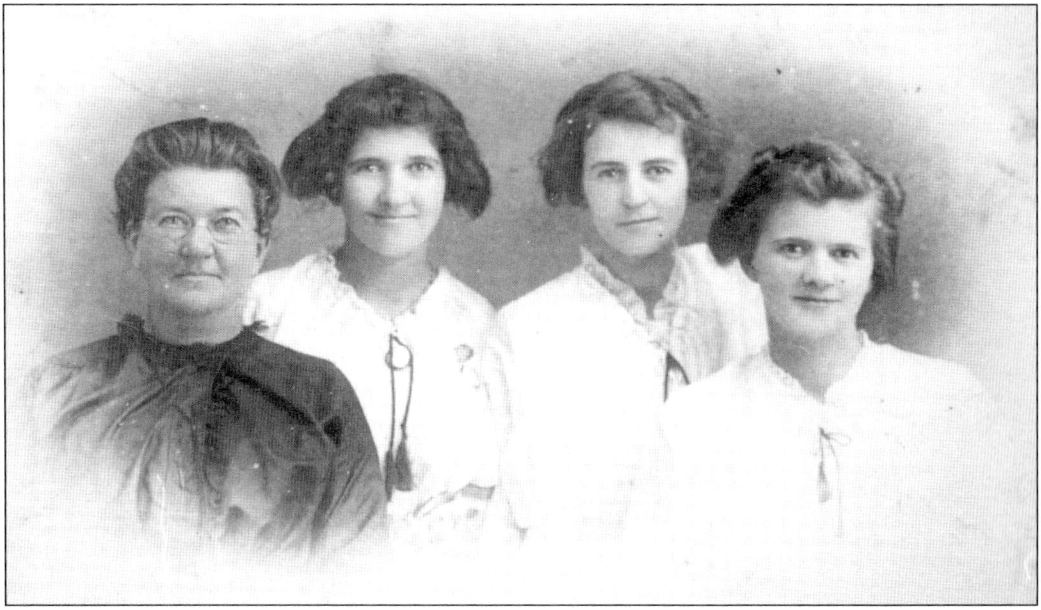

From left to right, Mary Druscilla Bassett Ramsey is pictured with her three daughters, Mary Wootsie R. Giles, Lucy Belle R. Joyce, and Nannie Laura R. Helms, around 1915. With the United States just a few years away from entering World War I and the coming of the industrial revolution in the form of furniture and textiles, this image reflects a more bucolic time in Henry County. (Courtesy of the Martha Jane Clark Collection of the Bassett Historical Center.)

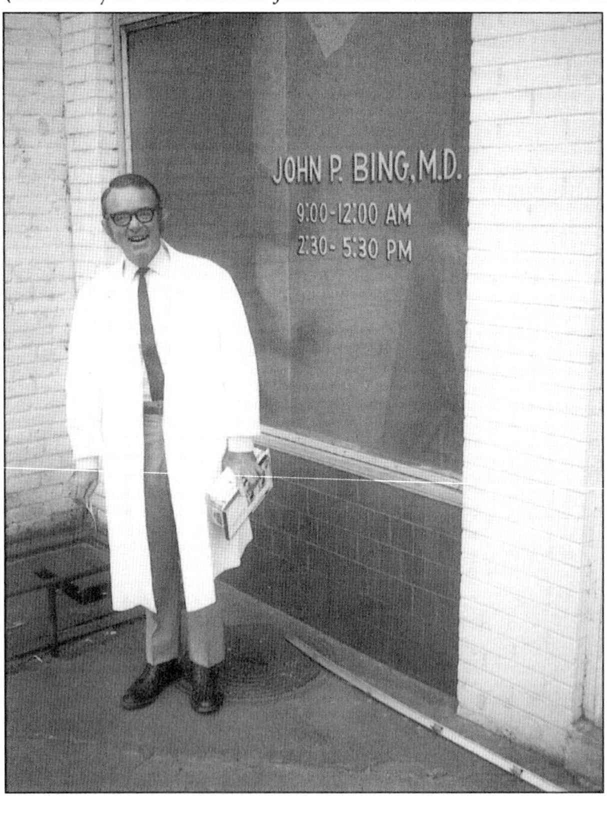

Dr. John P. Bing, shown outside his Bassett office in 1969, worked tirelessly collecting photographs. He called, cajoled, and brought photographs to the Bassett Historical Center to give the author over 1,700 images from which to choose the 200 photographs representing Henry County in this book. (Courtesy of John Bing.)

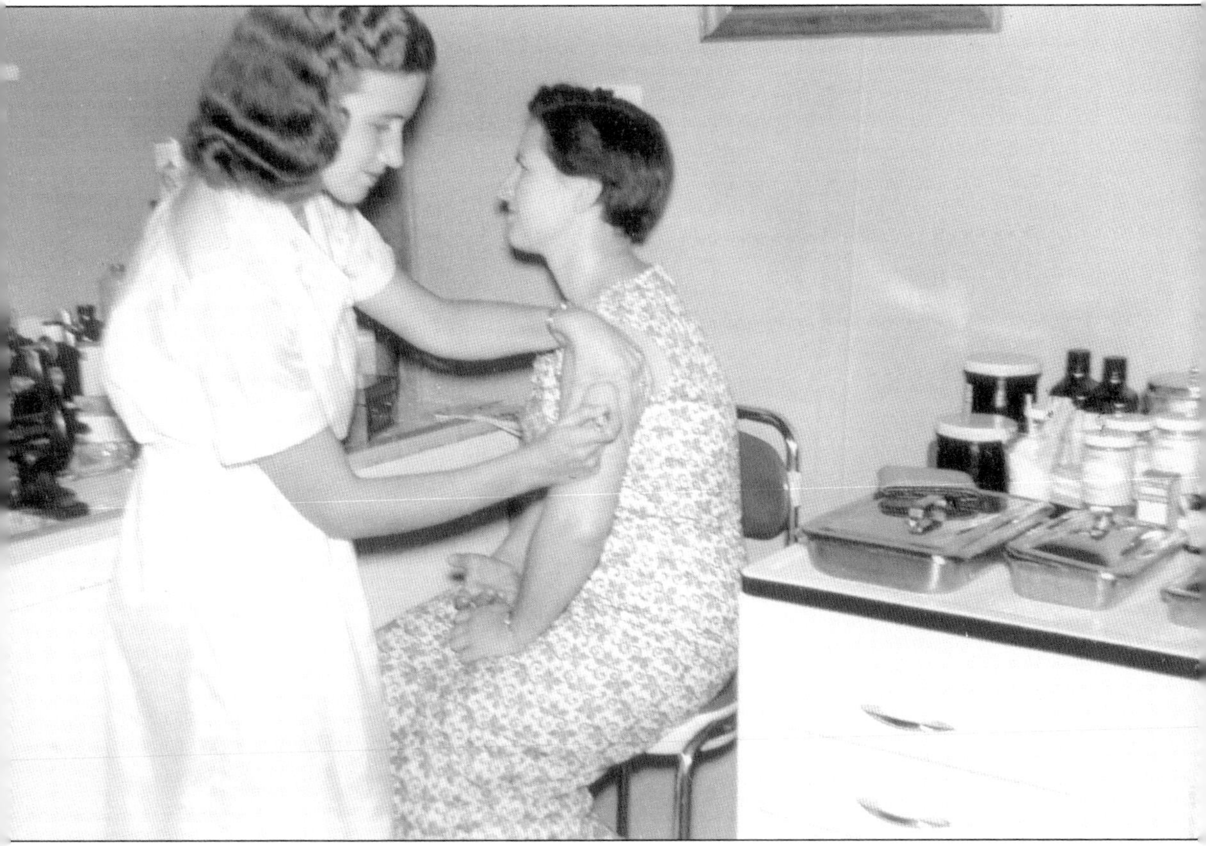

Registered nurse Marie Haynes Ashworth gives a shot to a patient in the office of Dr. John P. Bing in 1959. The office, in front of the Bassett Furniture Headquarters, was the site of Bing's practice for 20 years beginning in 1955. Marie worked there for one year. (Courtesy of Marie Ashworth.)

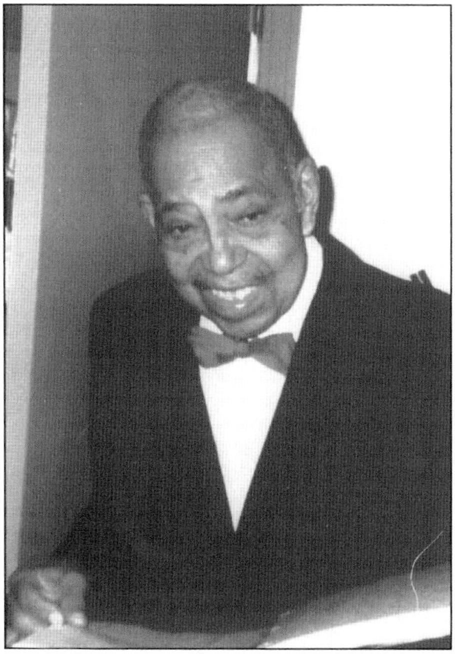

John Bruce Harris was the first African American principal in Henry County at Campbell Court School. Harris worked tirelessly to preserve the black history that continues today with efforts such as the Fayette Historical Initiative. He is compared often with O. E. Pilson, and both of their collections reside in the Bassett Historical Center. (Courtesy of the Bassett Historical Center.)

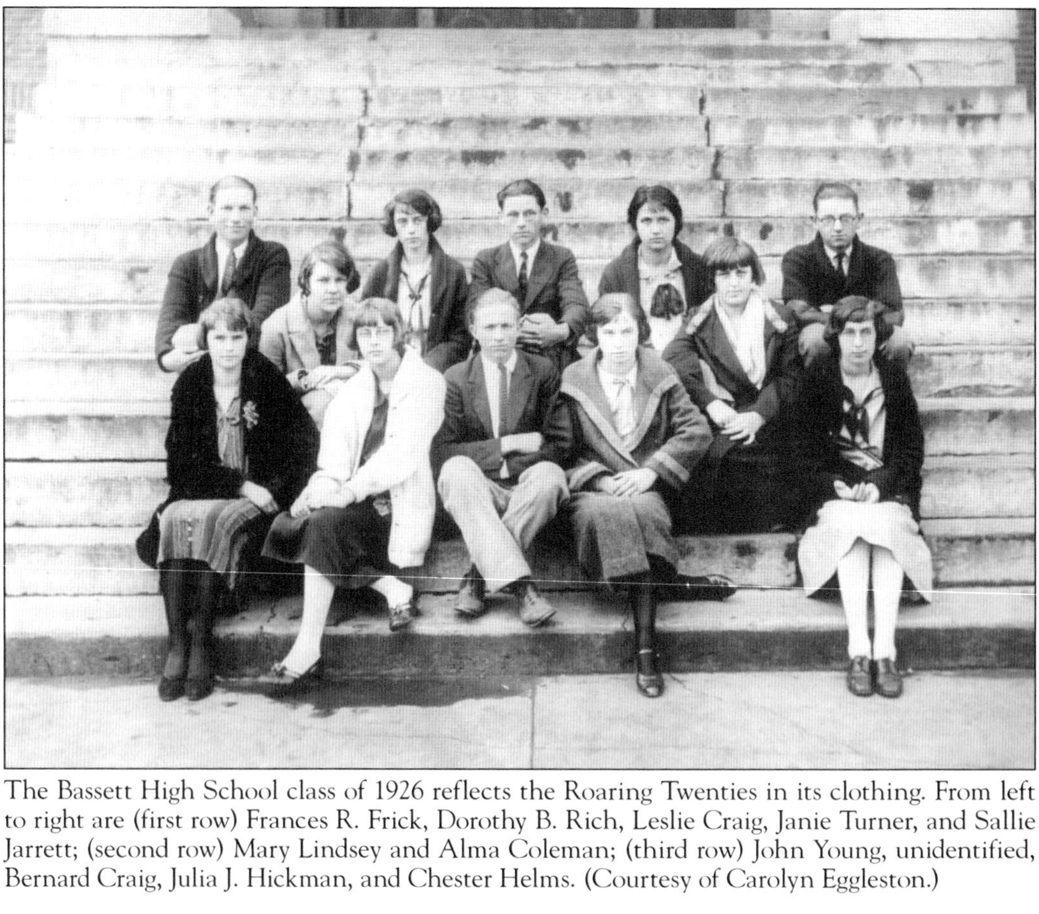

The Bassett High School class of 1926 reflects the Roaring Twenties in its clothing. From left to right are (first row) Frances R. Frick, Dorothy B. Rich, Leslie Craig, Janie Turner, and Sallie Jarrett; (second row) Mary Lindsey and Alma Coleman; (third row) John Young, unidentified, Bernard Craig, Julia J. Hickman, and Chester Helms. (Courtesy of Carolyn Eggleston.)

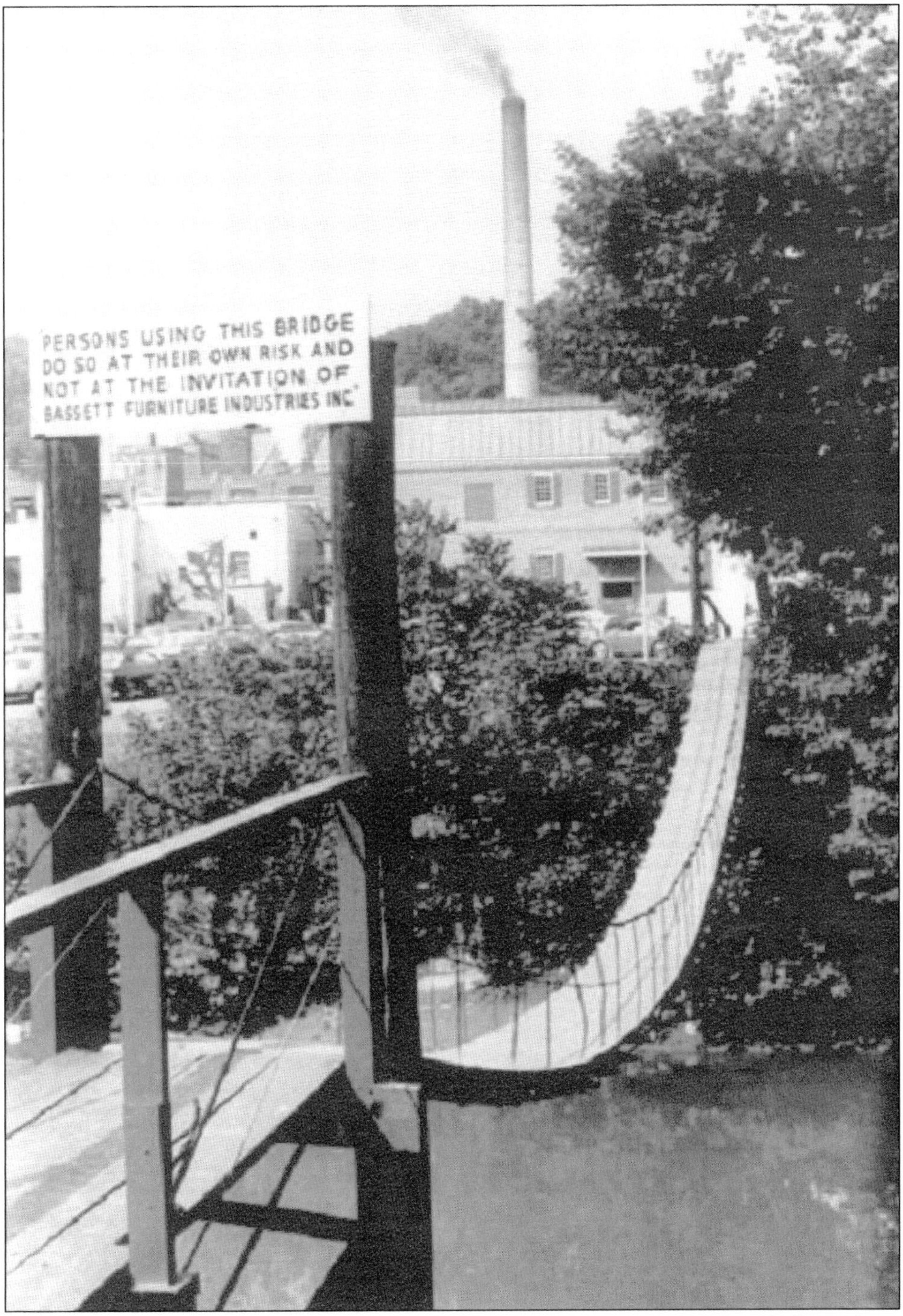

The three swinging bridges over the Smith River in Bassett were the main mode for pedestrians to cross. This bridge north of Bassett contains a strict warning to those brave enough to venture out over the waters of the stream first named Irwin, then Smith. In the watershed of the Dan River, the Smith begins its journey to Albemarle Sound in North Carolina in neighboring Patrick County, Virginia. (Courtesy of the Bassett Historical Center.)

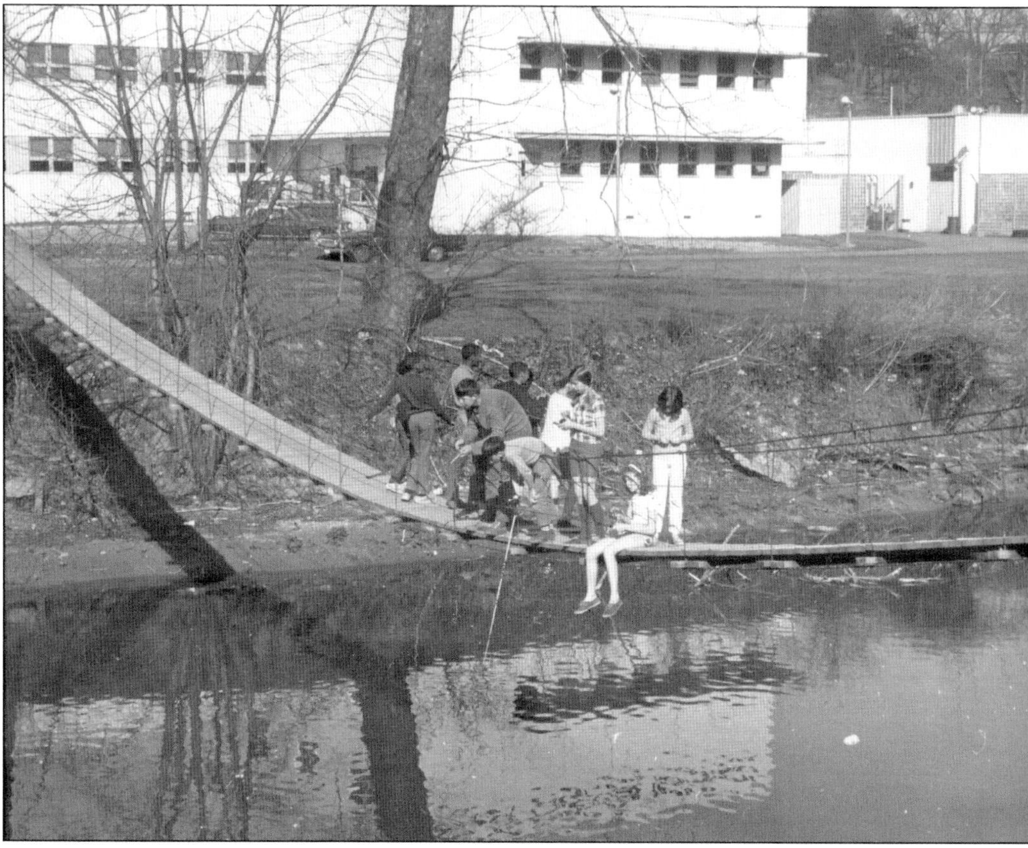

Another swinging bridge over the Smith River, behind the world headquarters of Bassett Furniture and just downstream from the Bassett Historical Center, was a popular place for children and adults to fish. Today the bridges are gone, but the center preserves the history surrounding them through the preservation of these images. (Courtesy of the Bassett Historical Center.)

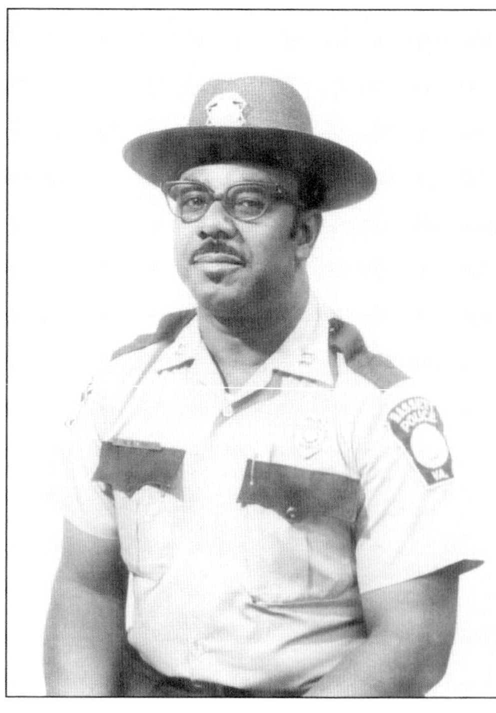

With 25 years of experience in law enforcement, Benjamin A. Smith was captain and investigator of the Bassett Police Department. The first African American to hold such a high place in Henry County law enforcement, he later worked as chief of security for Bassett Furniture Industries. He was married to Lois Pilson, and the couple had three daughters. (Courtesy of the Bassett Historical Center.)

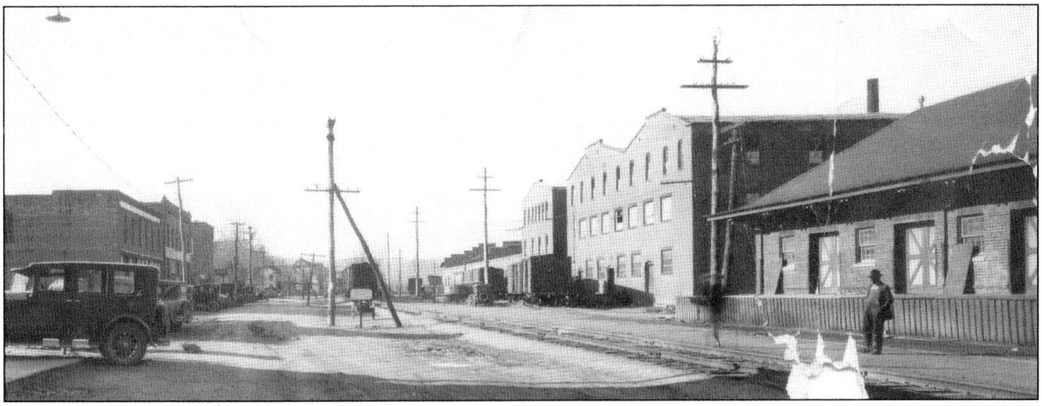

The growth of the furniture industry with the inception of Bassett Furniture Company in 1902 and the coming of the railroad in 1892 made Bassett grow. The train station built for loading cargo still stands today and is the focal point of history during the annual Bassett Heritage Festival each September. (Courtesy of the Bassett Historical Center.)

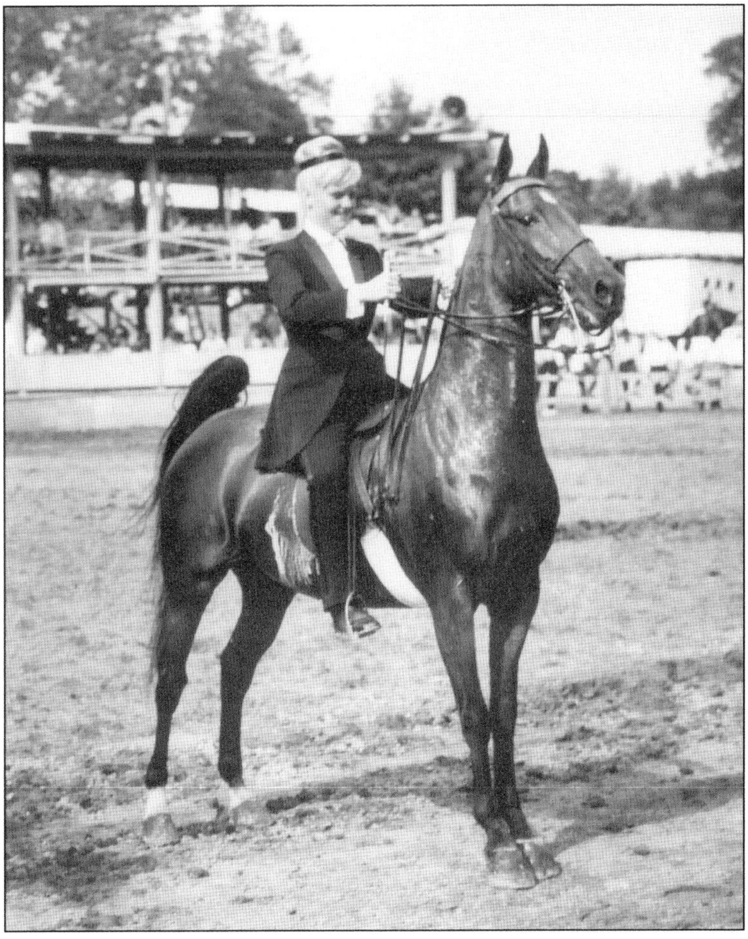

Dee Dee Bing Hennis, the daughter of Dr. John P. Bing and his wife, Joan, is pictured on Sassy Maid in the 1963 North Carolina State Amateur Equestrian Championship. Married to Dan Hennis, she lives near her parents in Bassett. She has two children, three stepchildren, two grandchildren, and five step-grandchildren. (Courtesy of John Bing.)

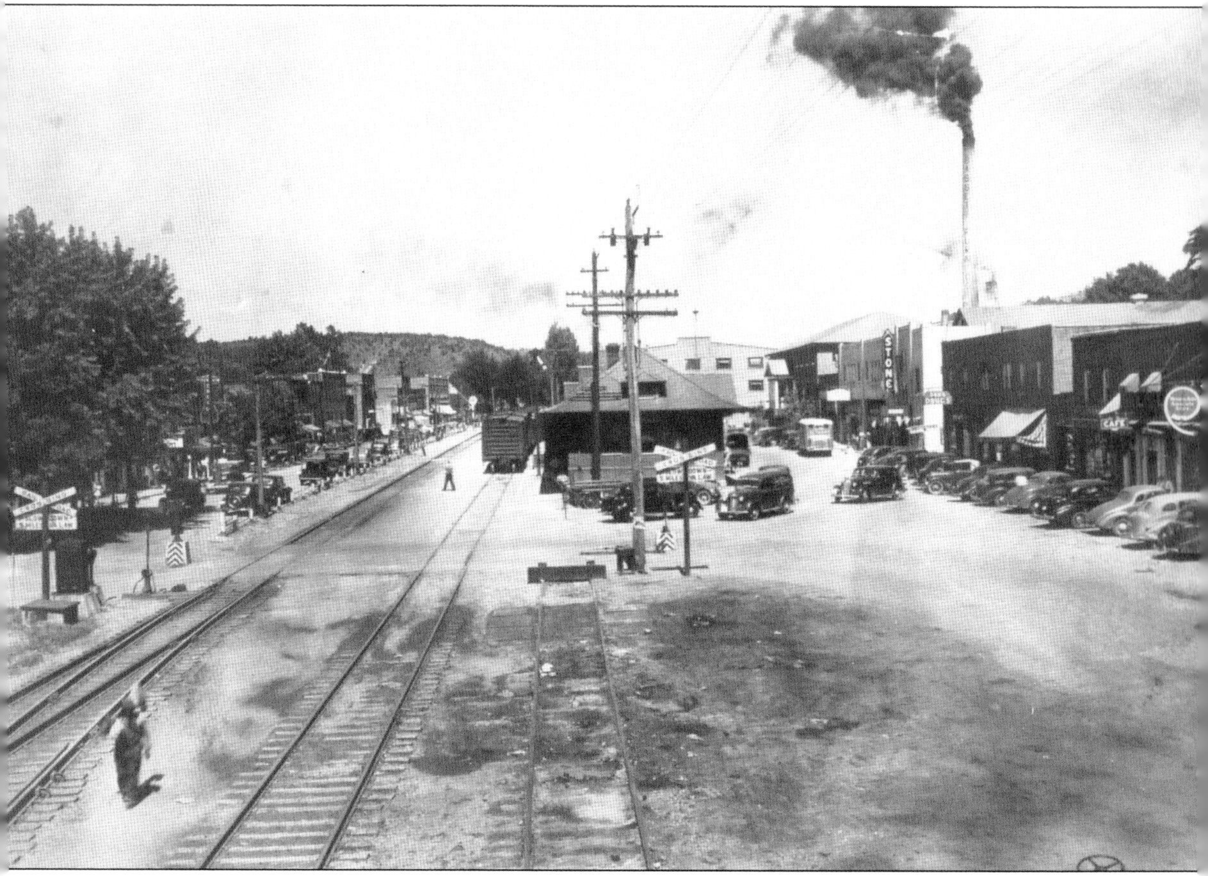

Bassett Furniture Company began as two sawmills providing crossties to the Norfolk and Western Railroad. The family began the furniture business when Charles, John, and Samuel Bassett, along with brother-in-law Reed L. Stone, came together in 1902. The result shown in this photograph is a boomtown, with factories belching smoke into the sky and commerce proceeding below. (Courtesy of the Bassett Historical Center.)

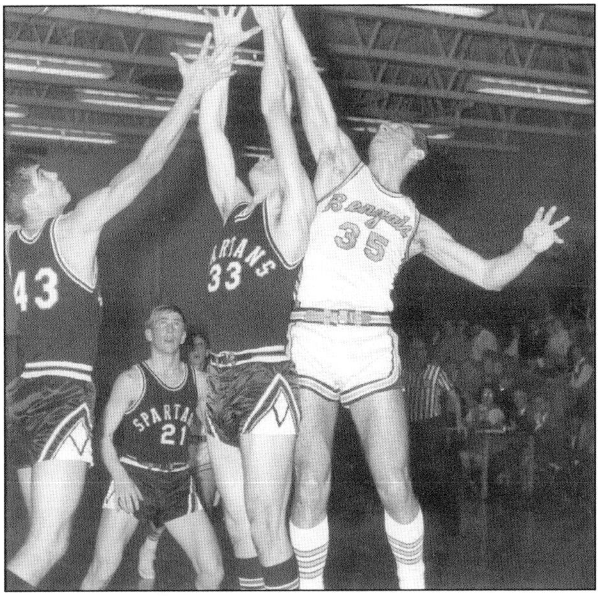

Donnie Doss (35) plays for John D. Bassett High School against Drewry Mason in the 1960s. The school, across the street diagonally from the Bassett Historical Center, became a middle school. David Wright, CEO of EMI Imaging, purchased and restored the building for public and business use. The Bassett Historical Center holds a history symposium in the auditorium. (Courtesy of the Bassett Historical Center.)

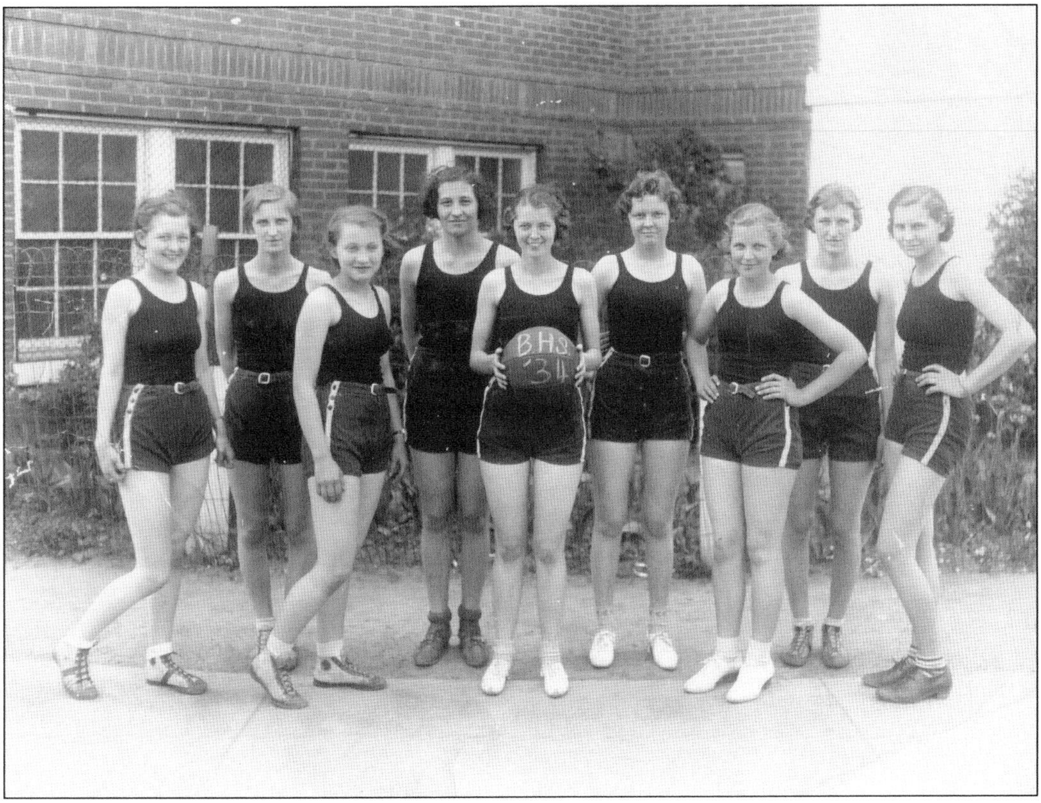

The 1934 girls basketball team of John D. Bassett High School included, from left to right, Margaret Holbrook, Cynthia Nolen, Galilee Smith Clark, Georgia Philpott Ingram, Marie Grogan Clay, Shine Jones Grogan, Ellery White Adams, Clovis Nolen, and Nellie Philpott Newman. In 2000, the successor Bassett High School won the girls state championship in basketball. (Courtesy of Galilee Clark.)

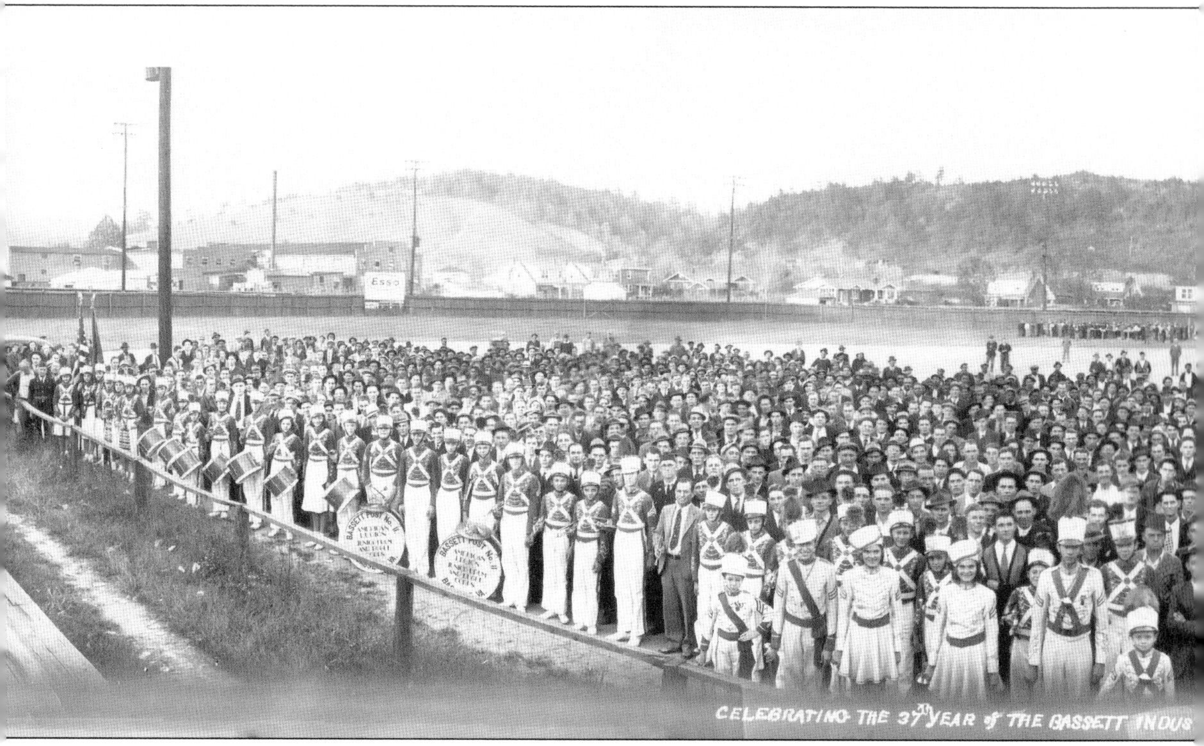

On October 22, 1938, the entire town of Bassett, including the American Legion Post No. 11 Junior Drum and Bugle Corps, came out to celebrate the 37th year of Bassett Industries. They held the celebration on the baseball field of the Bi-State Baseball League, which is still a baseball field today behind the Bassett Public Library, across the street from the Bassett Historical Center. Bassett Furniture expanded into J. D. Bassett Manufacturing, Bassett Mirror Company, and Bassett Chair Company. They acquired Craig Furniture in Martinsville, making it W. M. Bassett

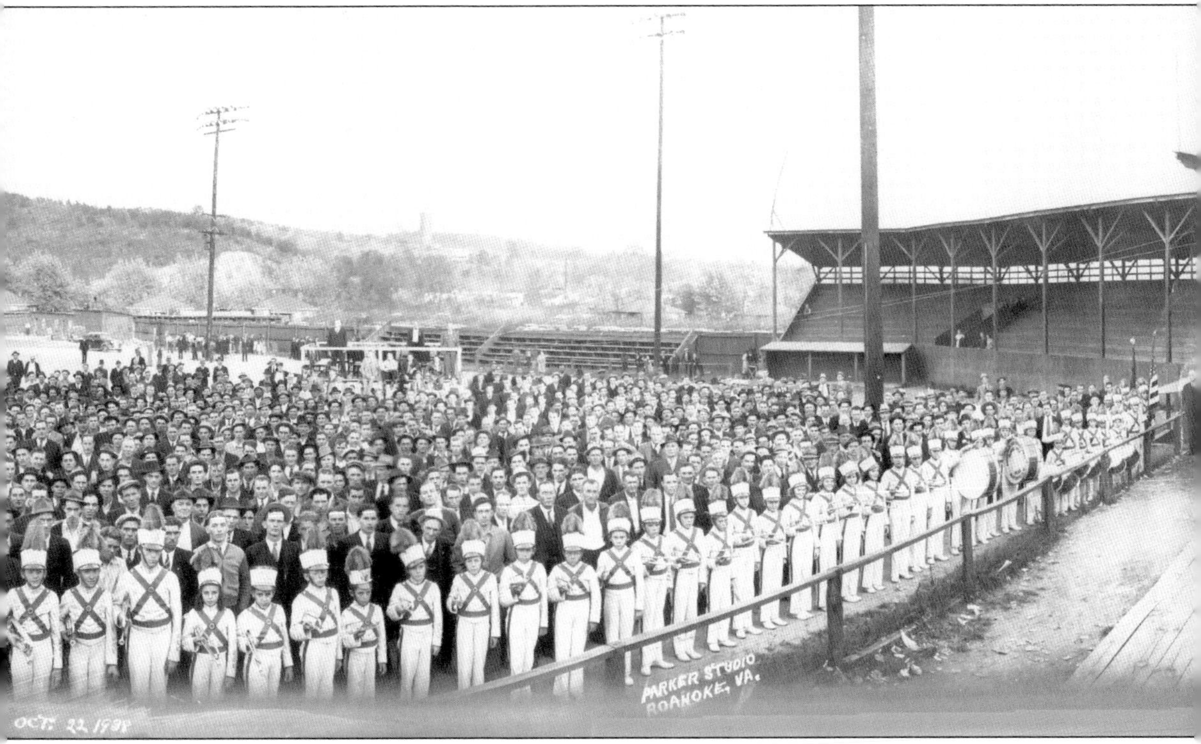

Furniture, and Ramsey Furniture, making it Bassett Superior Lines. Sons-in-law of the Bassett family Thomas Stanley and J. Clyde Hooker formed Stanley and Hooker Furniture Companies, which are both viable businesses today. Another son-in-law, Taylor Vaughan, and his brother started Vaughan Furniture. In 1938, a public stock offering raised over $2 million, giving Bassett Industries more reason to celebrate. (Courtesy of the Bassett Historical Center.)

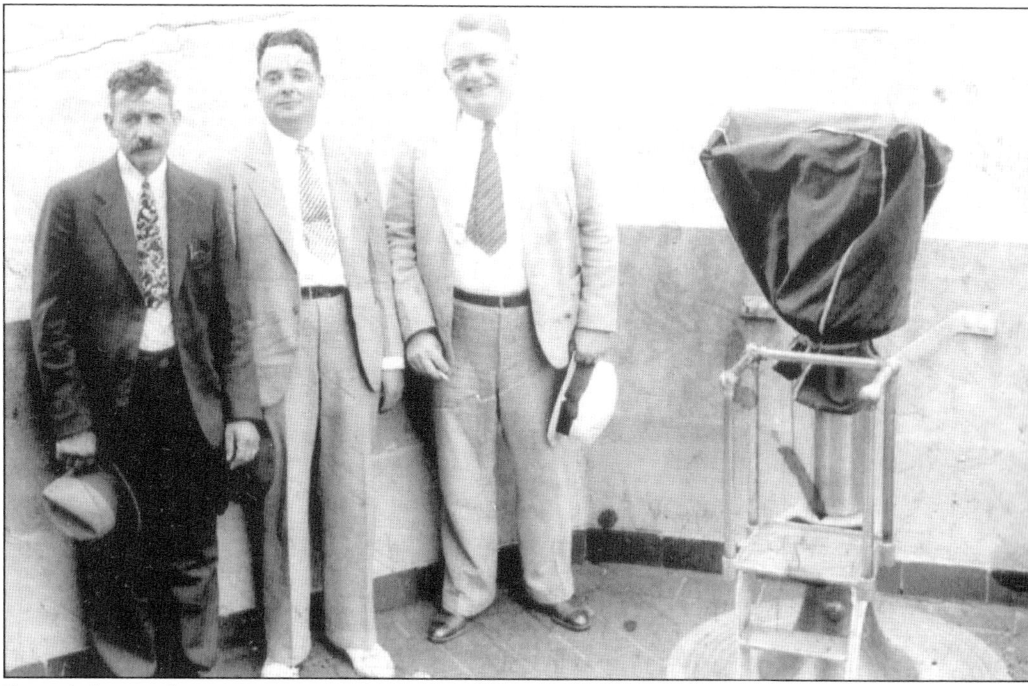

From left to right, P. M. "Doc" Ingram, Clenard Ingram, and Harold Stone are pictured at the 1939–1940 New York World's Fair. P. M. ran a grocery store in the south part of Bassett. Stone owned two grocery stores, one in the north and one in the south of the town. At the fair, the three Virginians got a look at the "World of Tomorrow" and the world of the immediate future, as World War II began during the fair. (Courtesy of Carolyn Eggleston.)

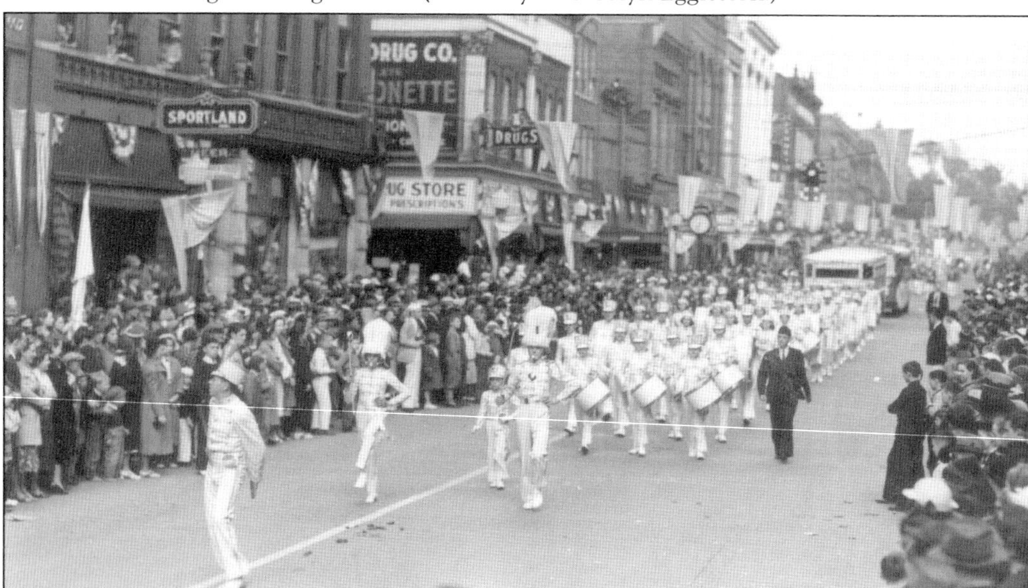

The John D. Bassett High School Drum and Bugle Corps marches in a parade, possibly in Roanoke, Virginia. Today the Bassett High School Bengal Band follows in the footsteps of those shown in this image. The new high school opened in 1978, and the older became a middle school. Two years later, the high school won the boys state track championship. (Courtesy of Rachel Koontz.)

Pictured from left to right, Virginia Belle Franklin Farmer, Codell Jones Wade, Marie Grogan Clay, and Jessie Williams Herman hitchhike and show a little leg and knee-length hose to entice a ride along a dirt road near Bassett. It is often a shock to think of one's parents as being young and goofing around with friends. (Courtesy of Paul Ross.)

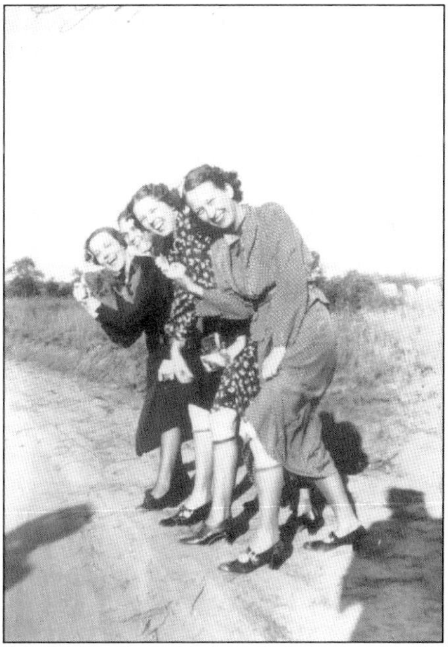

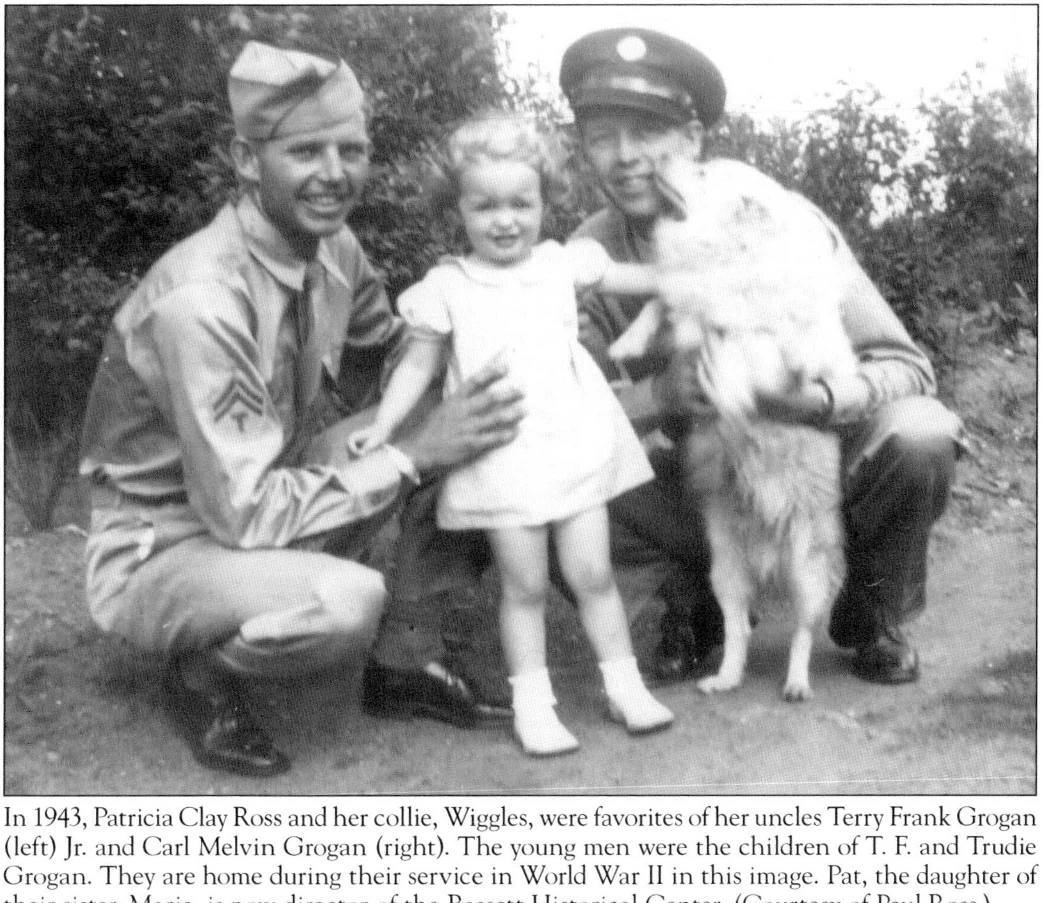

In 1943, Patricia Clay Ross and her collie, Wiggles, were favorites of her uncles Terry Frank Grogan (left) Jr. and Carl Melvin Grogan (right). The young men were the children of T. F. and Trudie Grogan. They are home during their service in World War II in this image. Pat, the daughter of their sister, Marie, is now director of the Bassett Historical Center. (Courtesy of Paul Ross.)

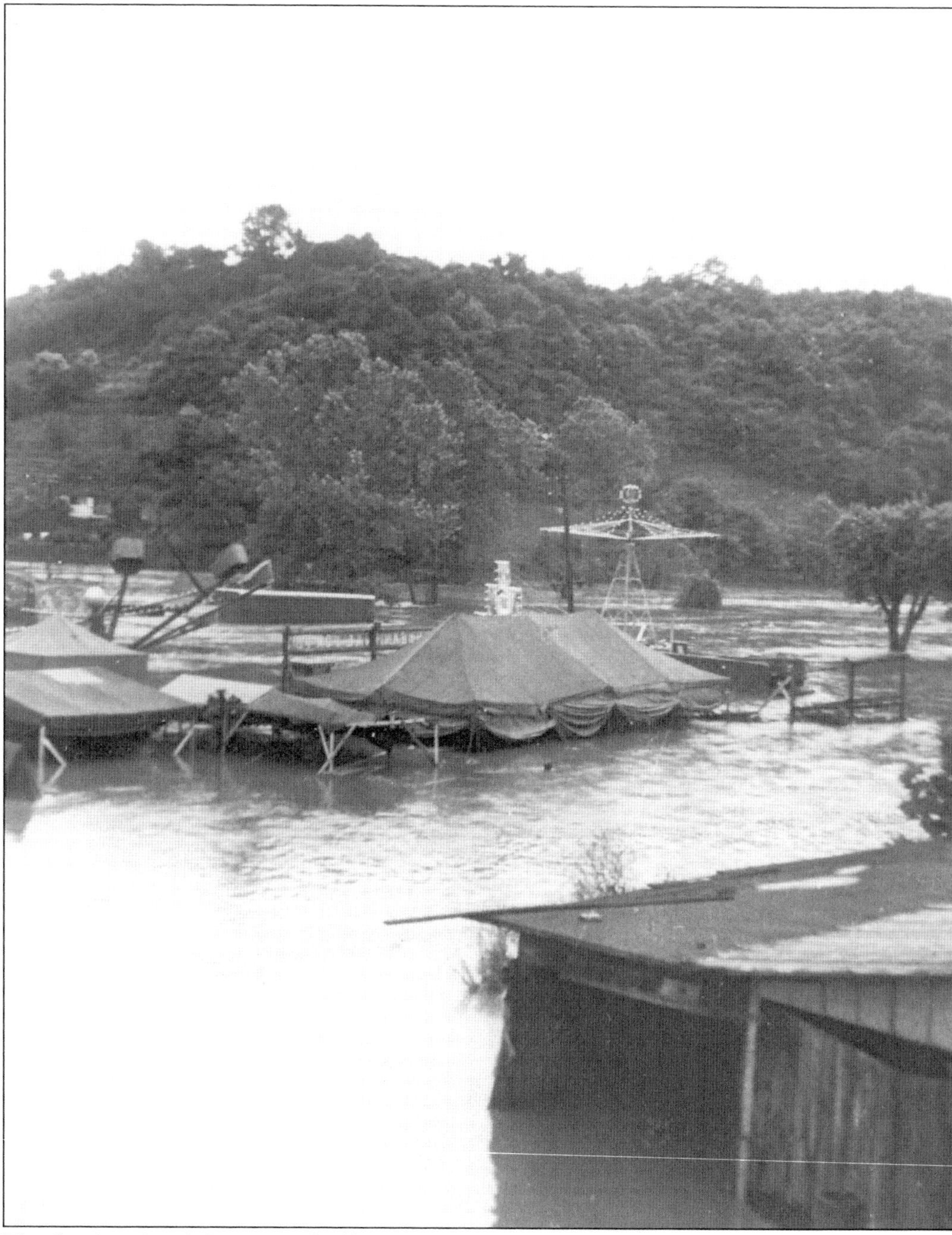

The flooding Smith River wreaked havoc on the town of Bassett many times over the years until the Philpott Reservoir was built. This 1940s carnival, warned of the impending flood, did not take it serious until it was too late to move to higher ground. Today the Philpott Dam controls the Smith River flow with daily releases of water. (Courtesy of Avis Turner.)

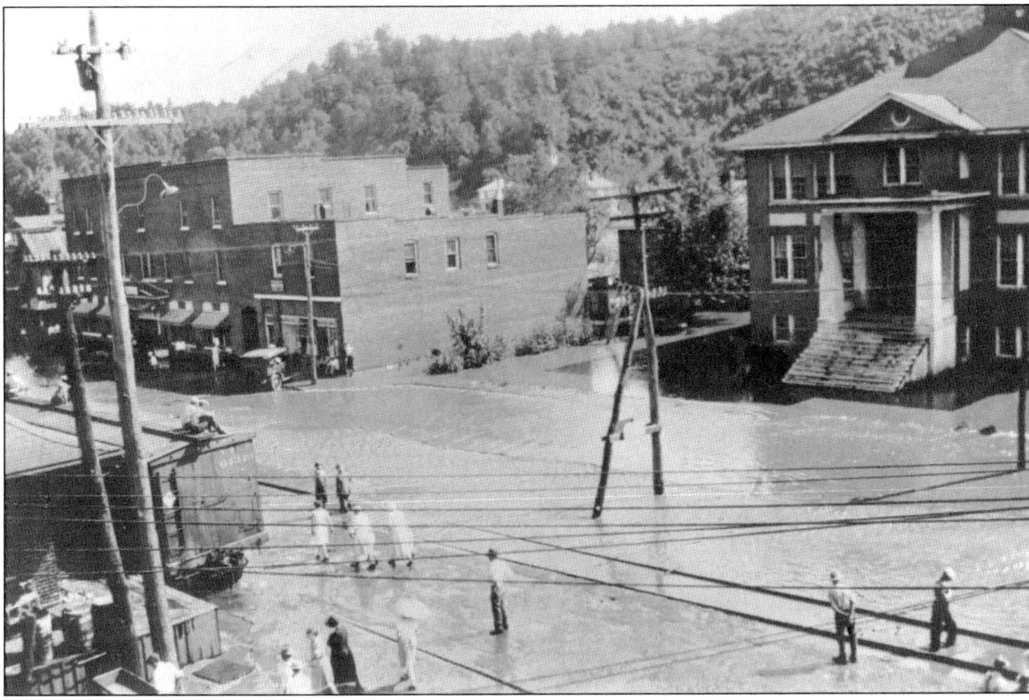

The original Bassett High School, shown in the right of this image, was not immune to the flooding Smith River. Notice the woman under an umbrella and men sitting on top of railroad cars while inspecting the rising waters before the Philpott Dam regulated the flow of the river. (Courtesy of C. M. Stafford.)

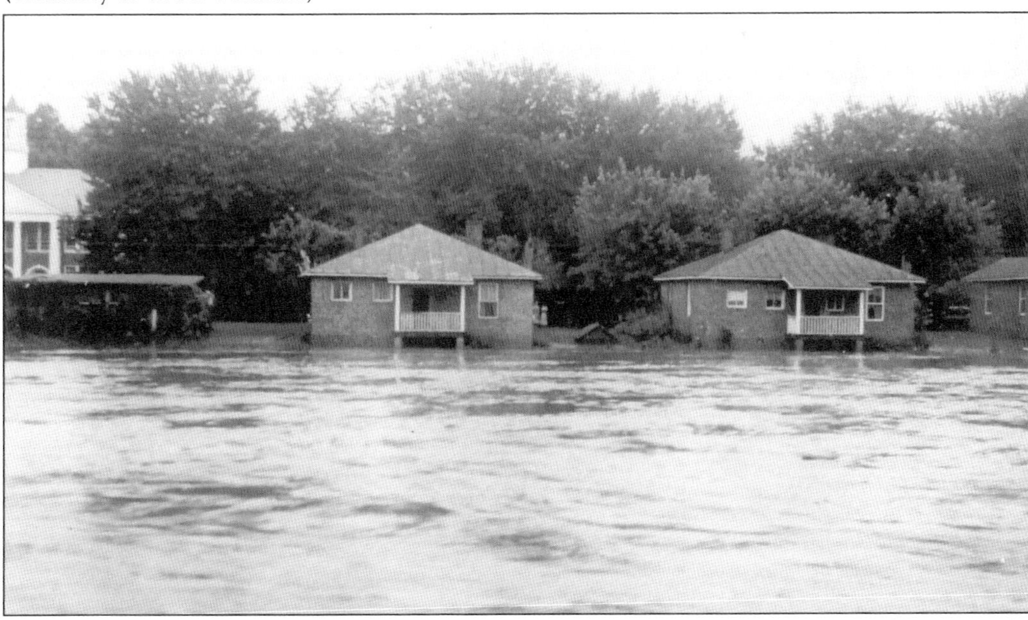

This image of the flooding Smith River shows the company houses of Bassett Industries at the location today of the Bassett Historical Center. John D. Bassett High School, at the left of this image, still stands at this location, owned today by EMI Imaging. When complete, the expansion of the center will fill this photograph. (Courtesy of Avis Turner.)

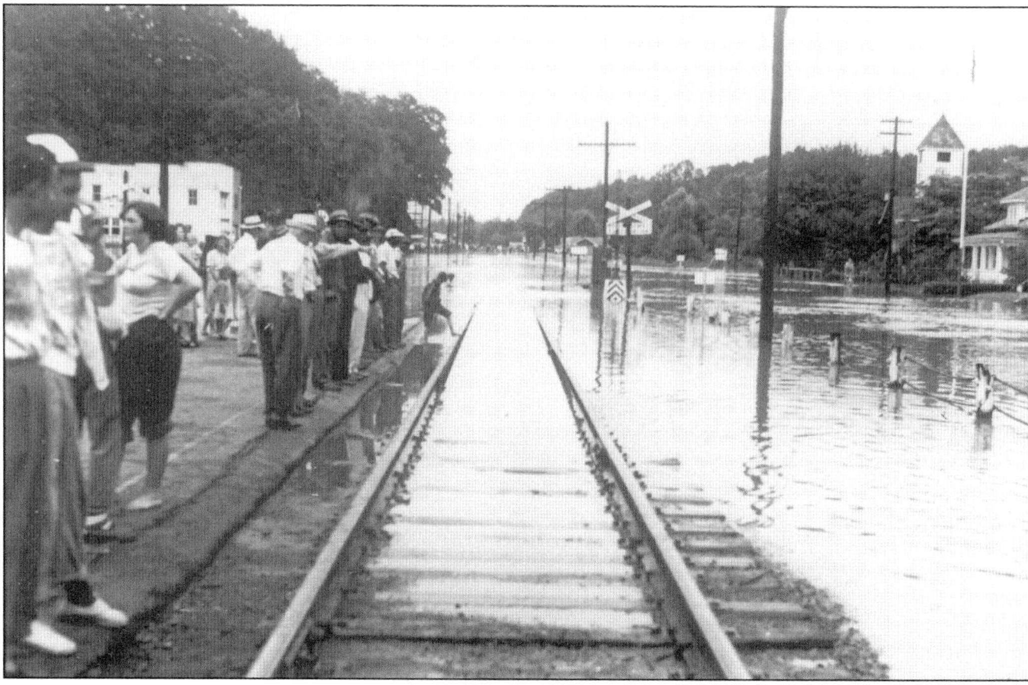

This 1940s image of the flooding Smith River in Bassett shows the tower of the First Baptist Church on the right and Lee Telephone Company, now Embarq and still present today, on the left. The riverbed is several hundred yards to the right of the railroad tracks, behind the tower and covered in water. (Courtesy of Avis Turner.)

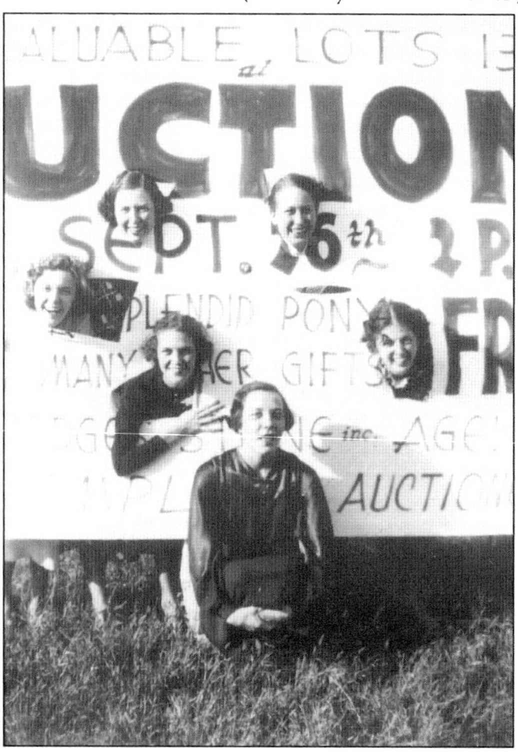

Either enticing visitors to an auction or having fun afterwards, pictured from top to bottom are Leila Grogan, Jessie Herman, Shine Jones, Codell Jones, Marie Grogan, and Virginia Belle Franklin, literally poking their heads through the sign directing visitors to a land auction. Marie married Charles Eugene "Gene" Clay, and they are the parents of Patricia Ross, director of the Bassett Historical Center. (Courtesy of Paul Ross.)

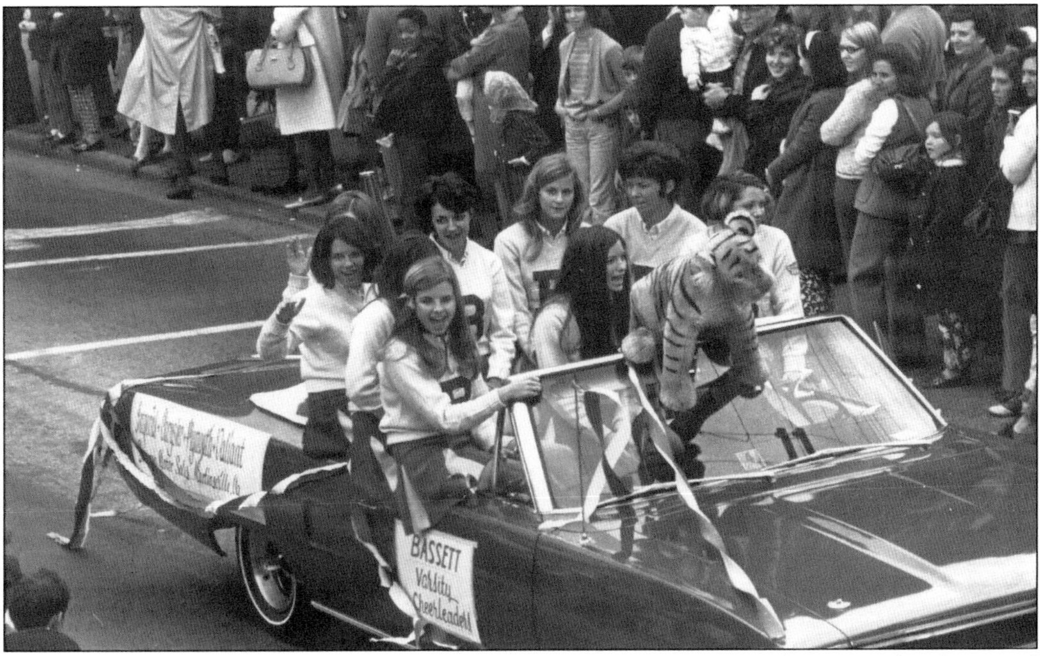

Sitting behind the Bassett Bengal mascot is senior cheerleader Pam Akers. Her family owned Akers Grocery Store in Bassett. That year, they cheered the Bassett Bengals on to win the 1970 Piedmont District Football Championship and were regional runners-up under coach Wayne Turner. Pam married attorney and Virginia delegate Ward Armstrong, and their two daughters were cheerleaders. (Courtesy of the Bassett Historical Center.)

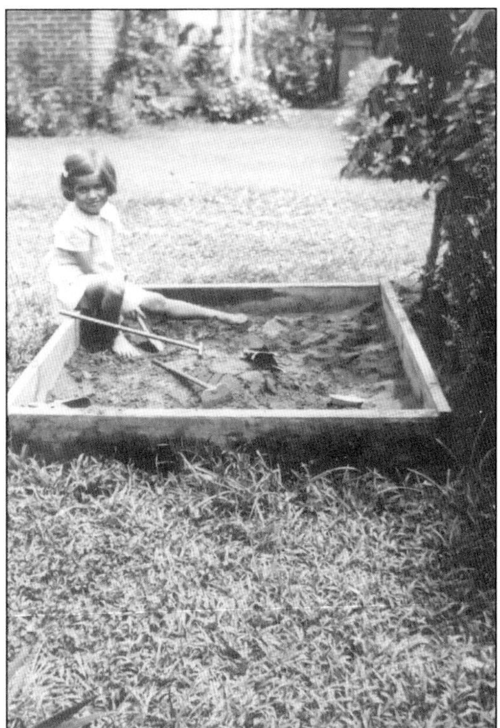

Avis Ellen Carter, the daughter of Clifford and Ida Hollandsworth Carter and wife of Elbert Turner, sits in a sandbox on Third Street in the northern part of Bassett, where the factory now rests along the Smith River. Avis donated many great photographs for this book, as she did for Images of America: *Patrick County*. (Courtesy of Avis Turner.)

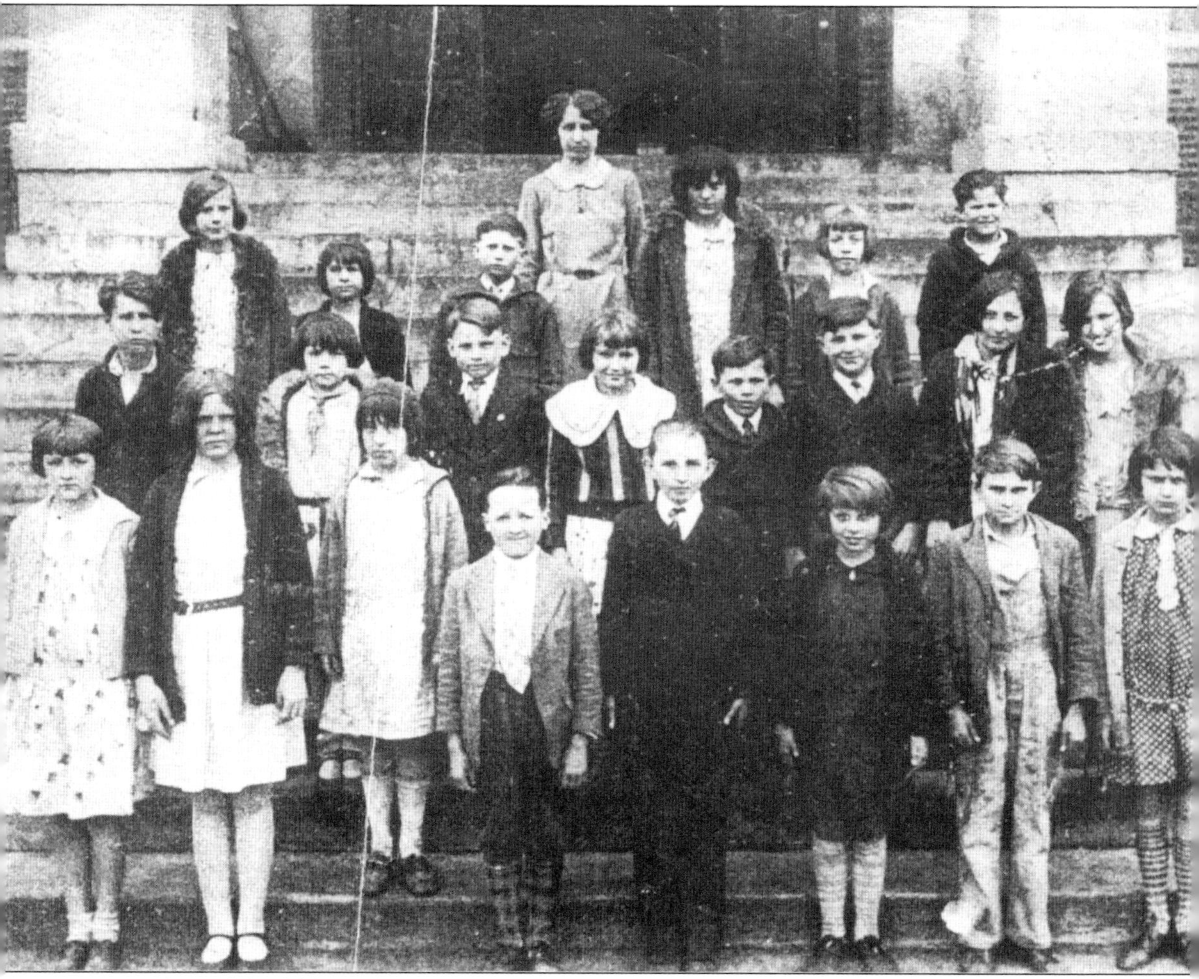

Members of the fifth grade class at Bassett High School in 1929 included, from left to right, (first row) Mrs. Charlie Waney, Mrs. Melvin Grogan, Mrs. Don Calaman, Billy Johnson, C. M. Stafford, unidentified, Cletus Turner and Mrs. Roy Beamer; (second row) Frank Ingram, unidentified, Robert LeFeaver, Mrs. Albert Clark, A. L. Philpott, John Helms, Mrs. Frank Ingram, and Mrs. Albert Williams; (third row) Mildred Ramsey, Ruby Southard, Johnny Ausborne, May Plybon, Virginia Crews, and S. K. McCall. (Courtesy of C. M. Stafford.)

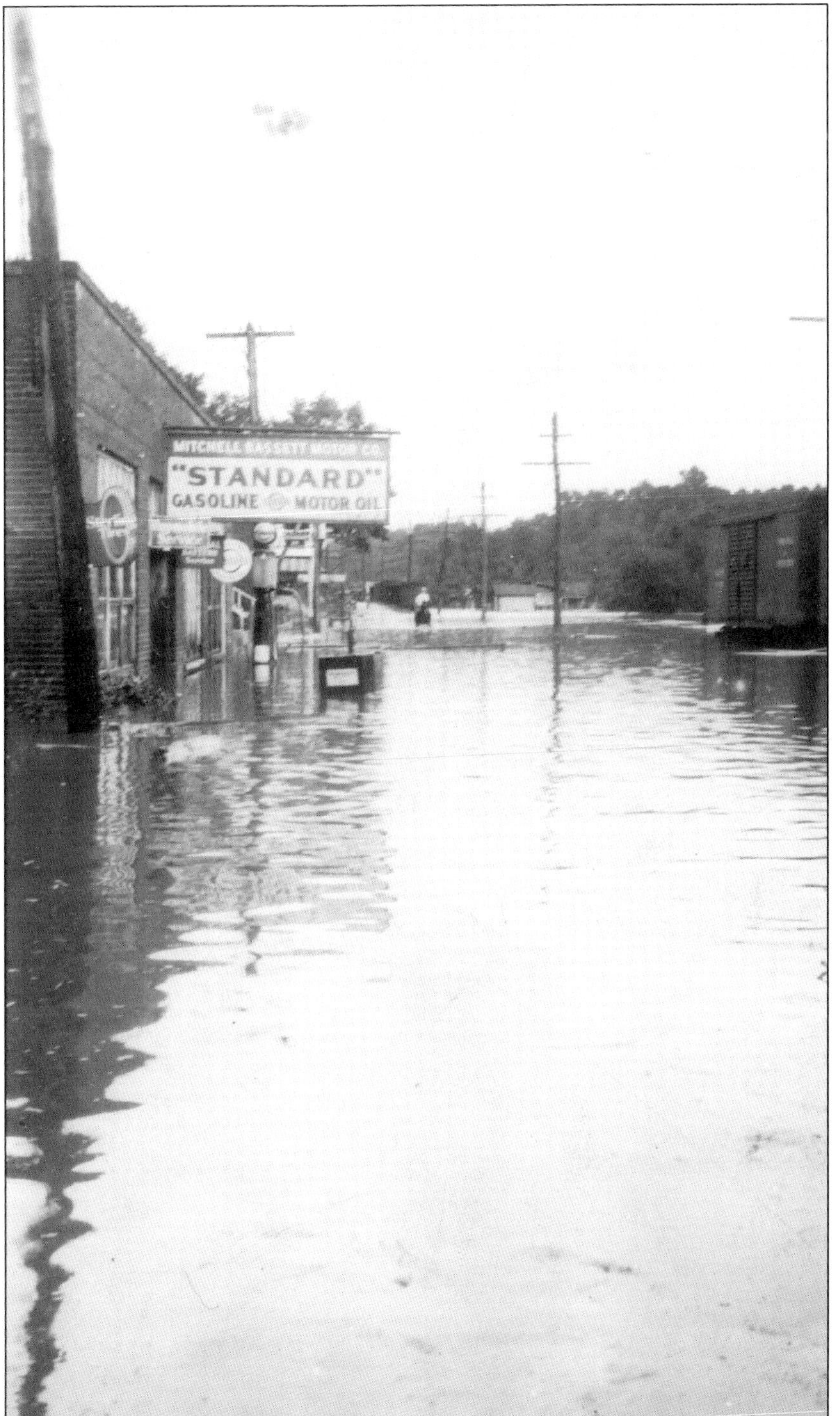

One of the worst floods along the Smith River was in 1937. This view of downtown Bassett looks south and east at Mitchell Bassett Motor Company. It is unclear whether the Standard Oil and Gas created an environmental hazard due to the flood, but the rising water eventually led to building a dam. (Courtesy of Posie Collins.)

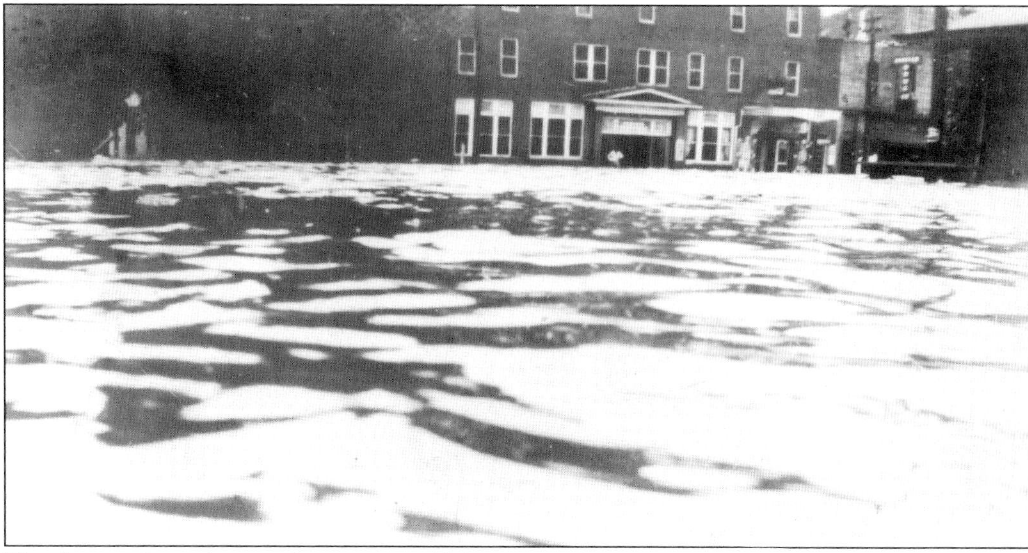

Floodwaters from the Smith River engulf the Riverside Hotel in downtown Bassett in this 1937 postcard image. In spite of the constant flooding of the town, the industrial growth of the furniture industry after the Great Depression and the coming world war continued to allow the community to rise again. (Courtesy of Juanita Wells.)

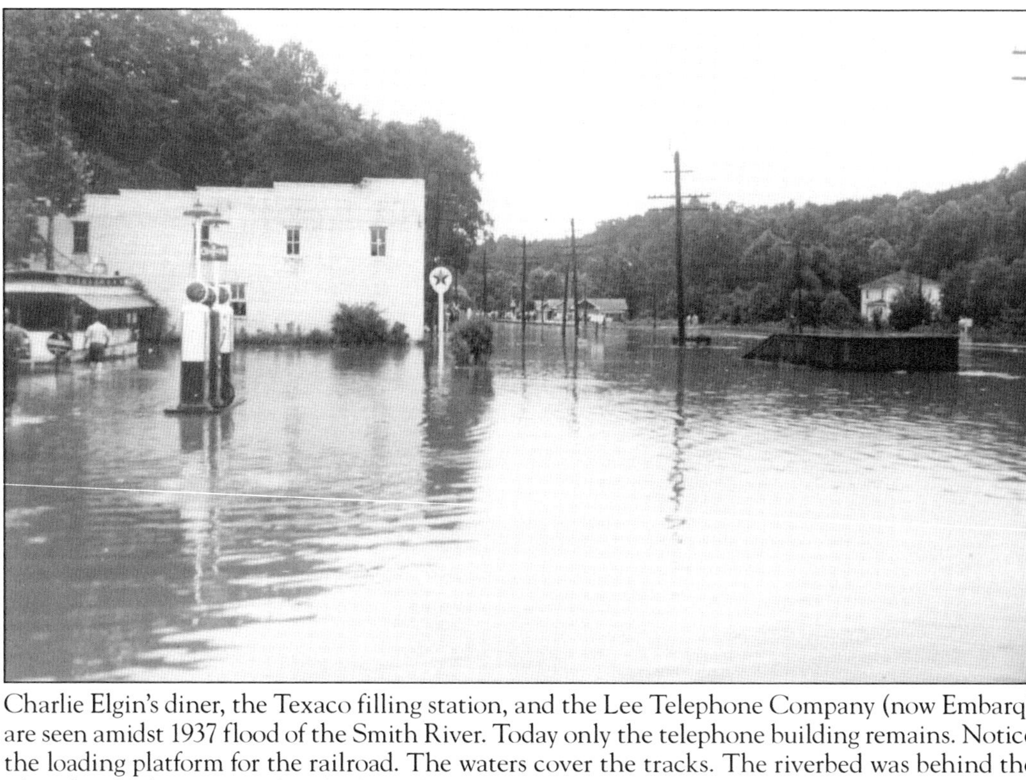

Charlie Elgin's diner, the Texaco filling station, and the Lee Telephone Company (now Embarq) are seen amidst 1937 flood of the Smith River. Today only the telephone building remains. Notice the loading platform for the railroad. The waters cover the tracks. The riverbed was behind the white house shown over the platform. (Courtesy of C. M. Stafford.)

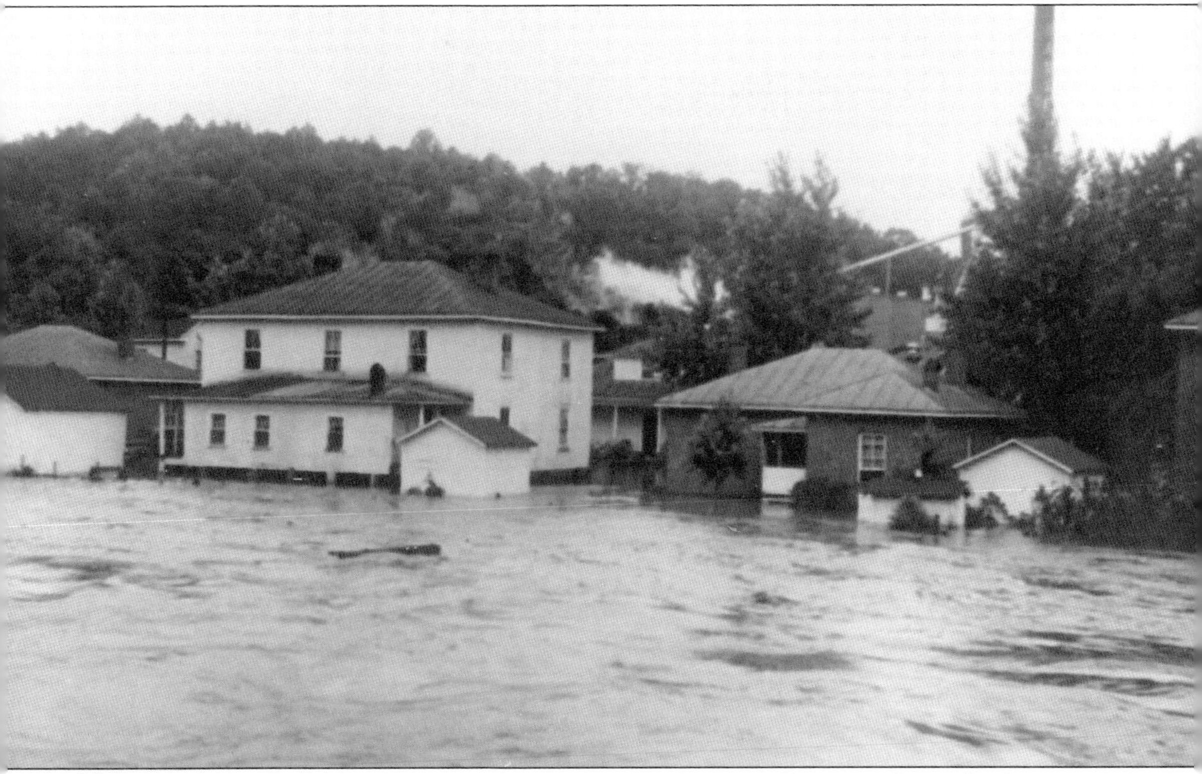

This image of the flooding Smith River in the northern section of Bassett shows the furniture plant across the river from the houses in the foreground. Bassett was the company town of Bassett Furniture Industries, and many of these company houses still remain today up and down Route 57, the Fairy Stone Highway, on both sides of the Bassett Historical Center. (Courtesy of C. M. Stafford.)

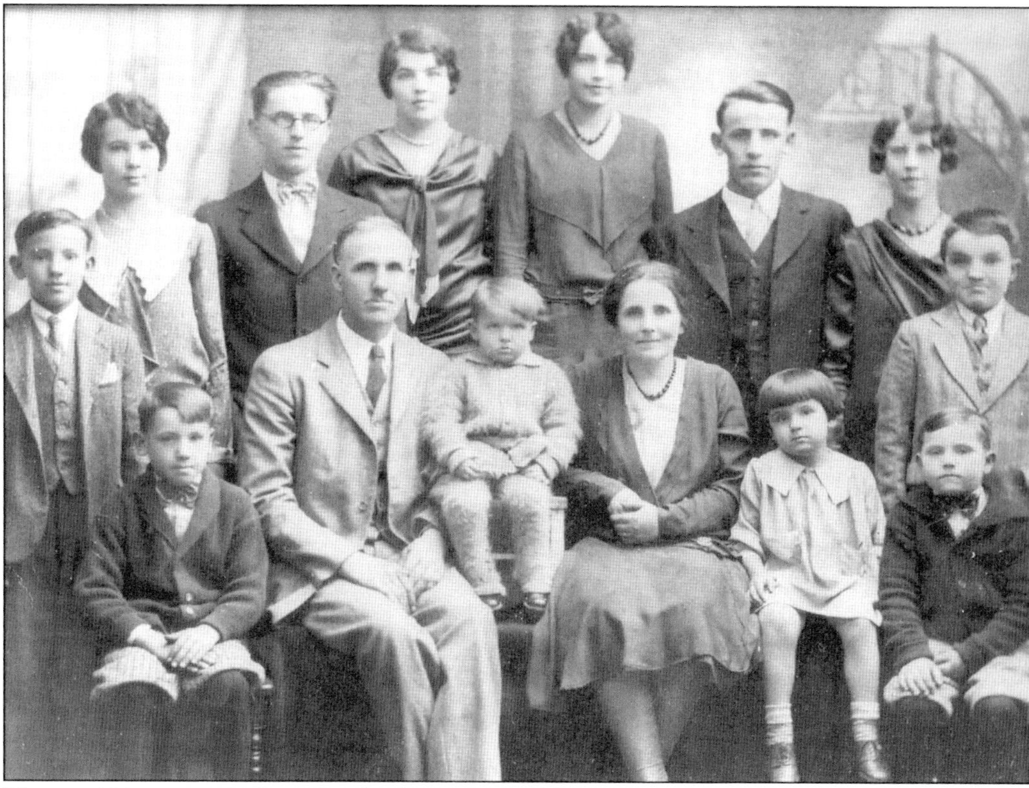

This *c.* 1930 image of Albert Frank Thomason and his wife, Cassie Metz Thomason, comes from the Bassett Forks area of Henry County. Pictured from left to right are their seven boys and five girls (first row) Harold, Wilson, Beatrice, and Dillard; (second row) O. C., Madoline, Ramey, Thelma, Glenwood, George, Celesta, and Simmons. (Courtesy of Betsy Whitlow.)

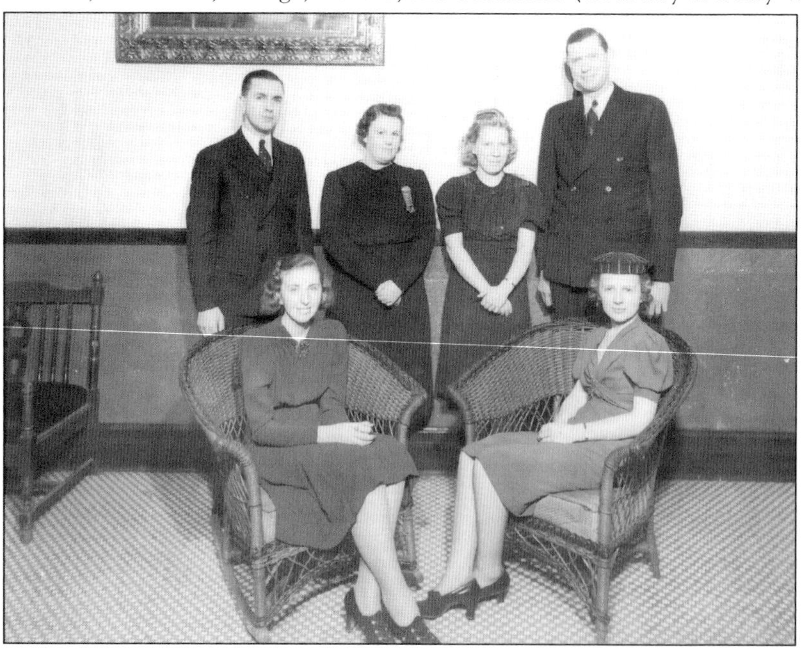

These students from the National Business College of Roanoke are in the lobby of Bassett's Riverside Hotel in the 1930s. From left to right are (sitting) Wilda Coleman and Agnes Park; (standing) Horace N. Wright, Nellie Haney, Ellen P. Gale, and Luther Baker. The furniture industry created a need for trained young people. (Courtesy Ross Gale.)

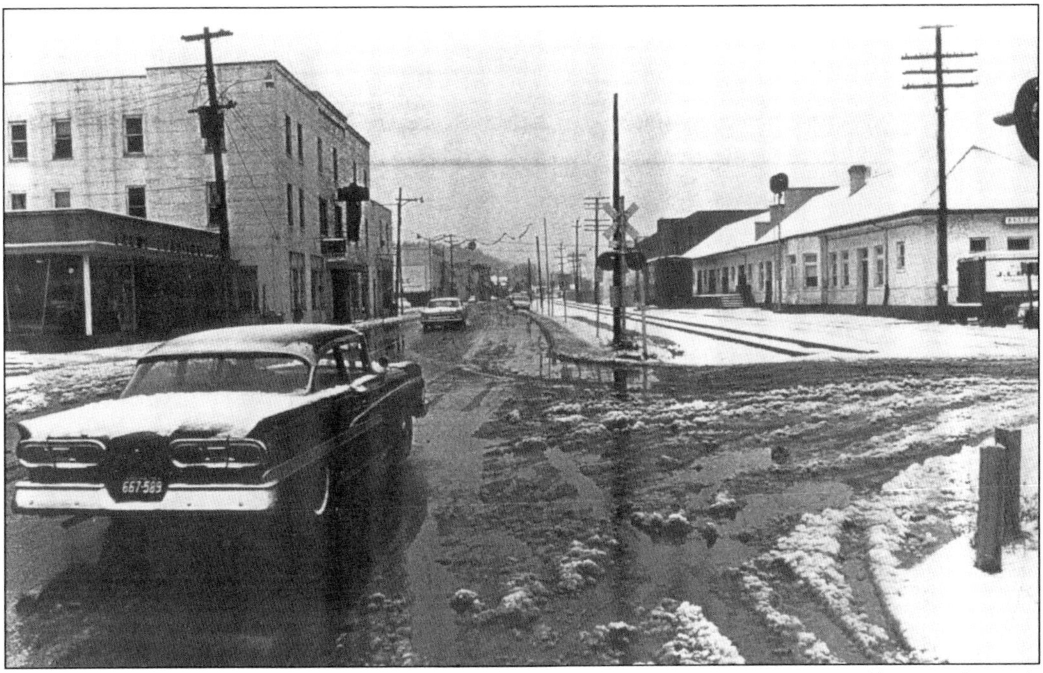

A winter view shows the downtown Bassett train station in the 1960s. Trains still come through daily headed for Winston-Salem, North Carolina, from Roanoke, Virginia, but sadly, with the loss of the local furniture industry, stops in Bassett are just part of history. The station opens now for the yearly Bassett Heritage Festival. (Courtesy of Kenney Kirkman.)

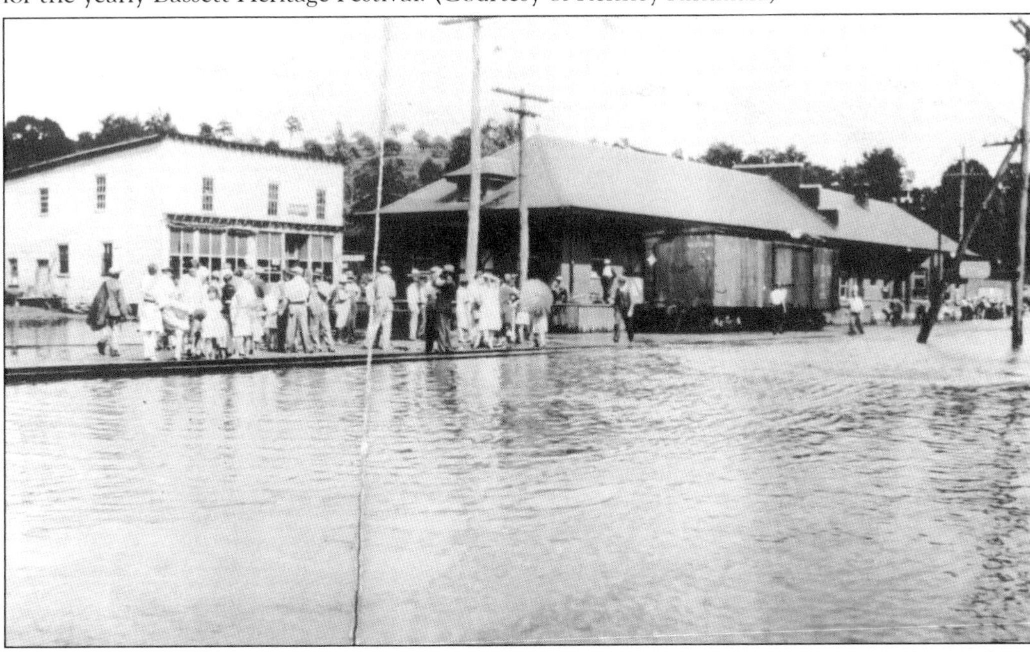

The flooding Smith River dominates the Bassett train station, covering the tracks in places in the downtown area in the 1940s. These Norfolk and Western (now the Norfolk Southern) tracks are still in use today, mainly carrying coal for the Duke Power Plant in North Carolina. (Courtesy of C. M. Stafford.)

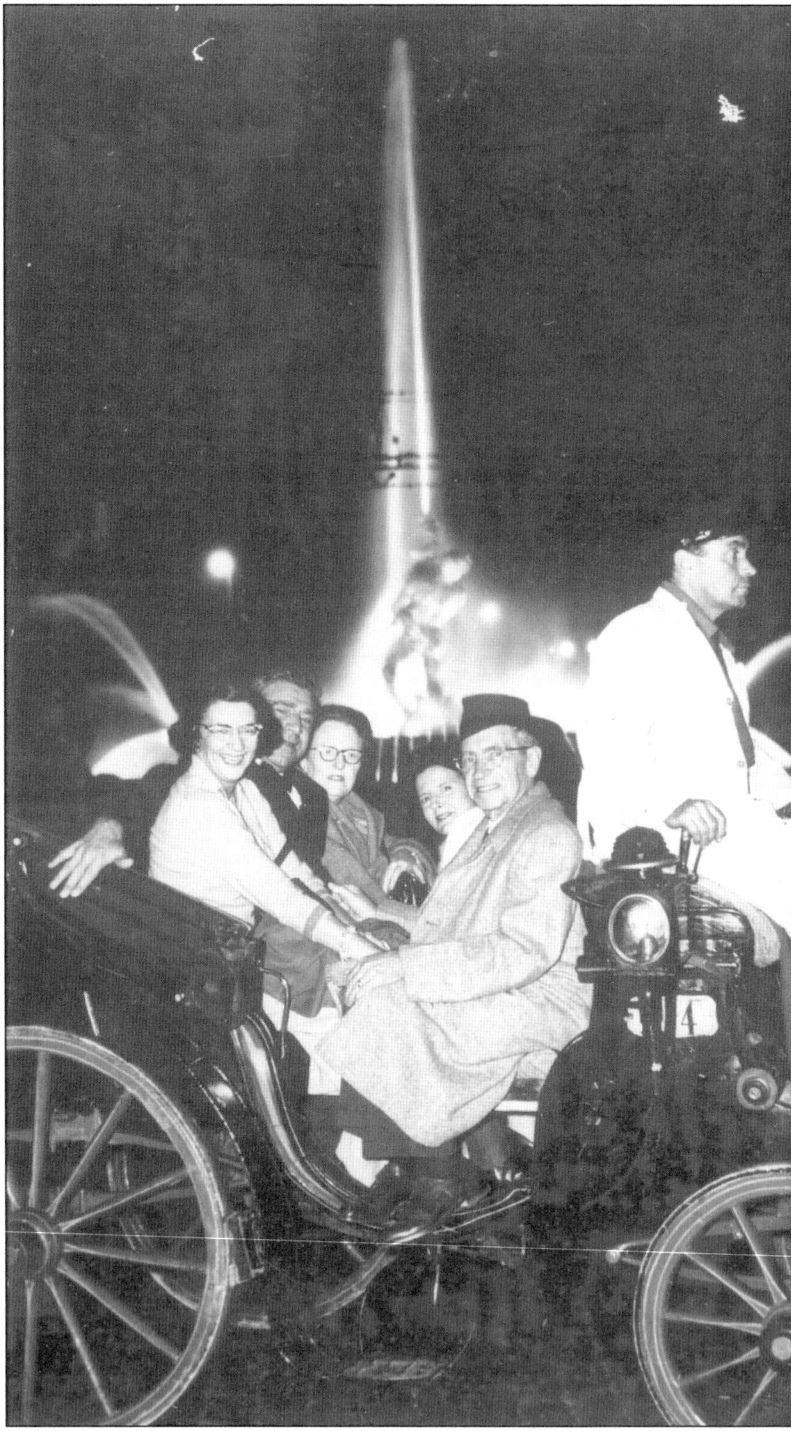

Helen Mildred Bassett is pictured in Rome, Italy, in the 1950s. She lived in Texas but traveled the world. The daughter of Samuel Henry and Eliza Joyce Bassett came back to Bassett for her final resting place. Her father, along with his brothers, John D. and Charles C., and brother-in-law Reed L. Stone, began Bassett Furniture Industries. (Courtesy of Posie Collins.)

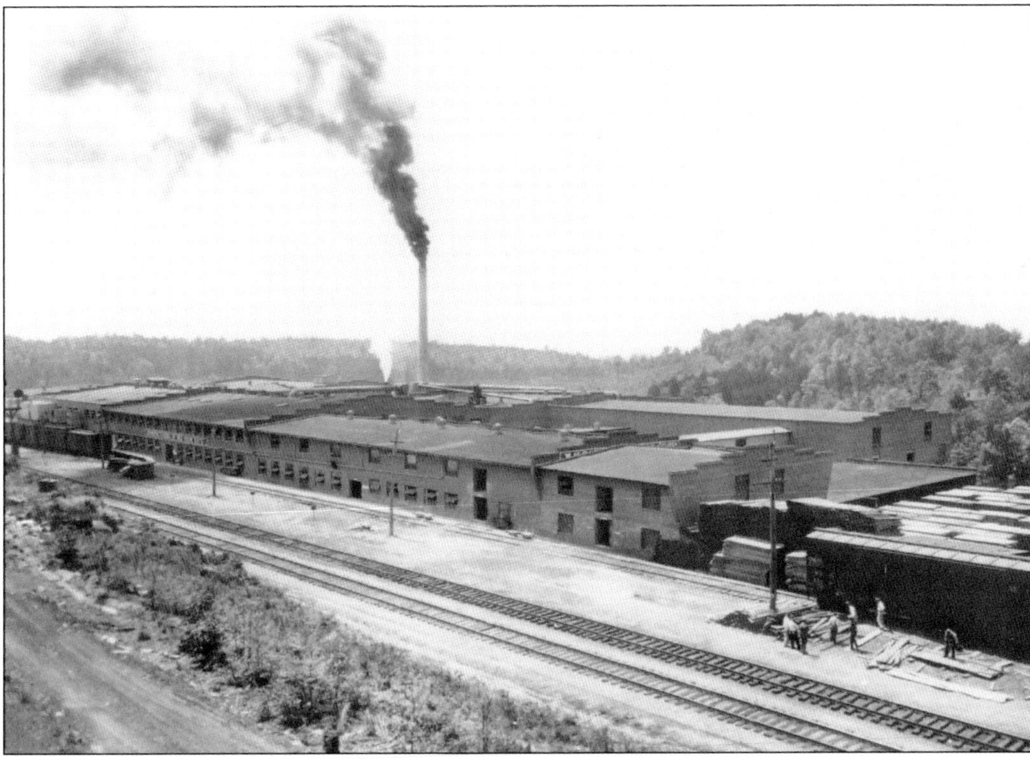

The W. M. Bassett Furniture Company of Martinsville is pictured in the early 1900s, probably after 1930. William M. Bassett expanded the family's furniture factories to nearby Martinsville by purchasing Craig Furniture in 1927. The son of John D. Bassett Sr. became unhappy with his position in the family company and branched out on his own. (Courtesy of Kenney Kirkman.)

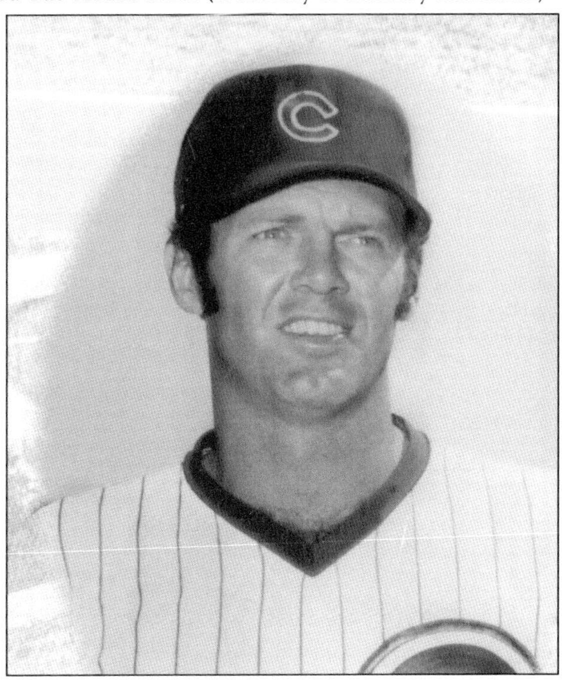

Randy Hundley of Bassett High School debuted for the San Francisco Giants in 1964. He played major league baseball for the San Diego Padres and Minnesota Twins but spent most of his career with the Chicago Cubs, where he played his last game in 1977. A Gold Glove catcher, he committed a National League record of only four errors in 1967. His son, Todd, played 15 years as a catcher, too. (Courtesy of the Bassett Historical Center.)

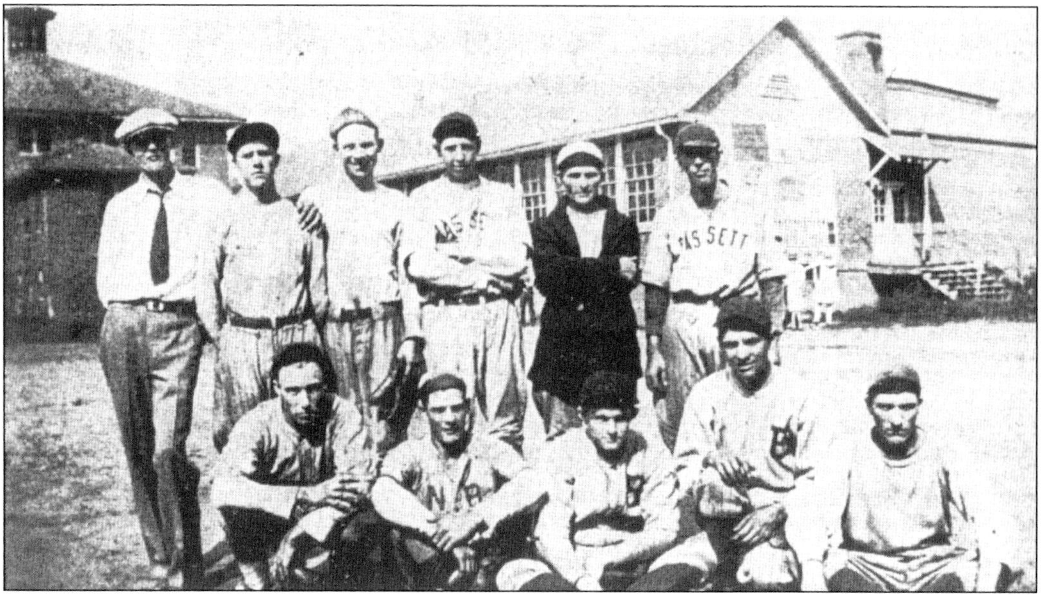

One of the first Henry County baseball teams was from Bassett in 1929. Among those identified are W. T. Carter, Howard Holbrook, Smiley Bullock, Trixie Bryant, Early Woody, Jubal Mitchell, George McCraw, Melvin Grogan, and Bill Beam. The county produced many professional players, such as the Detroit Tigers' Lou Whitaker. Today that tradition continues with the minor-league Martinsville Mustangs. (Courtesy of Teddy Compton.)

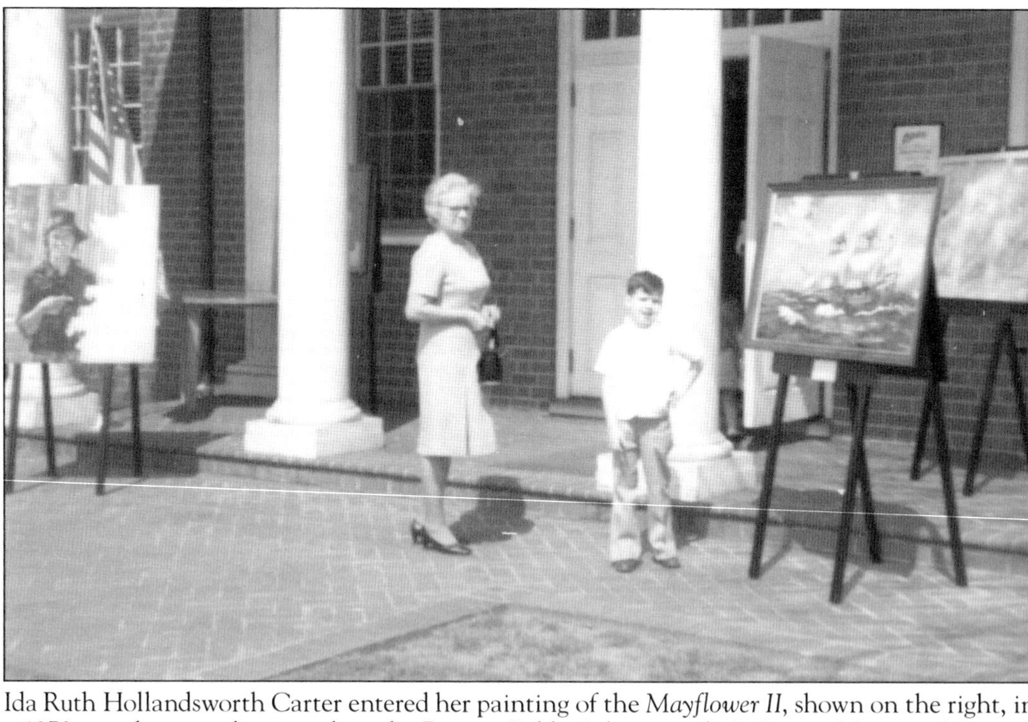

Ida Ruth Hollandsworth Carter entered her painting of the *Mayflower II*, shown on the right, in a 1970s art show at what was then the Bassett Public Library, today's Bassett Historical Center. She is with her grandson Mark Alan Turner. The library moved across the street, leaving the entire building to become the history library. (Courtesy of Avis Turner.)

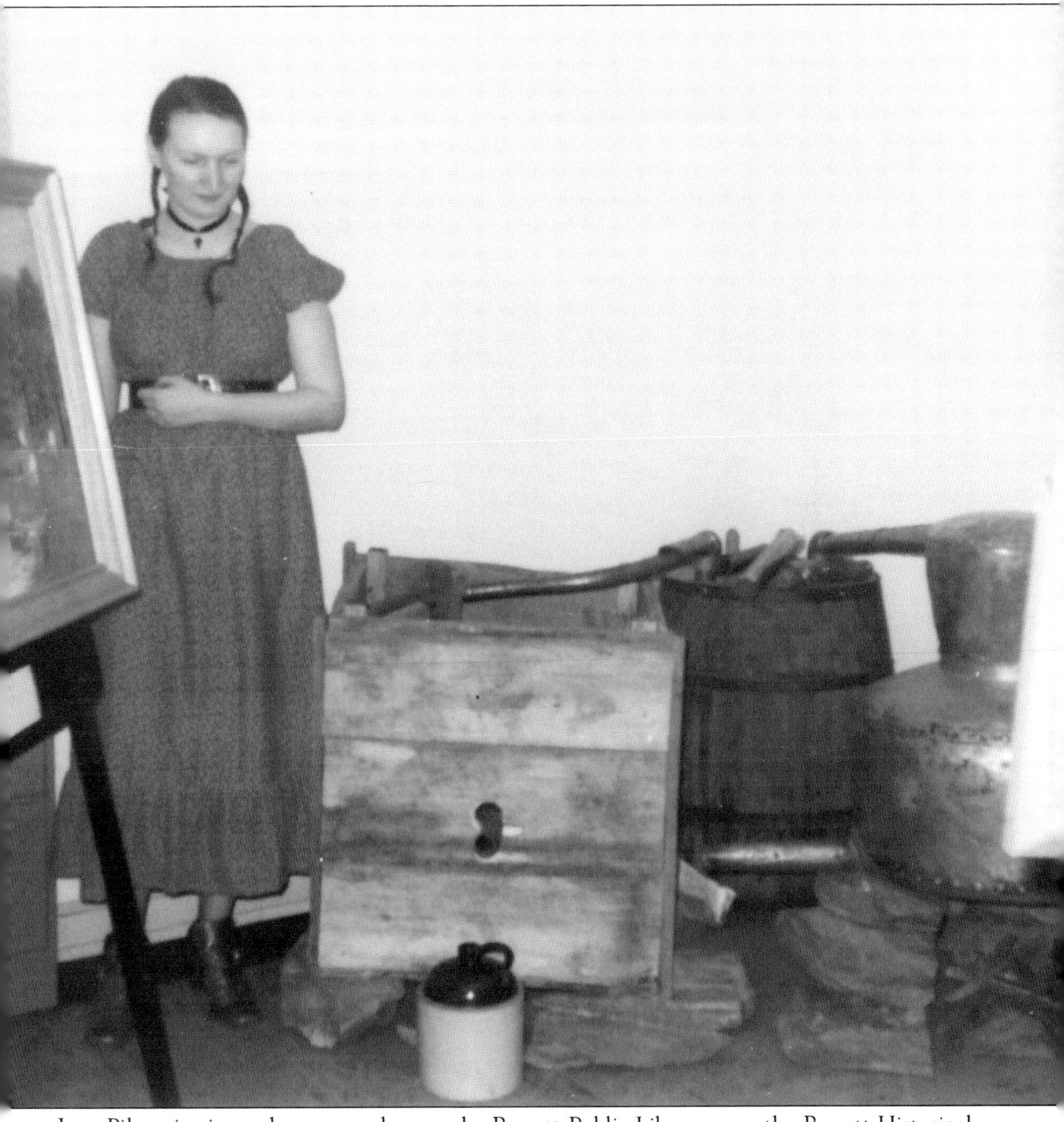

Jane Pilson is pictured at an art show at the Bassett Public Library, now the Bassett Historical Center, in the 1970s. The liquor still shown is on display in the library in the back room that contains information on military and native history. Jane is the daughter of Ophus Eugene Pilson, whose collection holds a special place in the library, residing in an entire room by itself. (Courtesy of Avis Turner.)

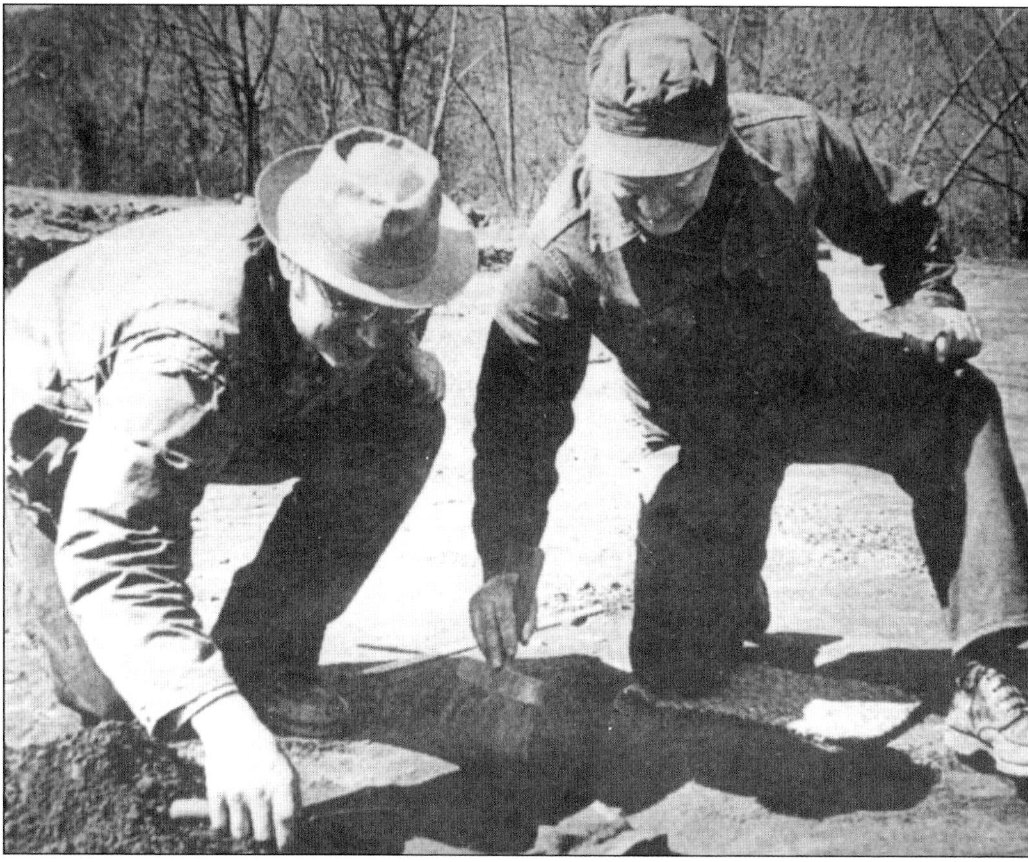

Wayne Clark (left), assistant archaeologist with the Virginia State Library, and Richard P. Gravely Jr. are pictured at the Koehler excavation along the Smith River in April 1976. Gravely's work on Henry County history, especially archaeology regarding native peoples, resides at the Library of Virginia and the University of North Carolina at Chapel Hill. (Courtesy of Avis Turner.)

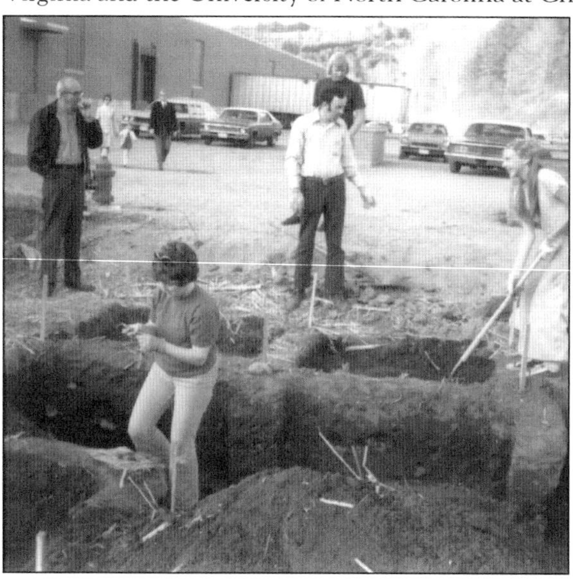

Jim and Brenda Childs (center) are pictured at an archaeological site titled the "Philpott Dig" in the northern part of Bassett behind the furniture factory in October 1974. This work uncovered the skeleton of a male 28 to 30 years old. The Bassett Historical Center contains an entire section on Native American history that includes books and artifacts. (Courtesy of Avis Turner.)

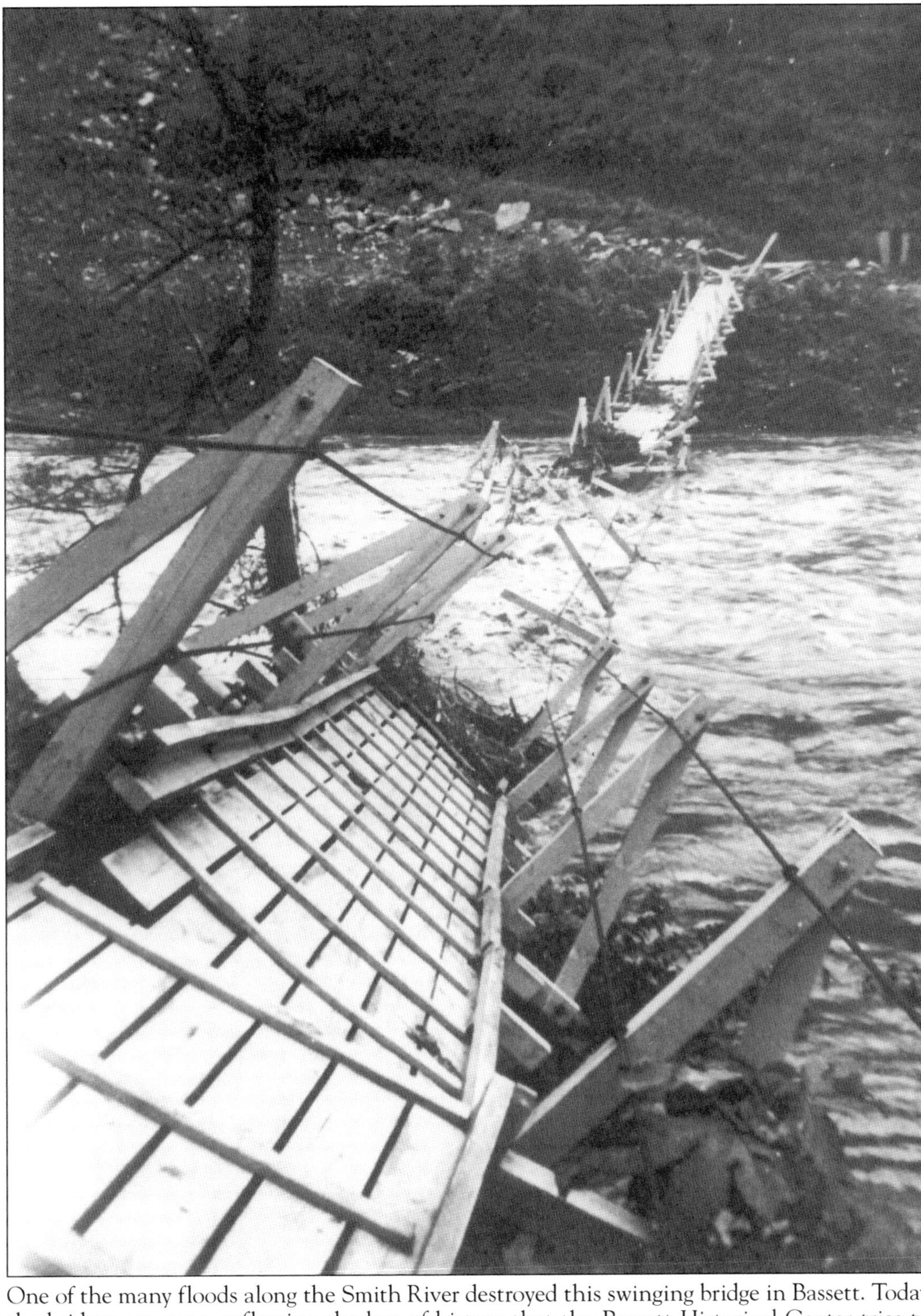

One of the many floods along the Smith River destroyed this swinging bridge in Bassett. Today the bridges are gone, reflecting the loss of history that the Bassett Historical Center tries to preserve. Bassett Furniture's headquarters and one factory still reside in the town, but the heyday of the industrial boom from 100 years ago is gone. (Courtesy of Avis Turner.)

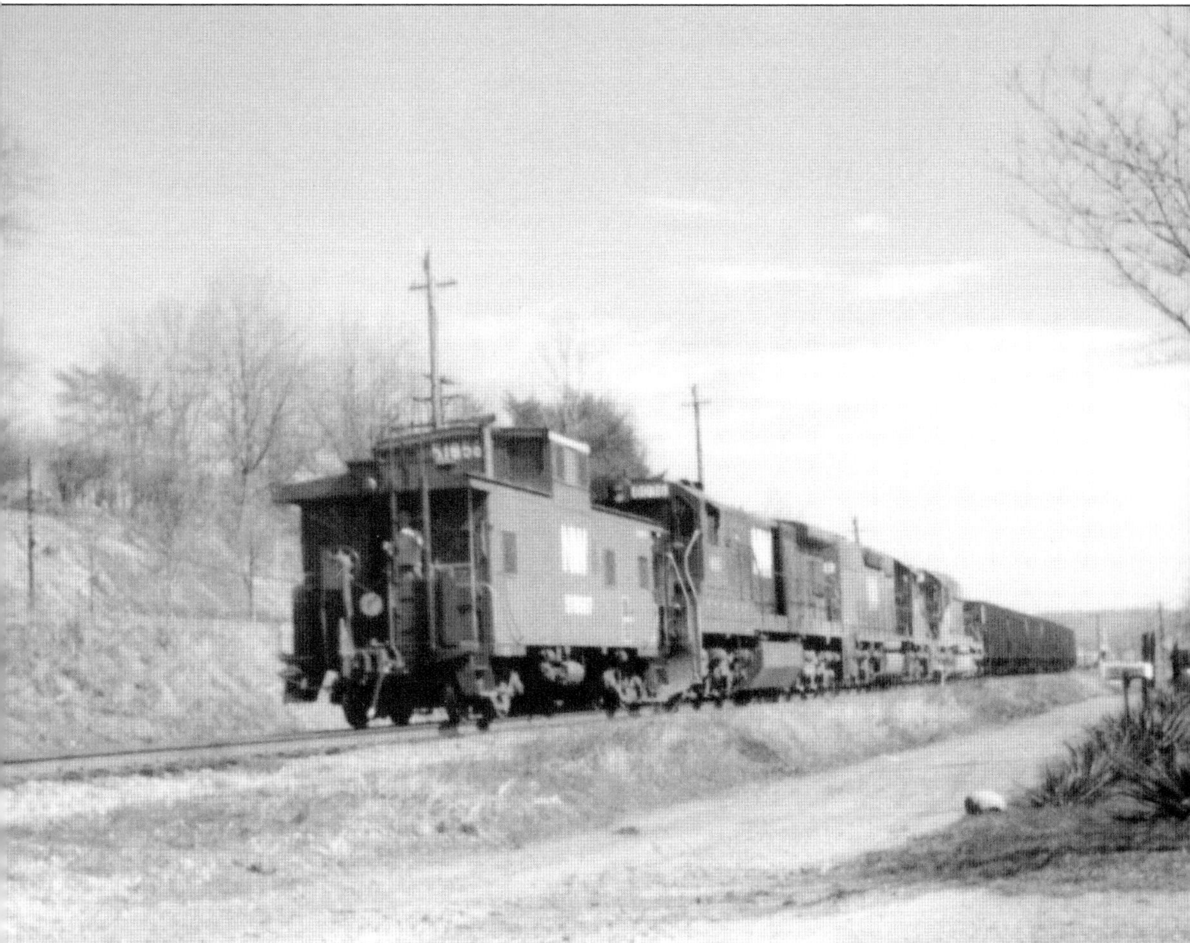

The rear of a southbound coal train rolling through Bassett in 1976 on the Norfolk and Western (now Norfolk Southern) Railway shows what once was and will never be again. A caboose, a sight seldom seen anymore, makes up the rear of the train as it passes through traveling between Roanoke, Virginia, and Winston-Salem, North Carolina. (Courtesy of Kenney Kirkman.)

Two

FIELDALE

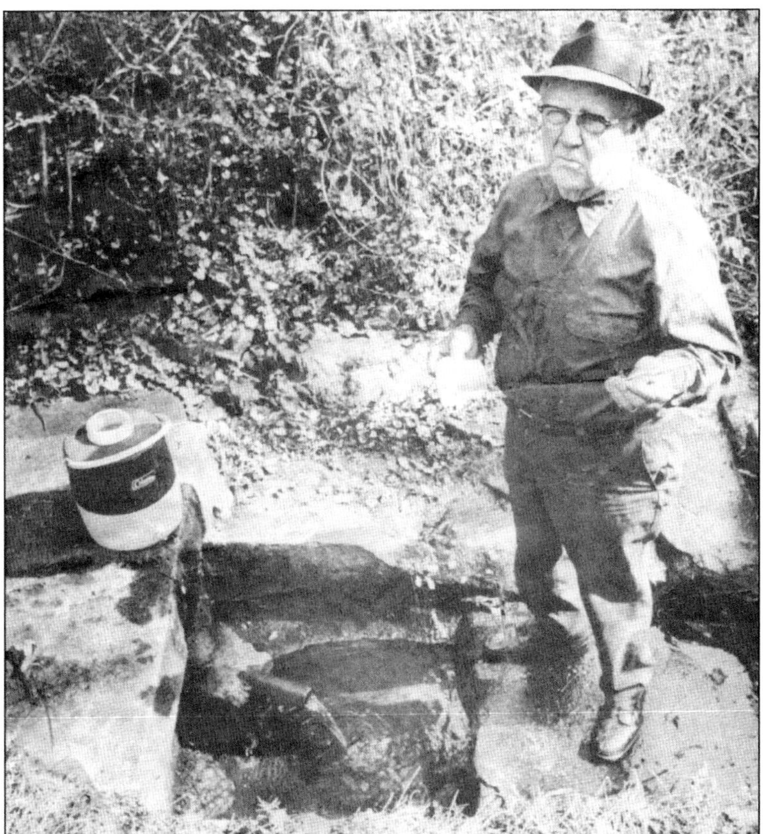

William Merriman is pictured at the Fieldale Spring. It was water that brought people to this part of Henry County to live, and it was water that brought industry in the form of the Marshall Field Company to Waller's Ford, which later became the town of Fieldale, on the Smith River. (Courtesy of Teddy Compton.)

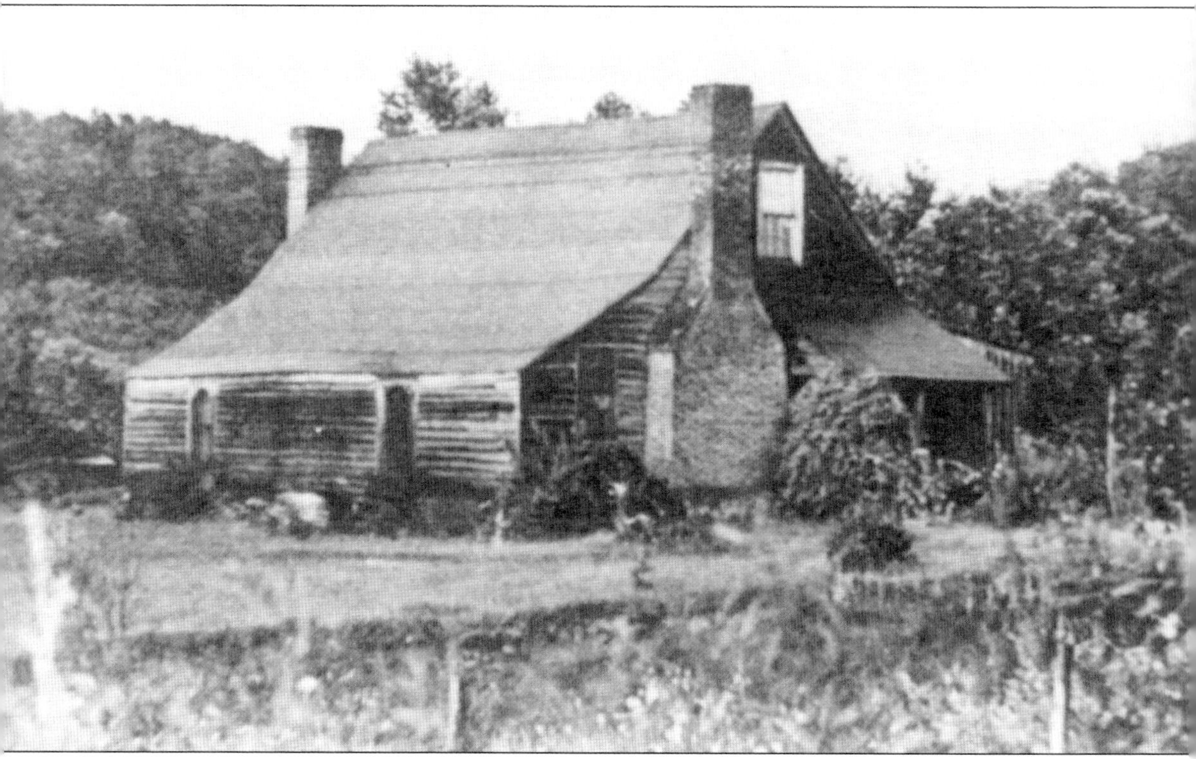

Fieldale was originally named Wallers for the Waller family, which had a plantation here. The house shown in this image and a ford on the river shared their name. It included the area from Beaver Creek north along the Smith River. Tradition holds that this was a mustering ground during the American Revolution. (Courtesy of Teddy Compton.)

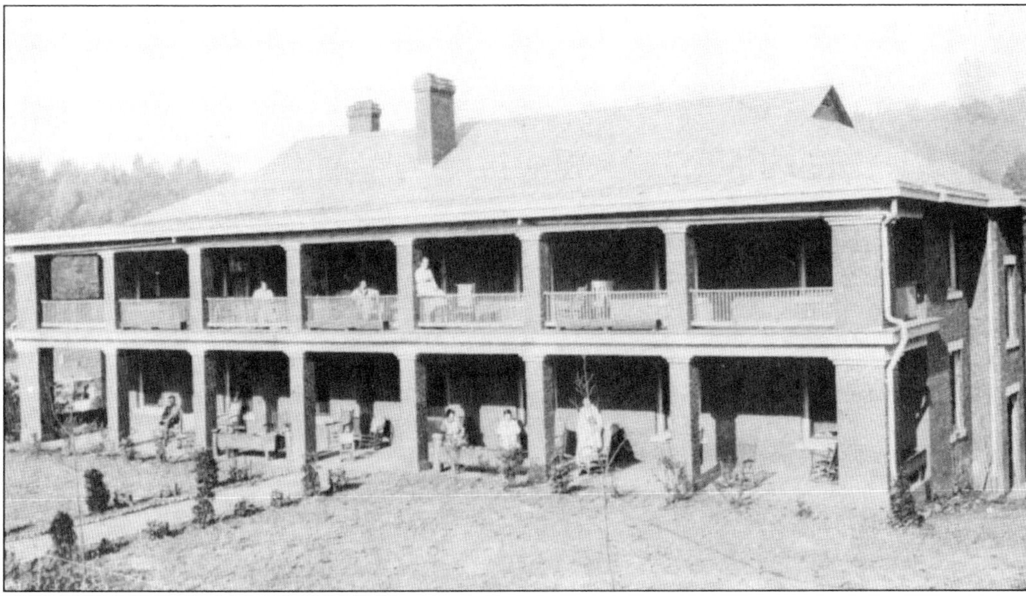

The Fieldale Hotel was one of the first buildings erected with the coming of the Marshall Field Company and the textile factory. Originally operated by Anna Stultz, it was a sign of the needs of a factory town and the many visitors that the new industry brought to the area. (Courtesy of Anne Copeland.)

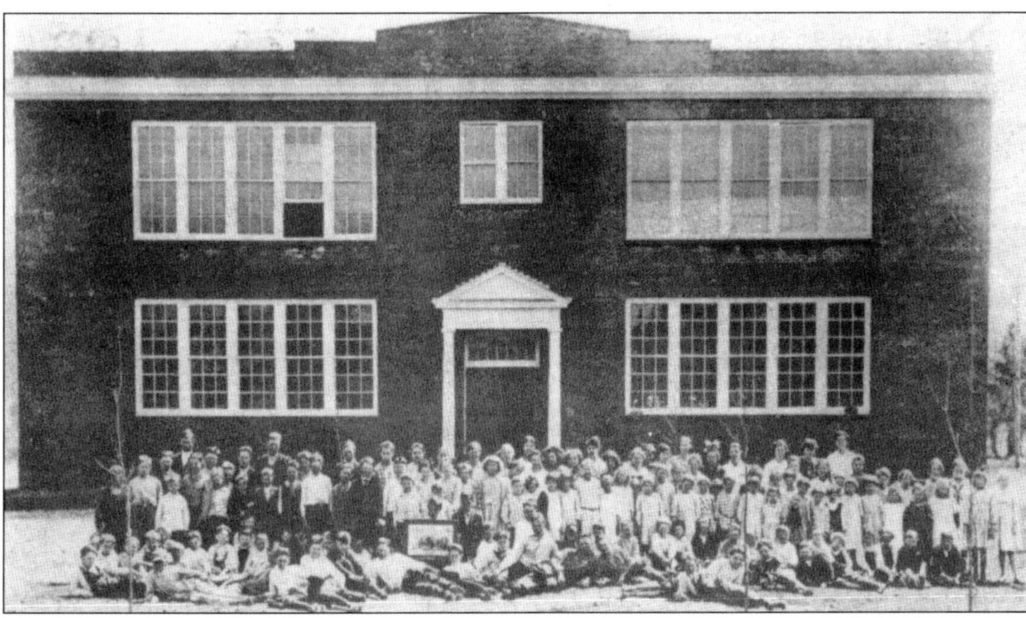

Fieldale Elementary School, built in 1921, was one of the benefits of Marshall Field Company coming to the area. The students threatened to strike after the removal of principal Marvin J. Lentz in 1932. After a public meeting, Lentz made a trip to Richmond to complete the state requirements needed to keep the job. (Courtesy of Anne Copeland.)

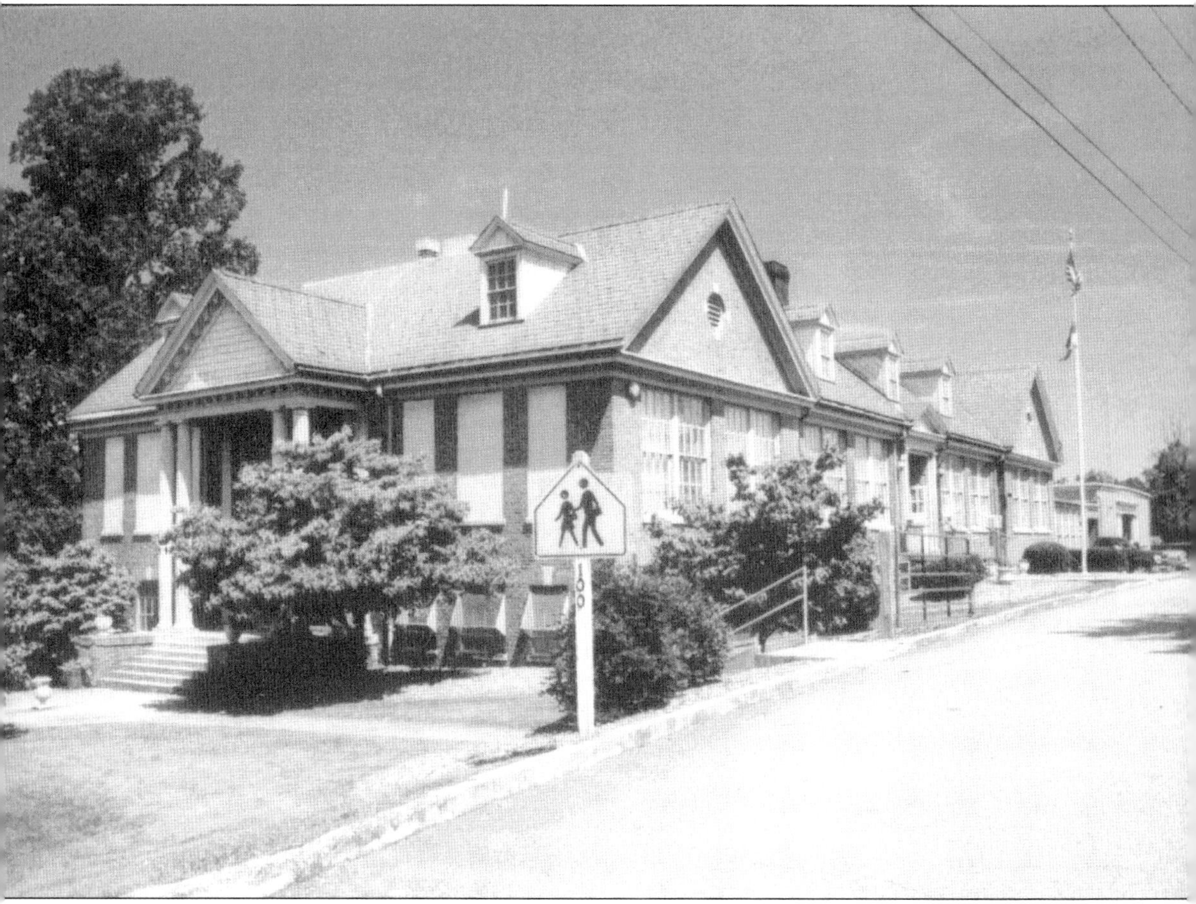

Built in 1942 and added to in 1953, Fieldale High School, the home of the Blue Devils, was one of the benefits of a being a company town. The first school, known as the Mountain Top School, began education in the community with the coming of Marshall Field Company. Fieldale High School became an elementary school. (Courtesy of Teddy Compton.)

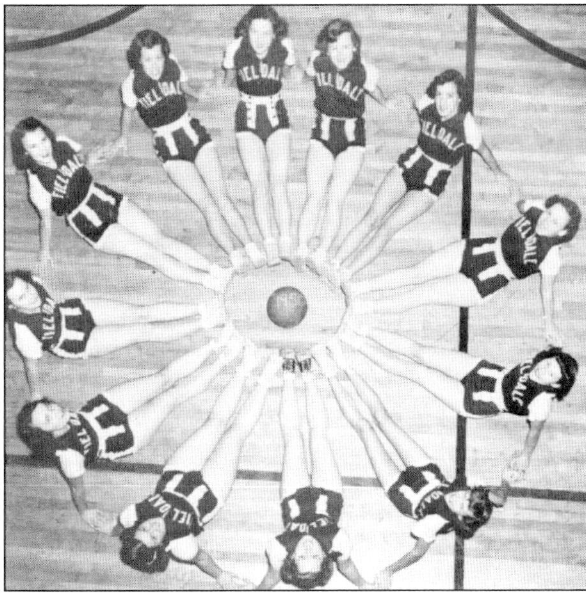

Boys and girls of the Fieldale High School played next door in the YMCA, now the community center and the site each May of the annual Fieldale Heritage Festival. Learn more about the festival at www.fieldaleheritagefestival.com. Marshall Field Company started the high school in 1931, with a four-year curriculum in place two years later, and the first building was in place by 1935. There were 358 elementary and 123 high school students by that time. Eventually, the Henry County School Board took over administration of the school. Fieldale High School merged and moved to become Fieldale-Collinsville High School, but with decreasing numbers, eventually the school merged with Bassett High School, ending the rivalry shown below in a 1961 game. (Above, courtesy of Teddy Compton; below, courtesy of Anne Copeland.)

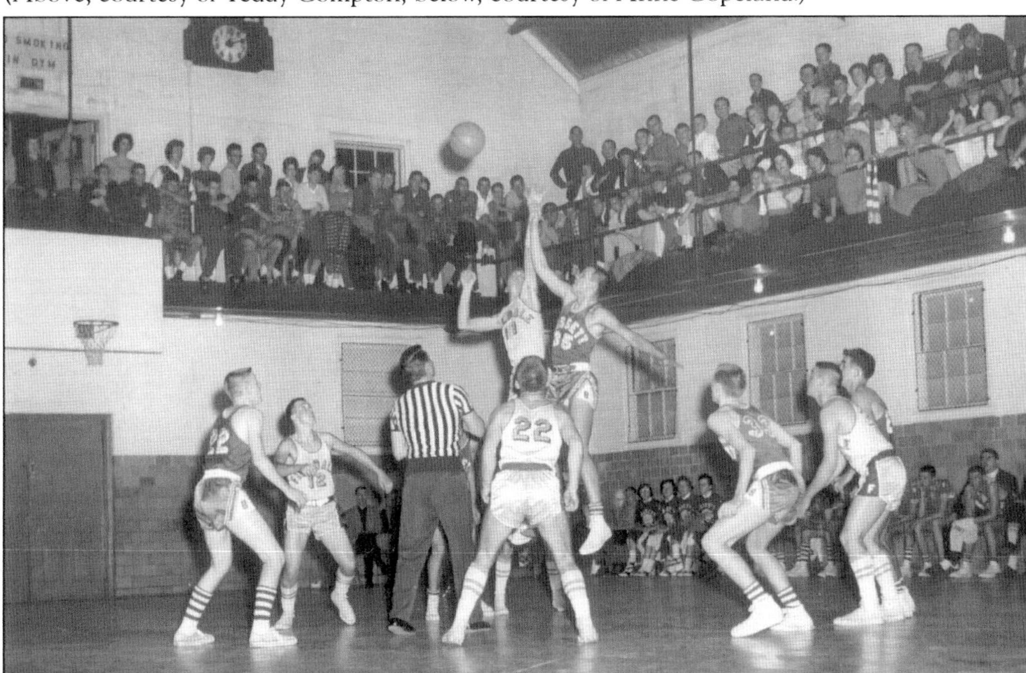

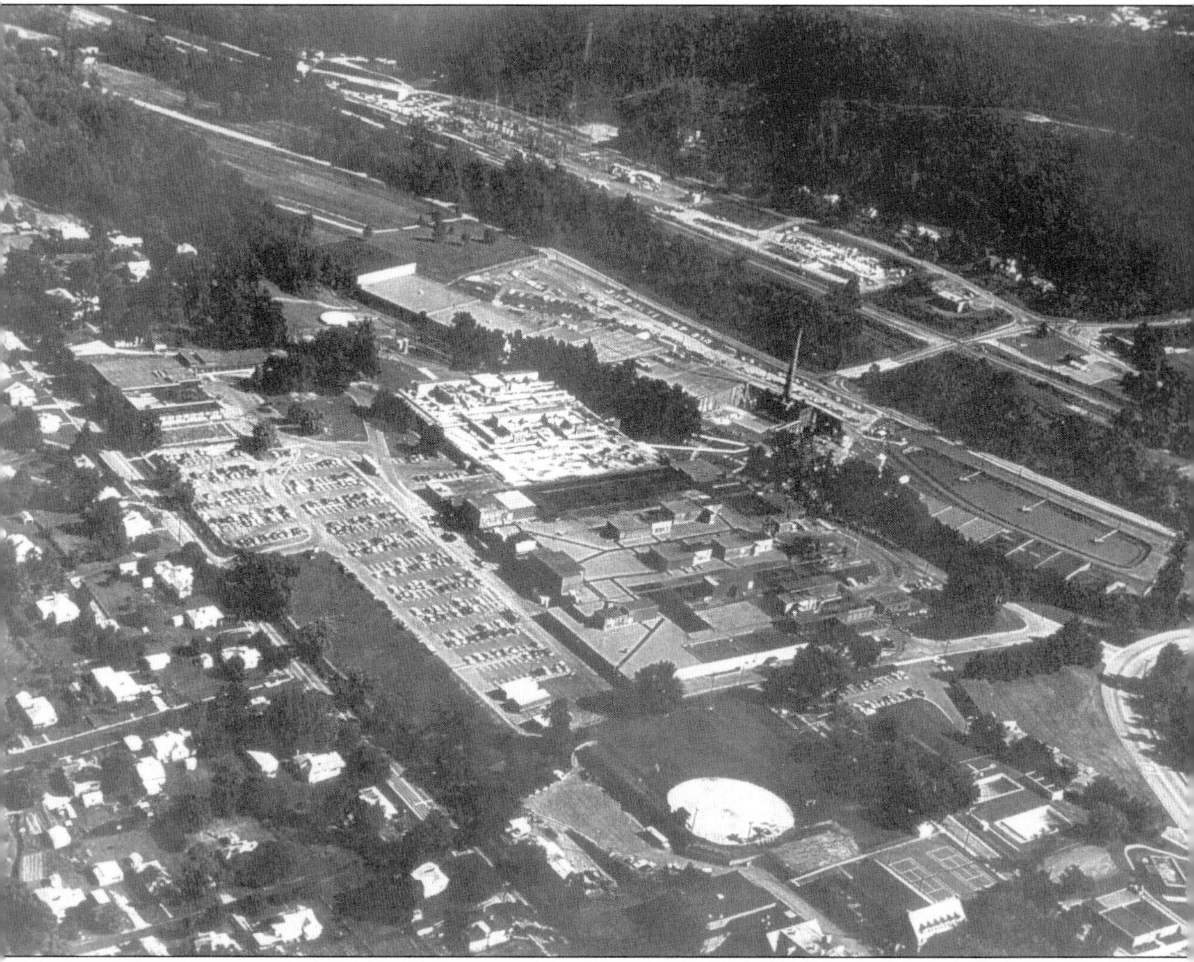

Beginning as Waller's Ford along the Smith River, Fieldale grew into a vibrant industrial complex with the coming of the Marshall Field Company in 1917. Lying between two railroad lines and the Smith River, Fieldcrest Mills produced textiles for nearly 80 years. This allowed schools, homes, and businesses to flourish in the small community during those years. (Courtesy of Teddy Compton.)

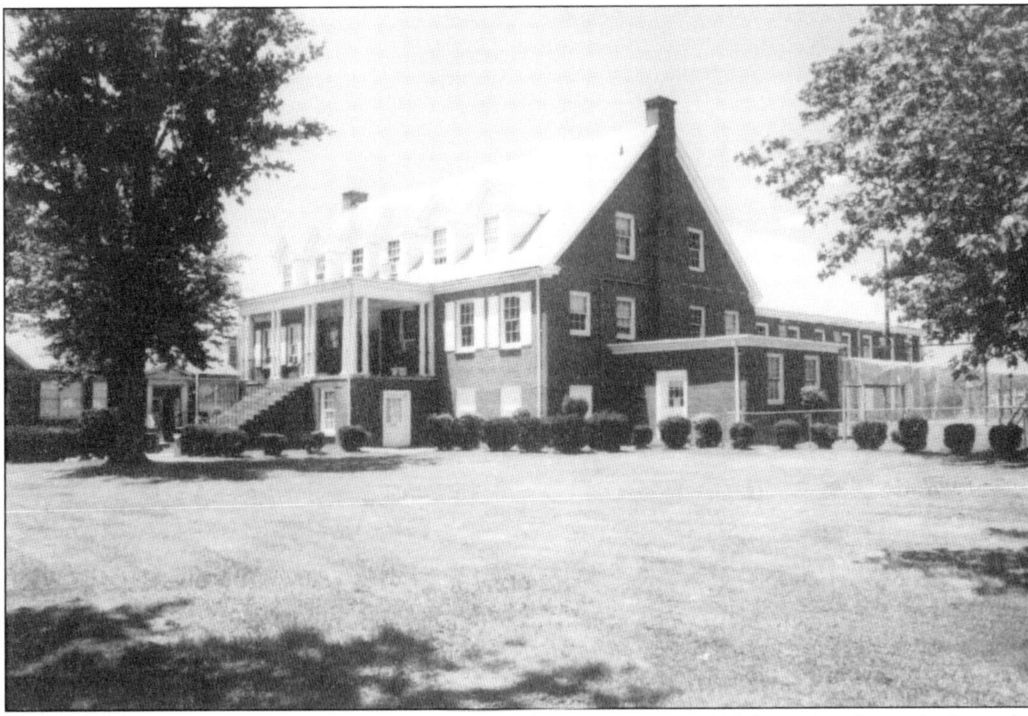

The Fieldale YMCA was built by Marshall Field Company in 1937 from funds made from the sale of a power plant to Appalachian Power Company. It was the site of basketball games for the neighboring high school. Now the community center, it is the site of the annual Fieldale Heritage Festival. (Courtesy of Teddy Compton.)

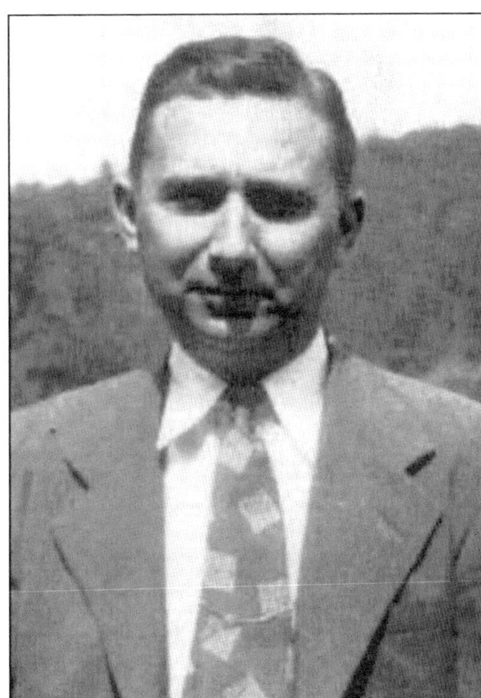

Fieldale High School principal Branch K. Rives received the Croix de Guerre with Silver Star from the Republic of France for his service in World War II. Given the medal for "outstanding service in a time of war," Rives acted as a liaison between the American and French troops during six months in 1945. (Courtesy of Teddy Compton.)

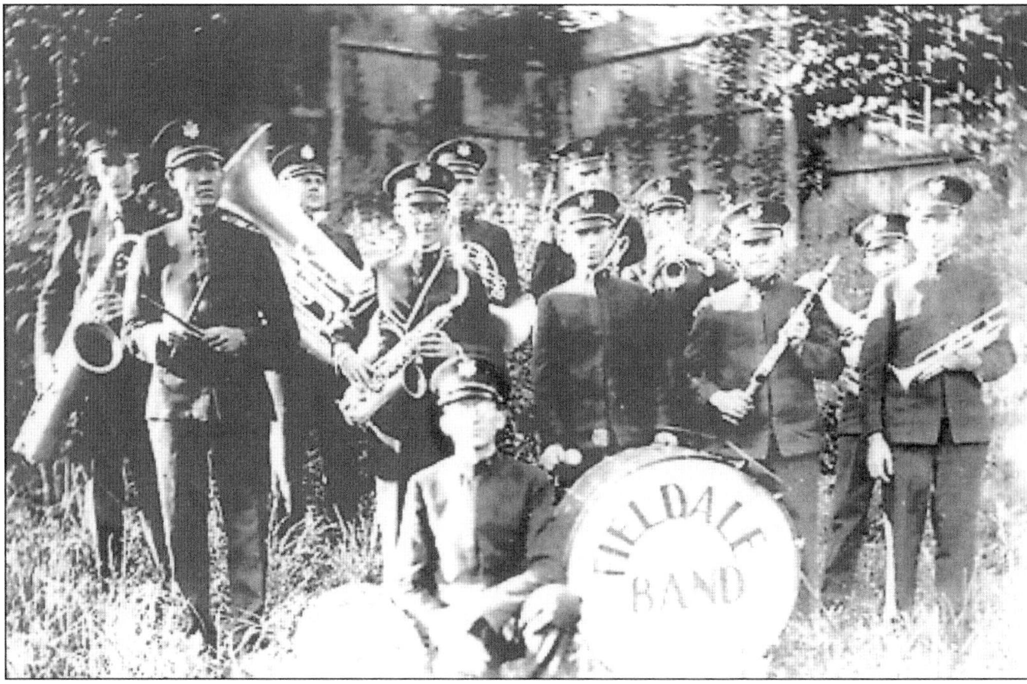

The Fieldale Community Band, pictured around 1930, echoed the theme "Happy Days Are Here Again." The only identified member is Lefty Harrington, standing second from the left with the saxophone and his famous smile, reflecting the economic good times in Fieldale. The company's economic influence lessened the impact of the Great Depression. (Courtesy of Teddy Compton.)

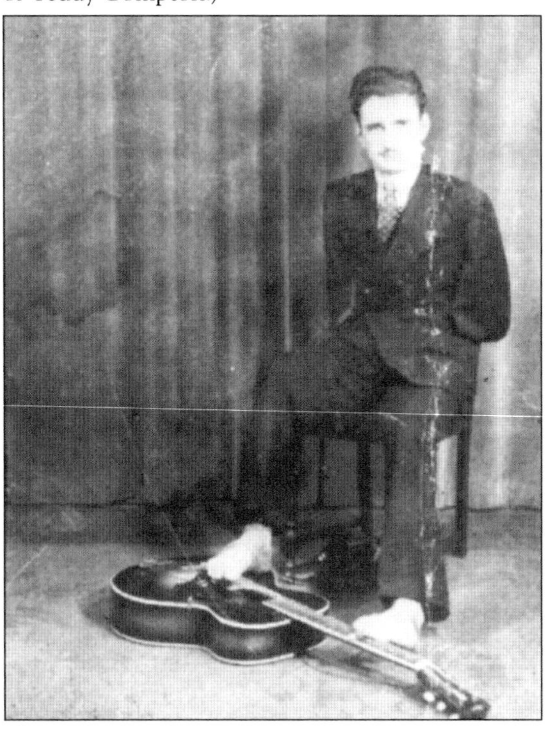

Born with no arms, Ray Meyers traveled the country playing the guitar with his feet. Among his stops was the Dale Theater in Fieldale. From Pennsylvania, Meyers drove without special equipment with driver's licenses in two different states. He smoked, shot guns, raised the hood of his car, and shook hands with his feet. (Courtesy of Teddy Compton.)

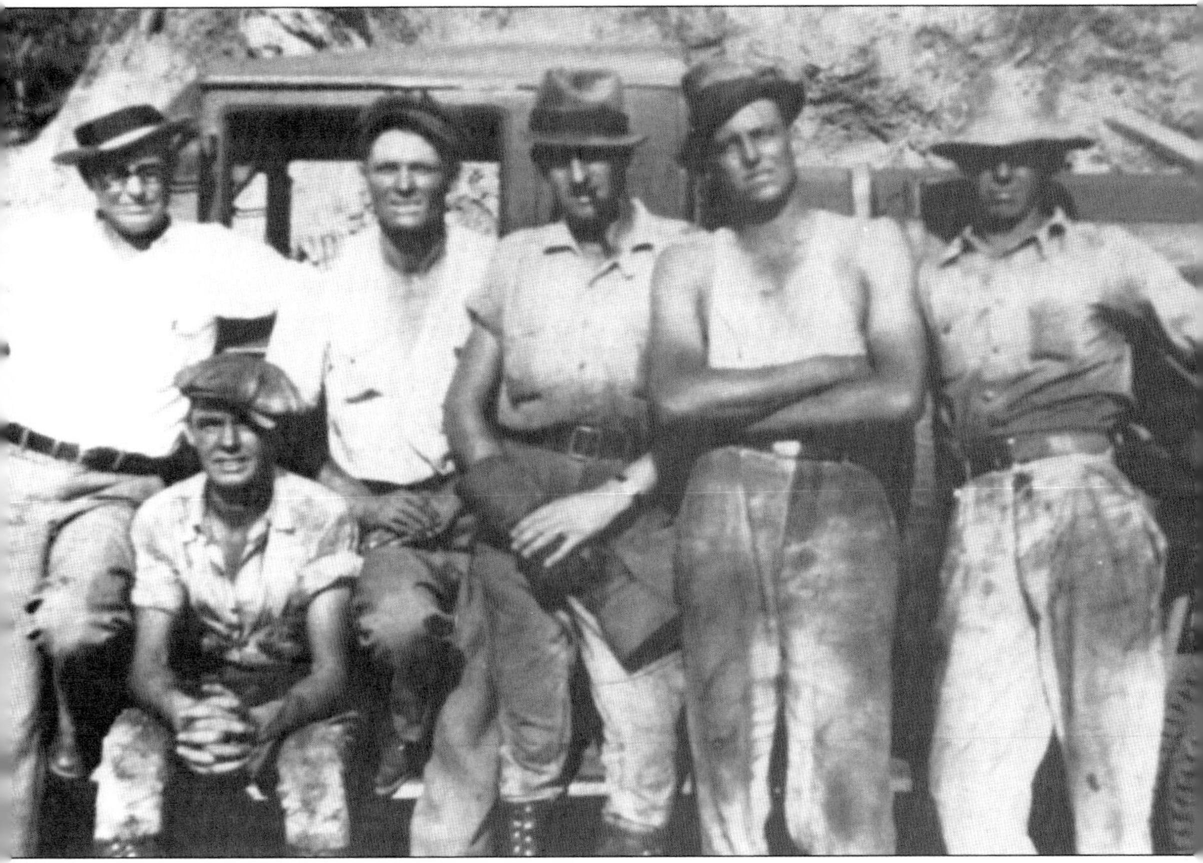

For the first 20 years of production, the mills of Marshall Field Company generated their own electrical power from steam. Fieldcrest Mills sold their power plant to Appalachian Power Company in 1937. The first work crew from Appalachian at Fieldale included J. H. Merriman, W. H. Beavers, Alonza Beheler, Willard Gourley, and Jamie DeShazo. (Courtesy of Teddy Compton.)

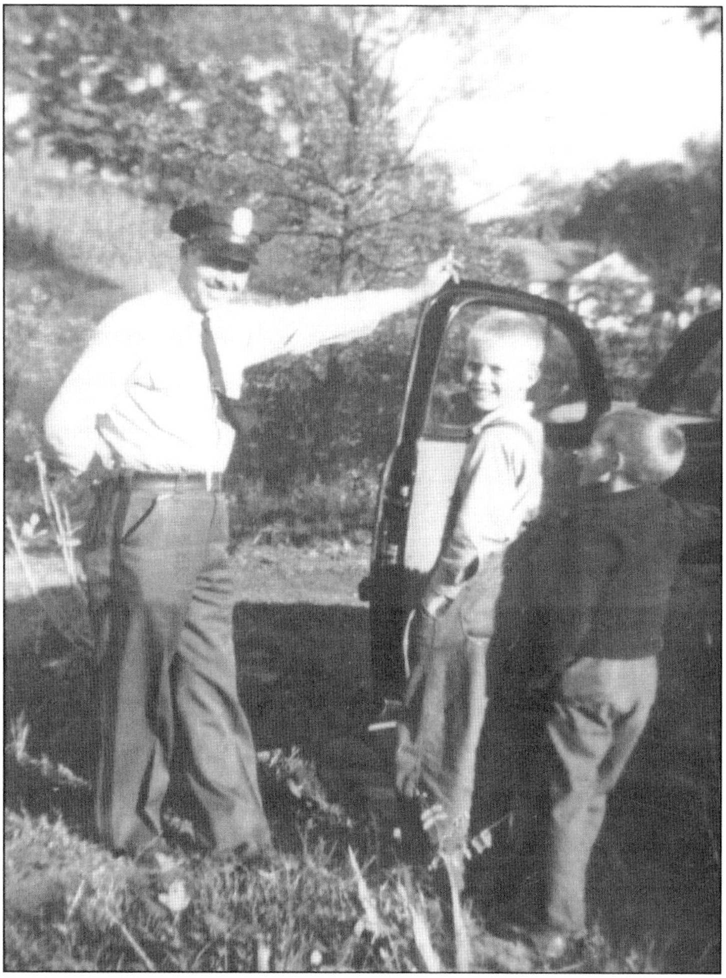

A company town needed law enforcement to keep control. Fieldale police officer John Johnston, shown with his sons Douglas (left) and Warren, represented this need. Sadly John Johnston lost his life in the line of duty along with Herman Ferguson. The first chief of police was H. W. Nester. Others who served were Jesse Stegall, J. W. Slaughter, James Compton, Herman Gray, Ralph Lawless, Jerry Harville, Paul Nichols, and Charlie Bradshaw. Looking like he is on the hunt for Bonnie and Clyde in the 1930s photograph below, Joseph Alfred Stegall served for 56 years in Fieldale. Starting in 1934, youngsters now grown remember his kindness when not directing mill or school traffic. (Above, courtesy of Teddy Compton; below, courtesy of Douglas Stegall.)

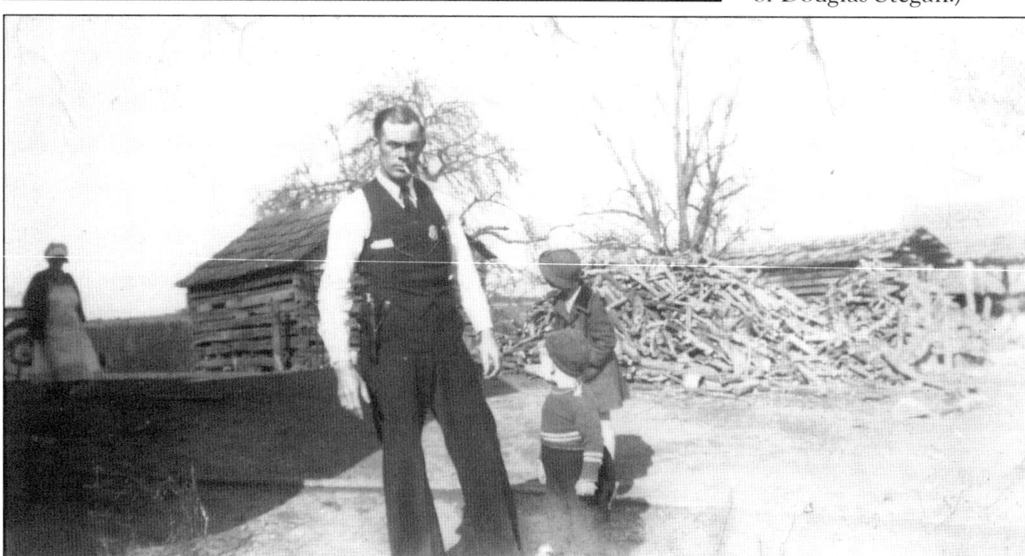

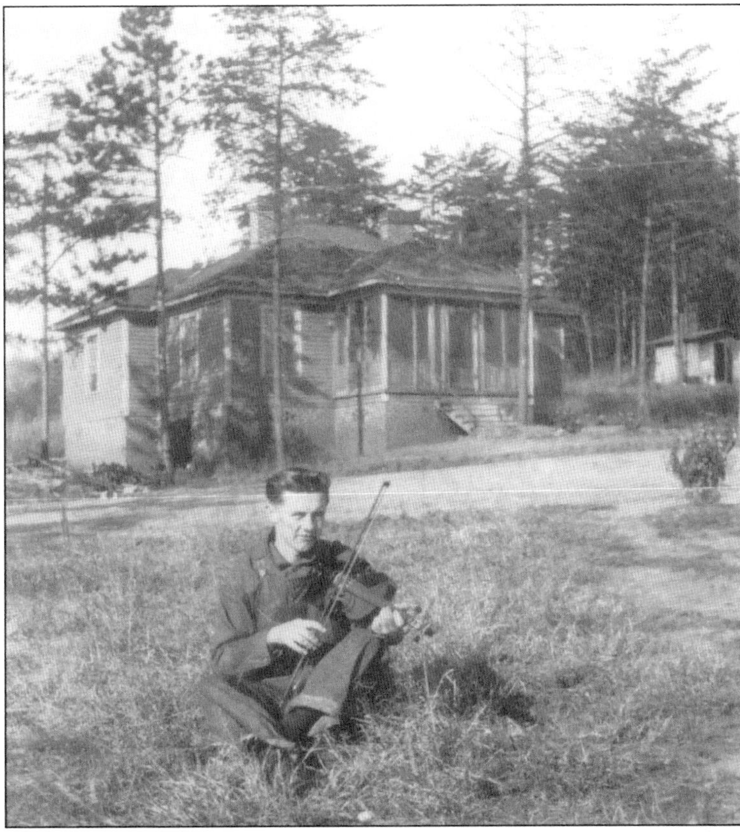

Playing his fiddle on Sawmill Hill, William Merriman began working at Fieldcrest Mills as a shipping clerk. The people of Fieldale entertained themselves with barbecues, parades and great Fourth of July celebrations. Music was and still is a big part of the culture, especially sawing on a fiddle during a bluegrass song. (Courtesy of Teddy Compton.)

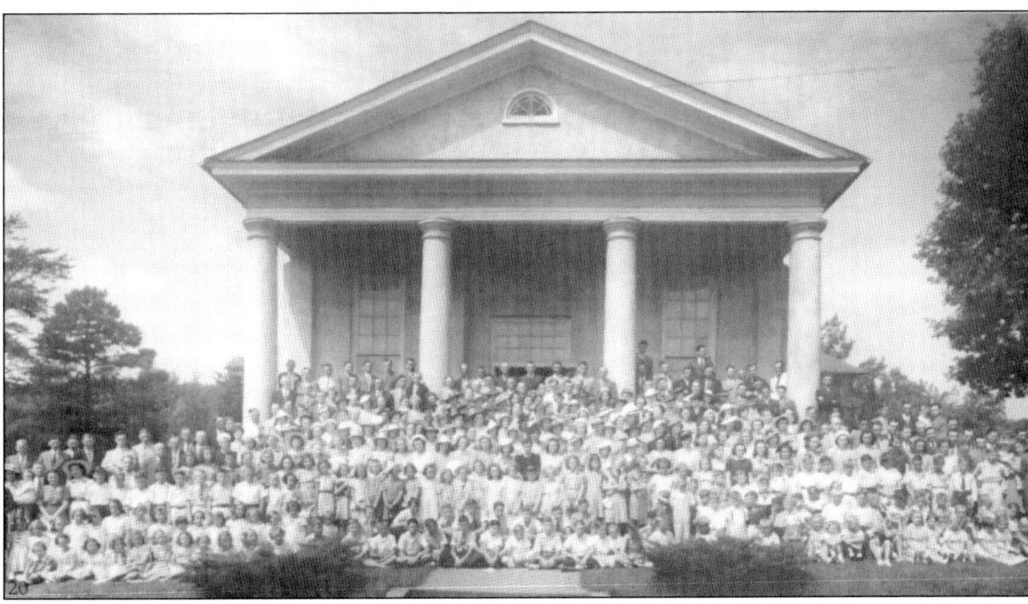

Completed in June 1920, Fieldale Baptist Church was a focal part of community life. It was constructed with help from Marshall Field Company, which deeded the church to the members in the 1950s. The company also deeded the Methodist church to its members and deeded the community recreational and community centers to the town. (Courtesy of Teddy Compton.)

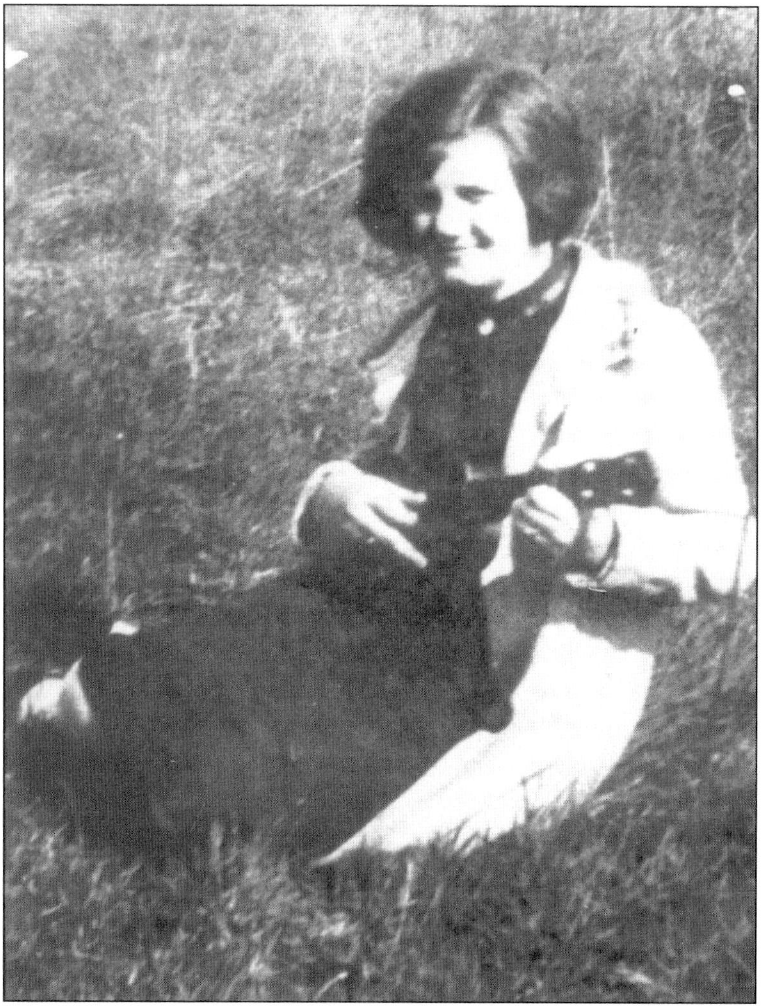

Virginia Merriman Compton wrote a history of Fieldale when not working for 38 years at Fieldcrest Mills handling the orders from Sears Roebuck and teaching Sunday school for 40 years. The daughter of Charles and Mary Lou Merriman, Virginia was the sister of William, George, Ernest, Lucy, Sue, and Polly. (Courtesy of Teddy Compton.)

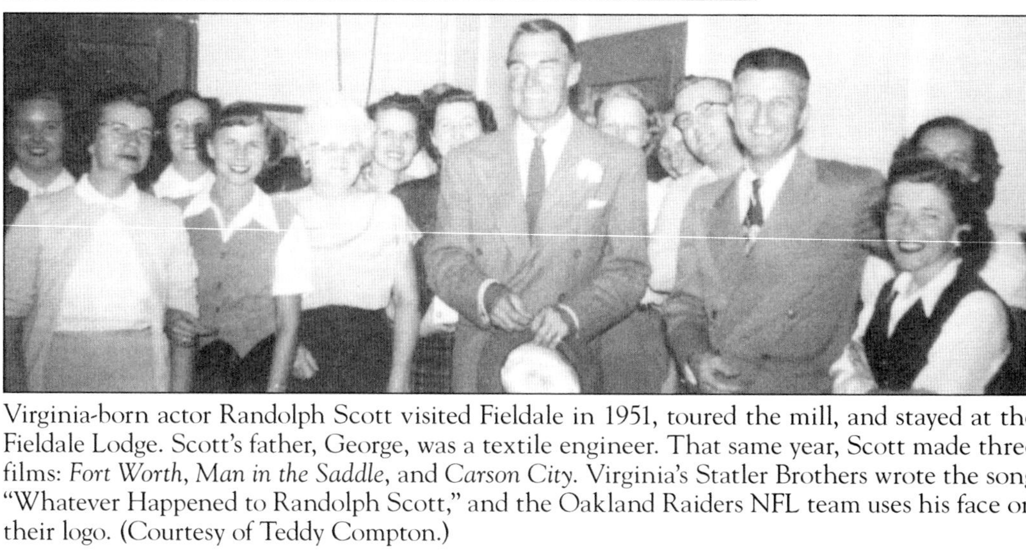

Virginia-born actor Randolph Scott visited Fieldale in 1951, toured the mill, and stayed at the Fieldale Lodge. Scott's father, George, was a textile engineer. That same year, Scott made three films: *Fort Worth*, *Man in the Saddle*, and *Carson City*. Virginia's Statler Brothers wrote the song "Whatever Happened to Randolph Scott," and the Oakland Raiders NFL team uses his face on their logo. (Courtesy of Teddy Compton.)

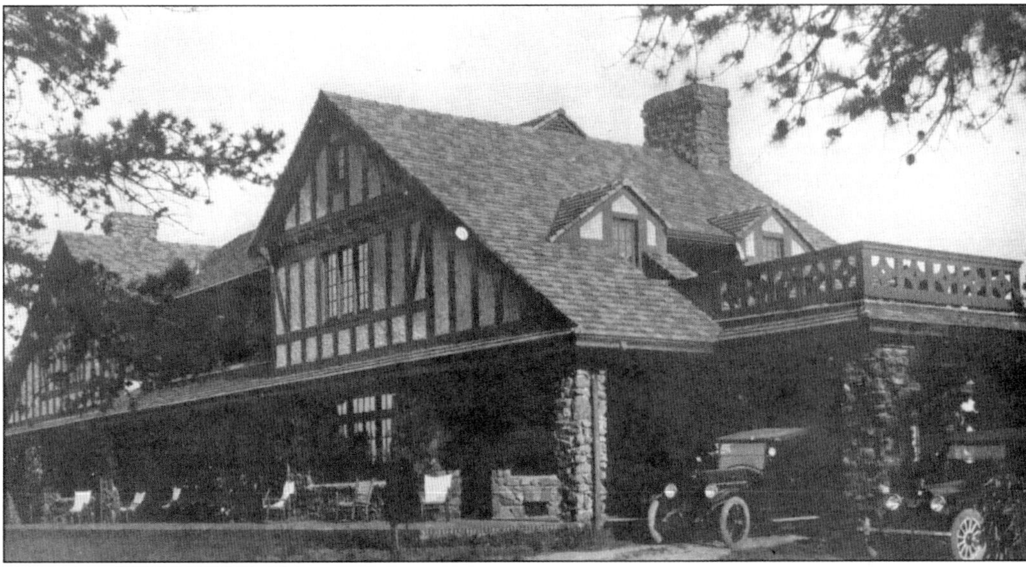

Marshall Field Company built the Marshall Field Company Clubhouse, now the Clubhouse Resort, to house company officials and guests. Affectionately called the Fieldale Lodge, the building sits on 448 acres of land. Construction began in 1917 with mules flattening the top of the mountain. Architect W. C. Northrup designed the English Tudor Revival country house at 8,500 square feet with seven second-floor bedrooms, six main rooms on the first floor, a billiard room, a sunroom, and east and west balconies. The house is on the National Register of Historic Places. Guests included actor Randolph Scott and Fieldcrest spokesperson and actor Mary Martin. It is now open for visitors again. (Courtesy of Anne Copeland.)

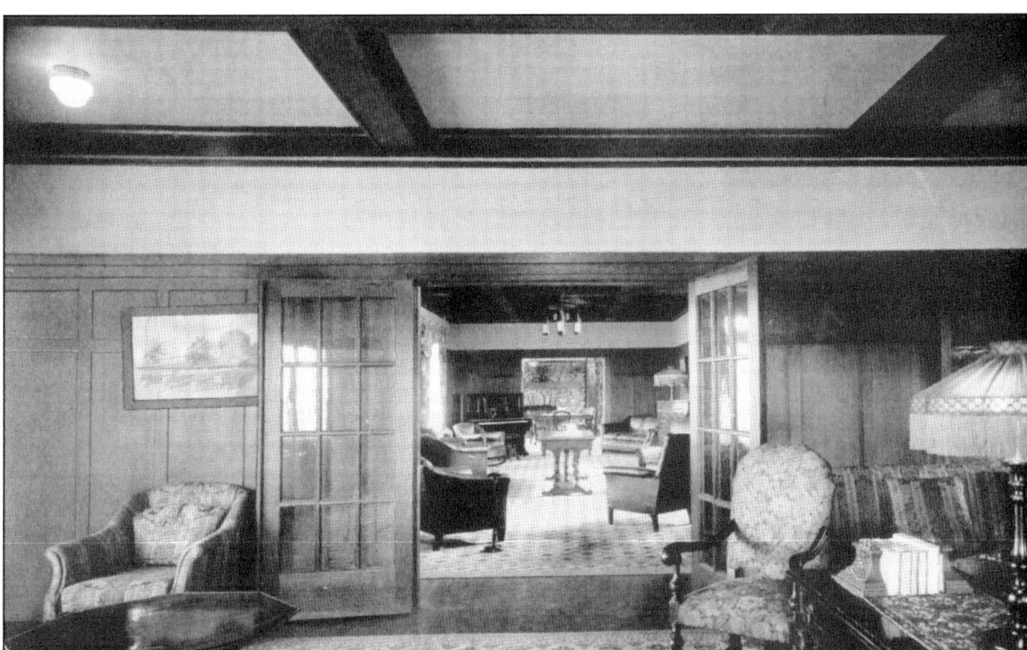

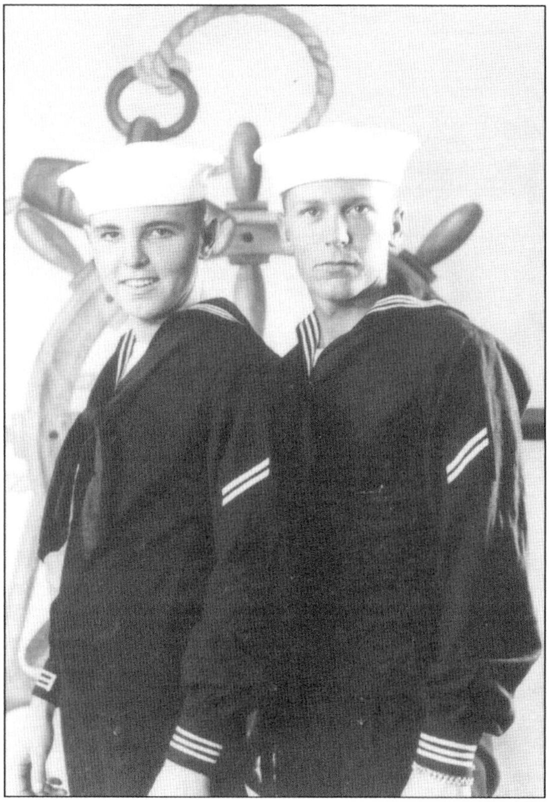

Fieldale's sons went off to war in World War II and Korea. Emory Pace Jr. (left), the son of Emory and Mattie Compton Pace, and Roy Harrell, the son of Gilbert Harrell, shown in this 1951 image, served in the U.S. Navy during the Korean War. Both came home to their parents. (Courtesy of Teddy Compton.)

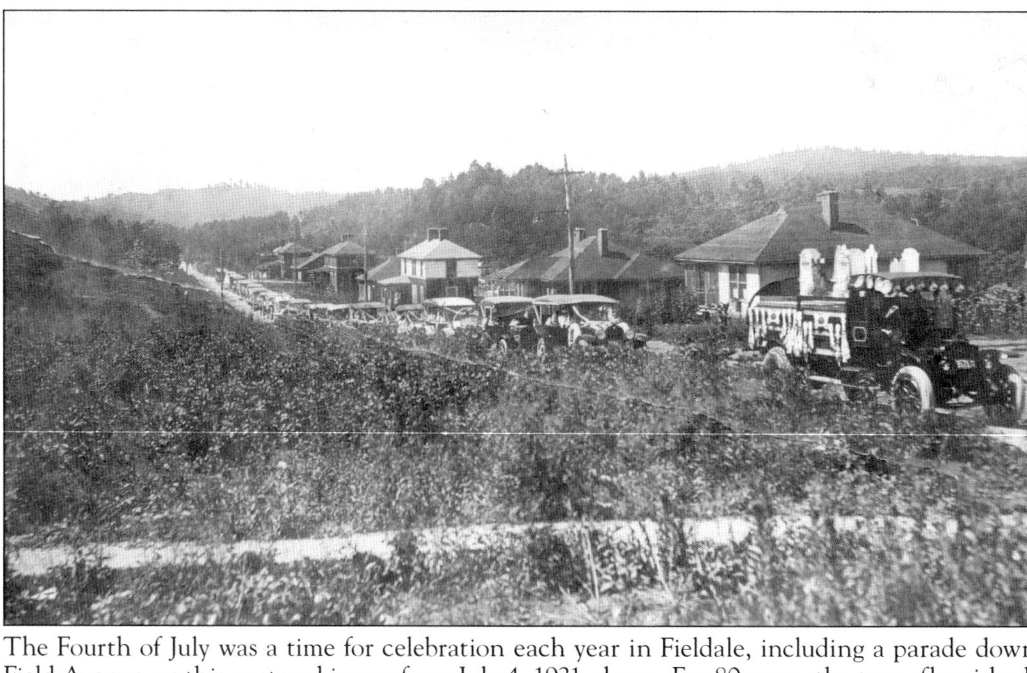

The Fourth of July was a time for celebration each year in Fieldale, including a parade down Field Avenue, as this postcard image from July 4, 1921, shows. For 80 years, the town flourished, insulated from the outside world by the economic security that a company town allowed, and the people enjoyed life. (Courtesy of Anne Copeland.)

After leaving Boones Mill in Franklin County at age 17, Cyrus D. Looney served in the U.S. Navy during World War I, as this image found in the library of the Fieldale Methodist Church shows. Looney came to Fieldale and worked 50 years for Marshall Field Company. He operated a saw-sharpening and woodworking shop after retiring. (Courtesy of Teddy Compton.)

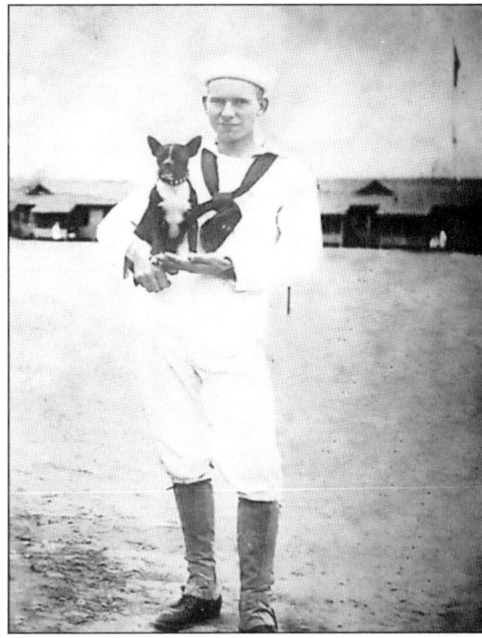

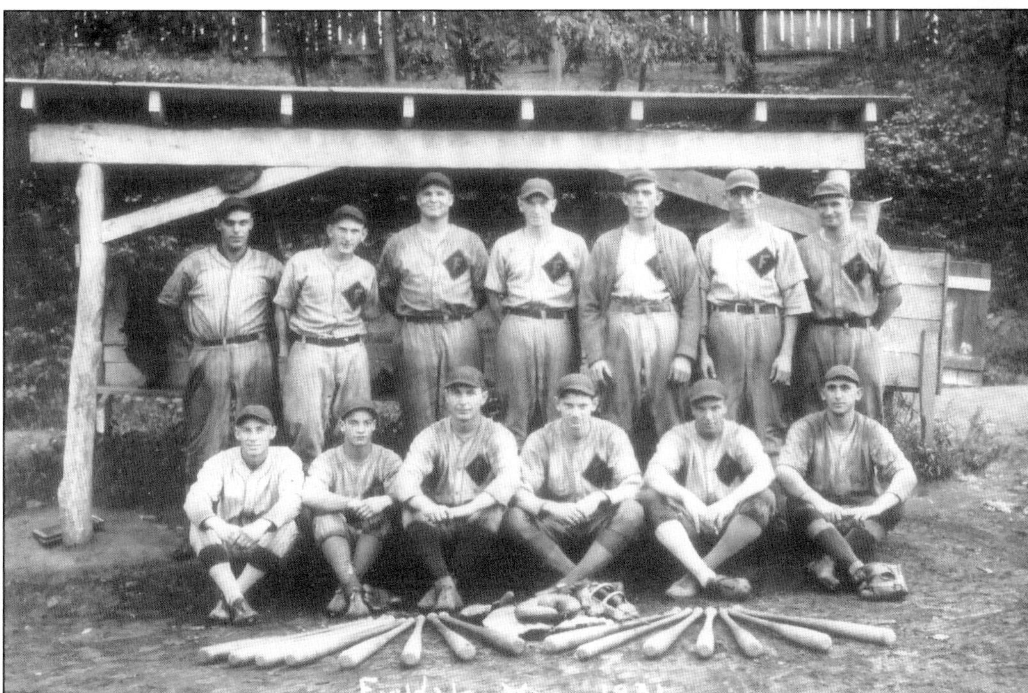

The Fieldale baseball team of 1931 played in the Bi-State League, which included teams from 10 towns North Carolina and 8 from Virginia. Teams from Henry County were the Fieldale Virginians (1934), Fieldale Towlers (1935–1936), Bassett Furnituremakers (1935–1940), and Martinsville Manufacturers (1934–1941). This photograph includes Hurst Morton, Frank Tipton, Clyde Joyce, J. Alfred Stegall, Lonnie Harrington, Turner Gilbert, Marvin Lentz, Paul Copeland, and Charlie Caudell. (Courtesy of Douglas Stegall.)

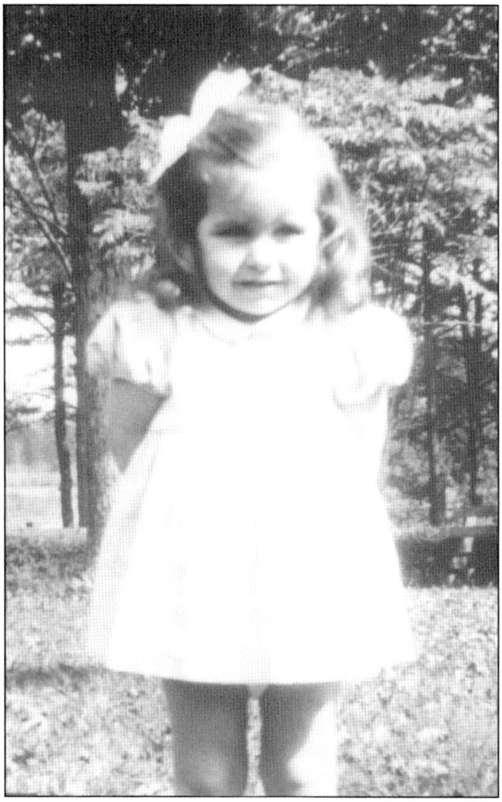

Mary Anne Copeland, the daughter of Eugene Herman and Mary Hurd Copeland, lives in the 1927 Plant Manager House in Fieldale. This image shows her at age three visiting her grandparent's home in Rangley with a 1936 Chevrolet in the background. It reflects the author's appreciation for her assistance with his work on history in her position at the Bassett Historical Center. She has the last word in this book. (Courtesy of Anne Copeland.)

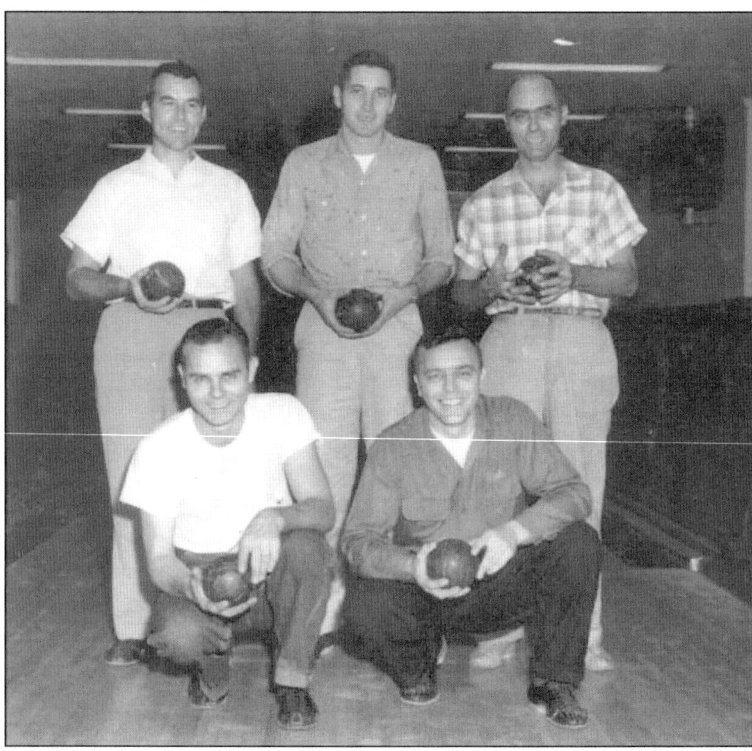

Duckpin bowling was an amusement for Fieldale residents like (first row, from left to right) George Horsley and Ned Horsley; (second row, from left to right) Lane Gusler, Doug Gilbert, and Mass Horsley. Among their nicknames were Wahoo, Hoyt, and Slingshot. They bowled in the YMCA (now the community center) in Fieldale. (Courtesy of Teddy Compton.)

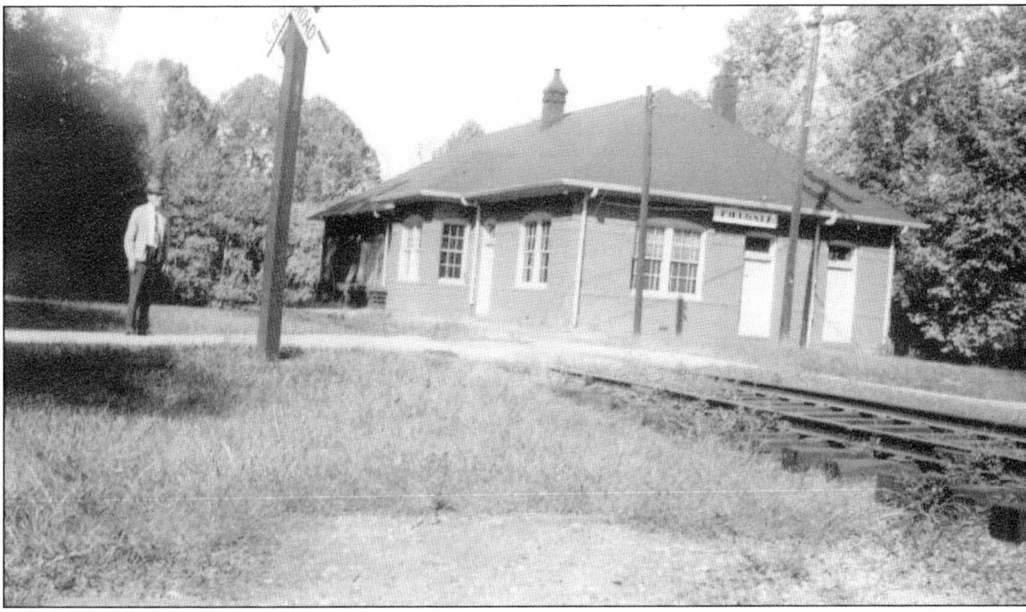

Fieldale used two railroads. The station above was for the Danville and Western, known as the "Dick and Willie." This building along the Smith River, still standing today, was for moving freight for the nearby Fieldcrest Mill, which was vital for the economic prosperity of the town. When the Smith River flooded, the mill offered prizes to the townspeople who washed and cleaned the most towels. The Norfolk and Western Railway, and the Danville and Western used the station below at nearby Koehler jointly for many years, but it was torn down around 1973. (Courtesy of Douglas Stegall.)

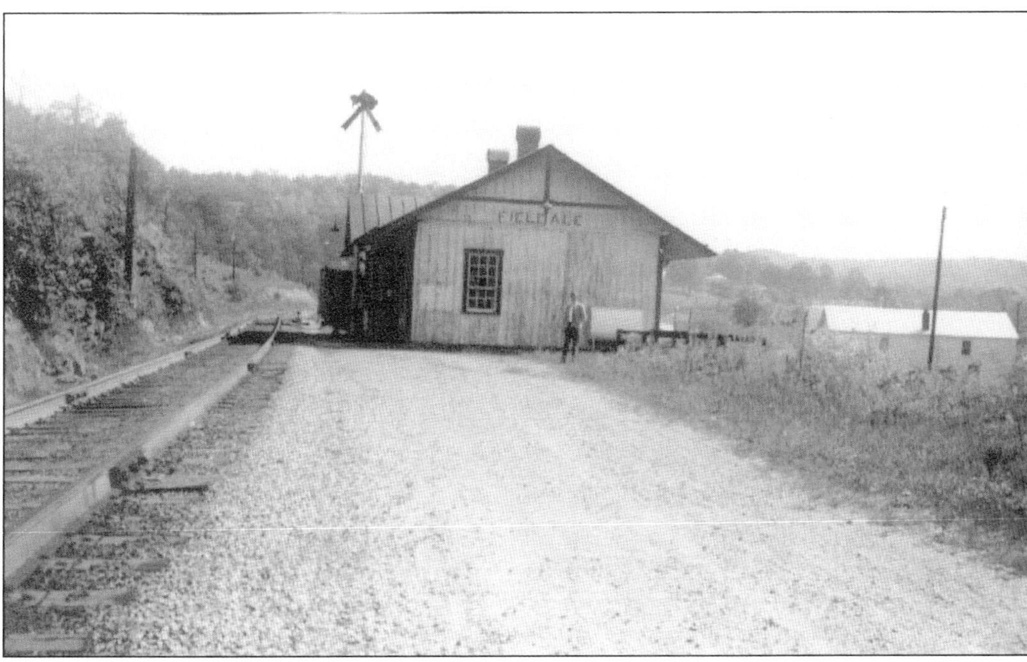

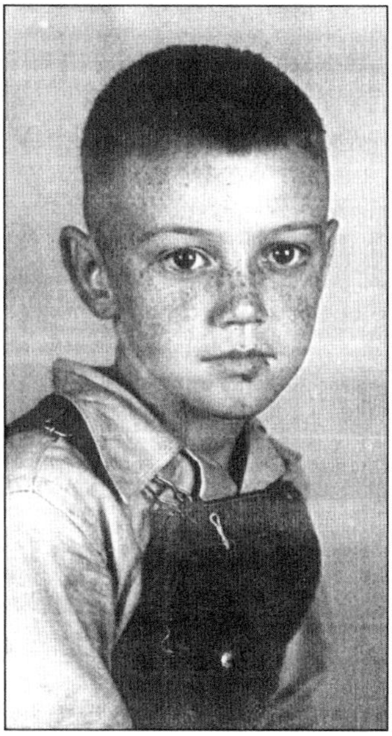

Teddy Compton, pictured in the fourth grade at Fieldale Elementary School, was the son of the previously mentioned Virginia Compton. He grew up to work at DuPont in Martinsville and married Margaret Creasy. He volunteers at the Bassett Historical Center, and this book would not exist without his assistance by sharing his large collection of photographs. (Courtesy of Teddy Compton.)

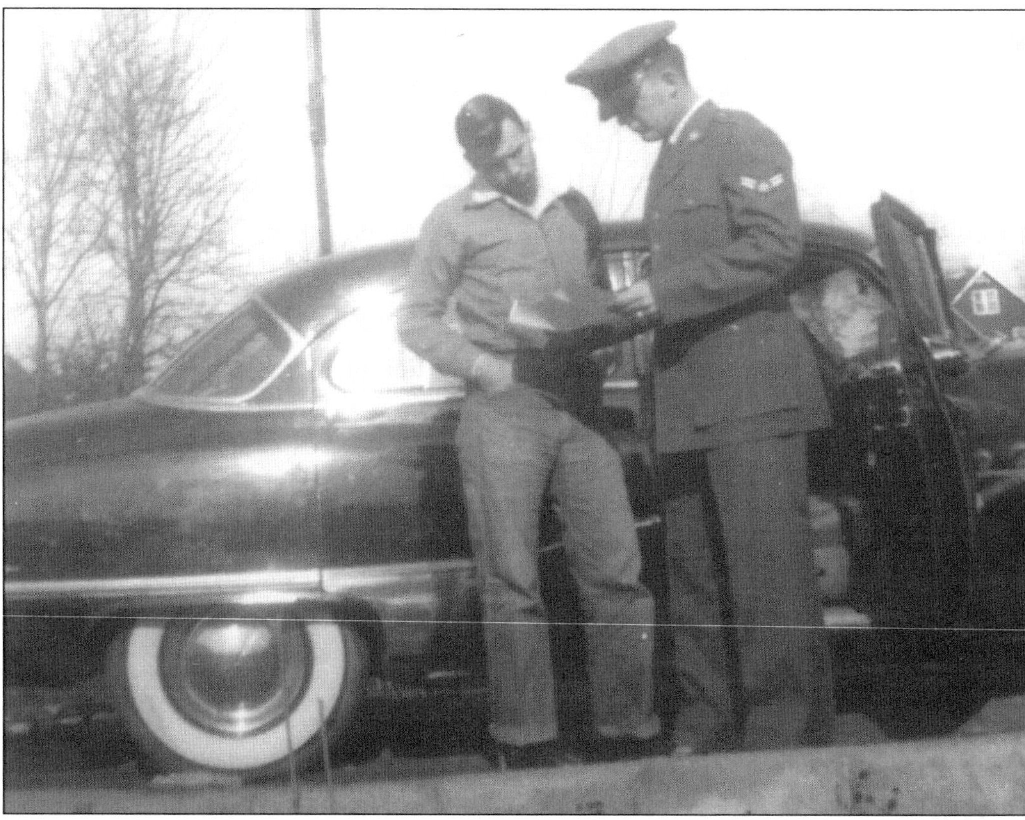

Continuing a long line of men from Fieldale to serve in the armed forces of the United States, Ronald Derl Compton of the U.S. Air Force shows Alton Wilkinson of the U.S. Navy his orders in this 1954 image. Ronnie was the son of Virginia Compton and sibling of Jenna Lou and Teddy Compton. (Courtesy of Teddy Compton.)

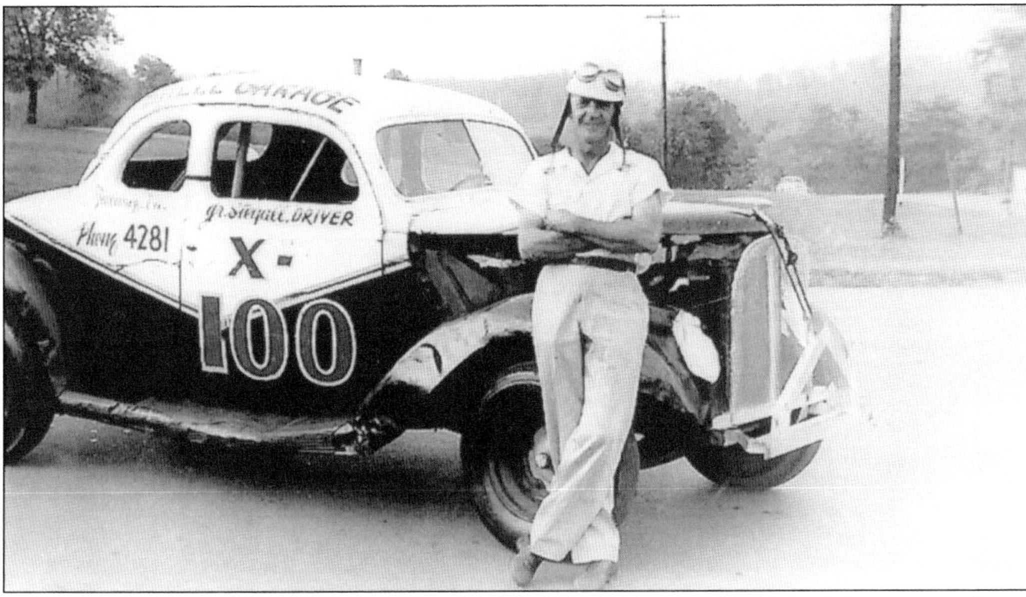

Percy James Adams is pictured at his Fieldale Shell filling station in 1950s with his racecar, driven by Junior Stegall. Adams left to become a special officer for the Stanleytown police. Dirt-track racing continues at Oak Level Raceway in northern Henry County as it has since 1978, with six classes of cars every Friday night. (Courtesy of Teddy Compton.)

Emory Goode started as foreman of the packing and shipping department and became superintendent of the Fieldcrest Hosiery Mill in 1933. Goode managed it for the next 22 years, until the mill closed. He went into the insurance business until 1979, when he died at Fieldale Baptist Church, where he worshipped. (Courtesy of Teddy Compton.)

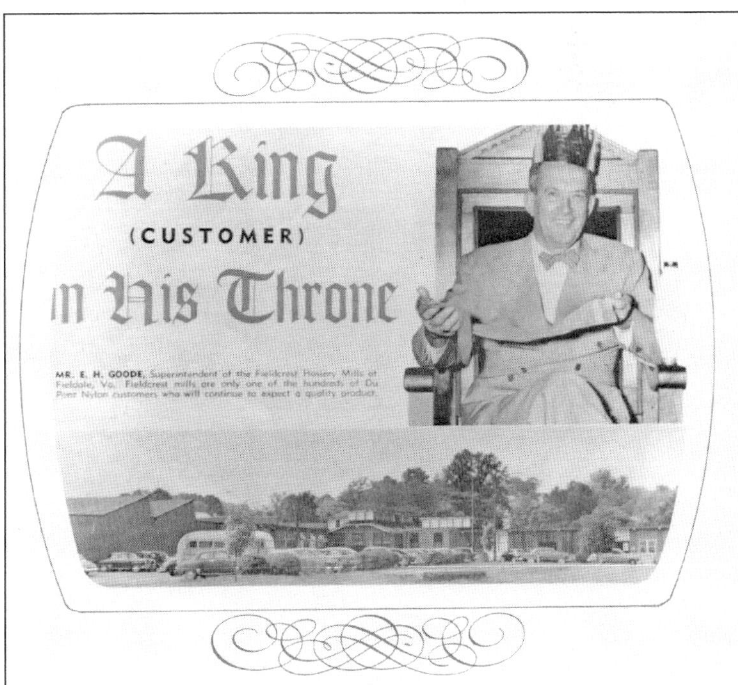

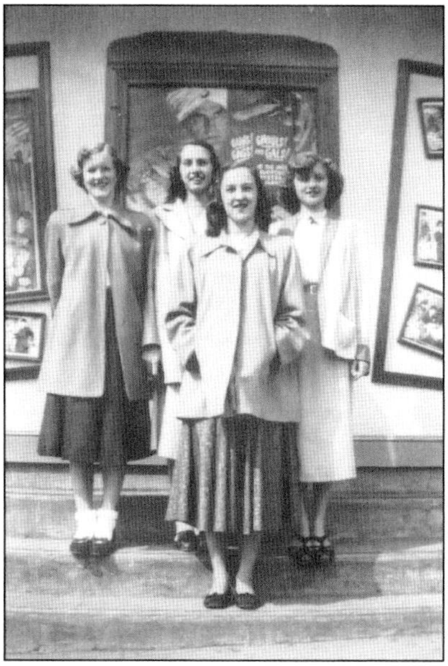

The Dale Theater was the center of entertainment in Fieldale, as these ladies could attest. Pictured from left to right are Molly Shelton, Loretta Pruitt, Becky Wilkinson, and Jean Graham. The theater served other purposes, such as the site of a 1932 meeting to avert a strike of the local high school students, who threatened to walk out when the Henry County School Board replaced principal Marvin Lentz. (Courtesy of Teddy Compton.)

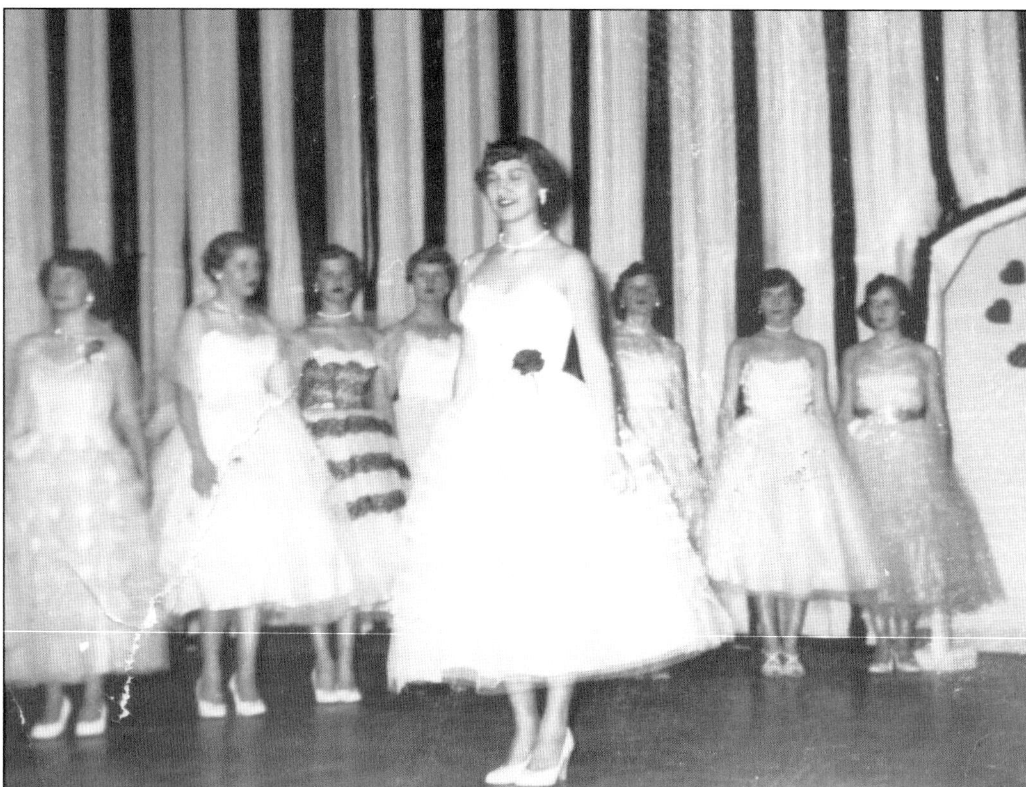

Looking like the actress that shares her name, Joan Allen was the first runner-up in the Fieldale High School Beauty Pageant in 1955. Others in the photograph include Betty Turner (third from left) and Elvena Plaster (fourth from left). Joan and Jesse Frith's daughter, Joella, competed in beauty pageants like her mother, receiving Miss Congeniality in the Little Miss Martinsville Pageant. (Courtesy of Joan Frith.)

Maude Franklin Childress (1904–1990) grew up in Martinsville but moved to Fieldale. This image of her from the 1920s reflects the flapper style before the Great Depression, which did not influence the company town on the Smith River as other places in the country suffered through economic downturns. (Courtesy of Anne Copeland.)

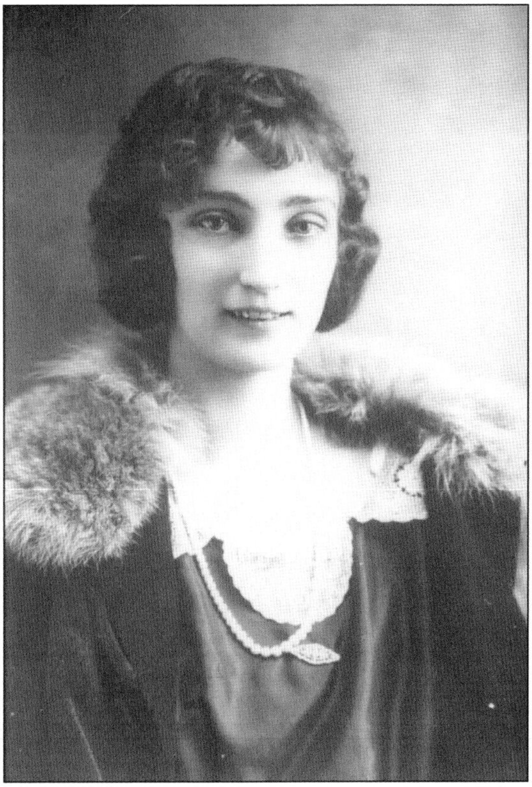

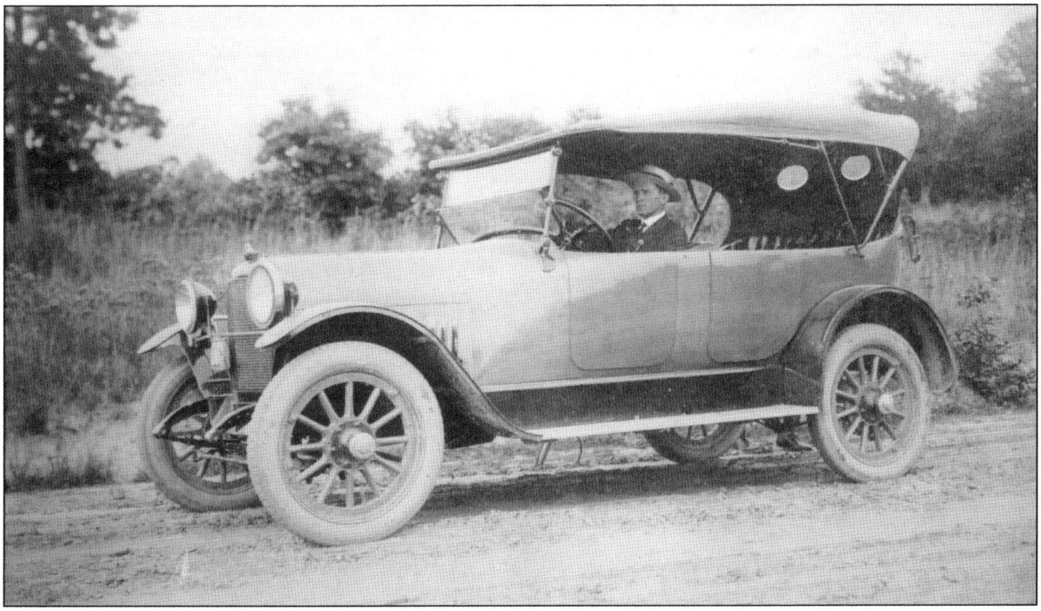

With the coming of the Marshall Field Company, the need for better transportation including trains, planes, and automobiles came to Fieldale and Henry County. George Cabell Davis (1881–1968), the son of John William and Betty Turner Davis, is making his way around the dirt roads of Henry County. Access to the factory made better roads a necessity. The first hard-surfaced road built in Henry County was from Martinsville to Fieldale. (Courtesy of Anne Copeland.)

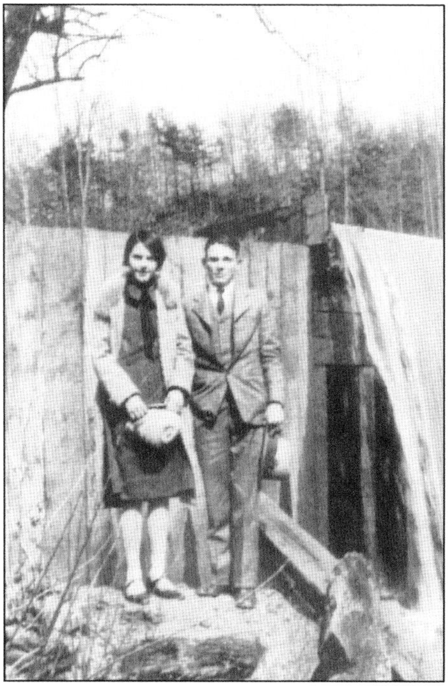

Before Marshall Field Company made towels at Fieldale, industry in the form of grist and sawmills lined the Smith River and its tributaries. This image from 1930 shows Harvie and Glenwood Prillaman at the Rough and Ready Mill, which was built along Reed Creek to grind grain for local farmers. (Courtesy of Betsy Whitlow.)

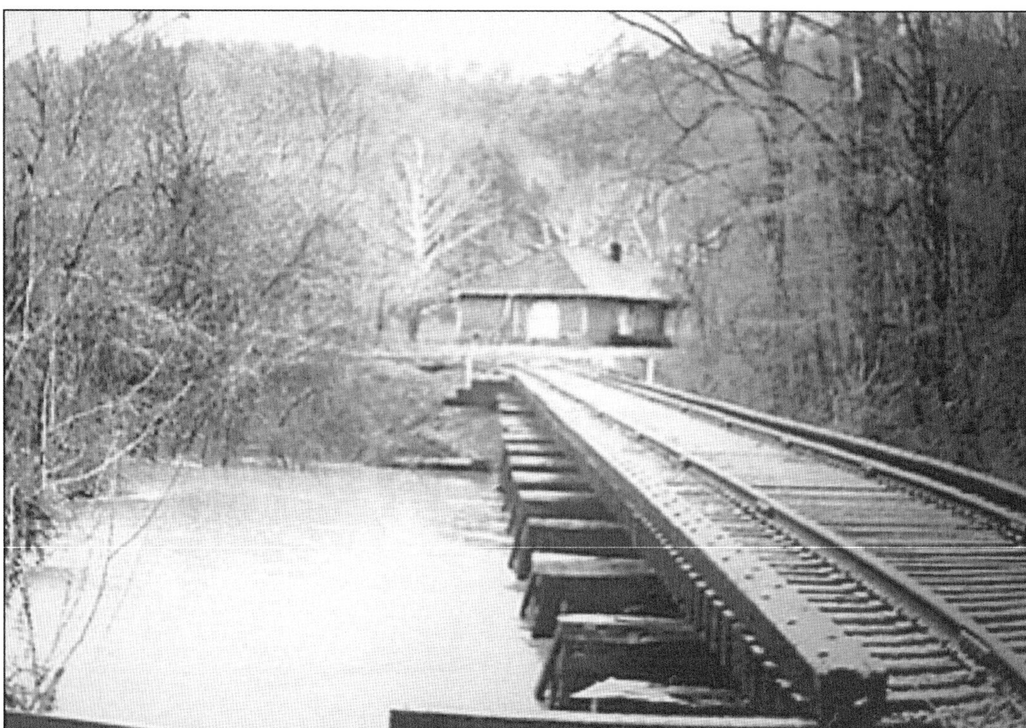

The Danville and Western Railroad, known locally as the "Dick and Willie," ran from Danville to Stuart, Virginia. This station served the railroad along the Smith River at Fieldale. The original plan linked the railroad with rail service along the New River, but due to financial problems, the railroad never went further west. (Courtesy of Teddy Compton.)

This image of J. William Merriman riding his horse with his 1933 Buick in the background reflects the changes he witnessed in his life. Merriman began his career at the mill in Fieldale on October 11, 1920, and stayed on the payroll until he retired as foreman of the packing, stock room, shipping, and storage department in 1968. (Courtesy of Teddy Compton.)

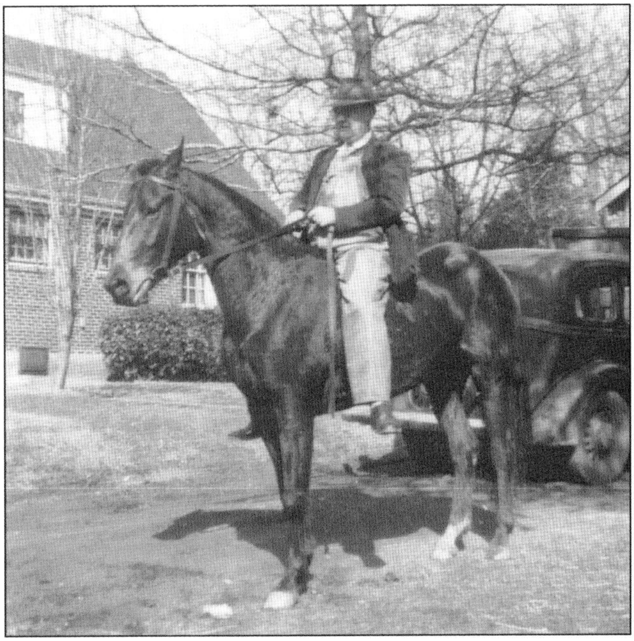

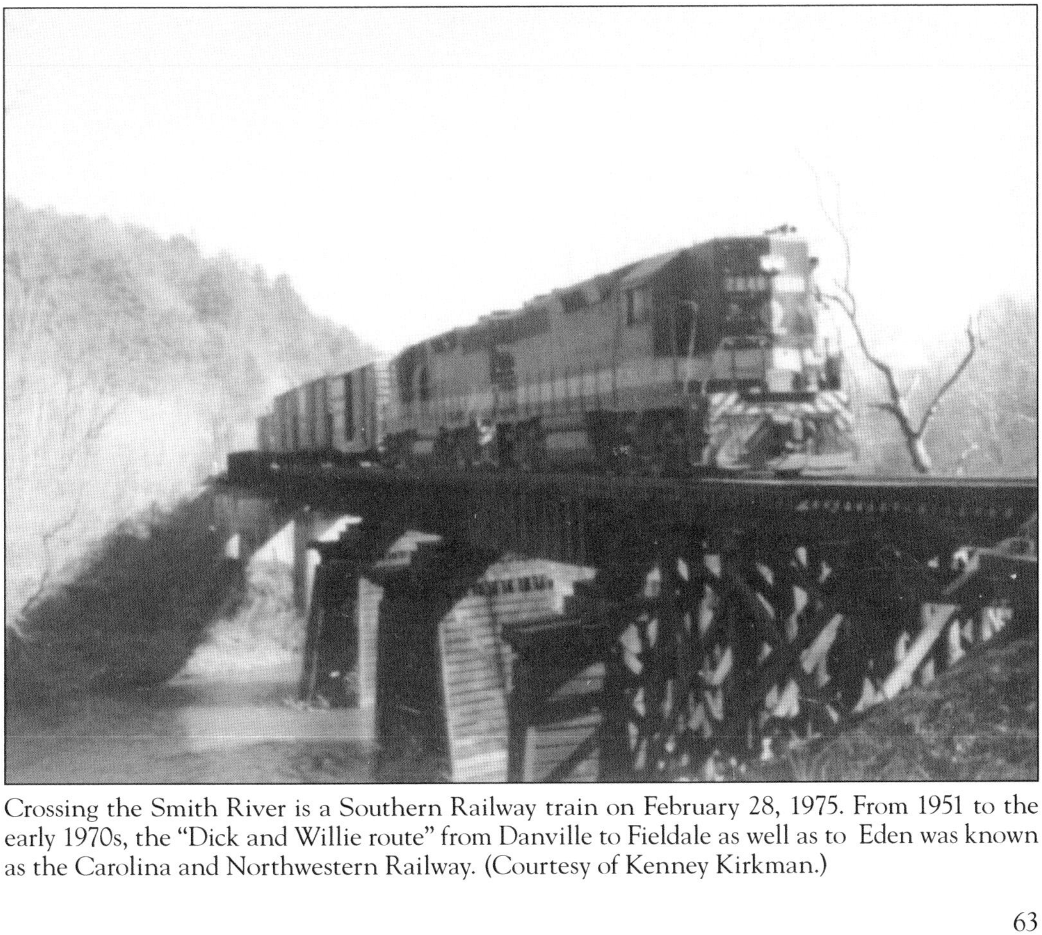

Crossing the Smith River is a Southern Railway train on February 28, 1975. From 1951 to the early 1970s, the "Dick and Willie route" from Danville to Fieldale as well as to Eden was known as the Carolina and Northwestern Railway. (Courtesy of Kenney Kirkman.)

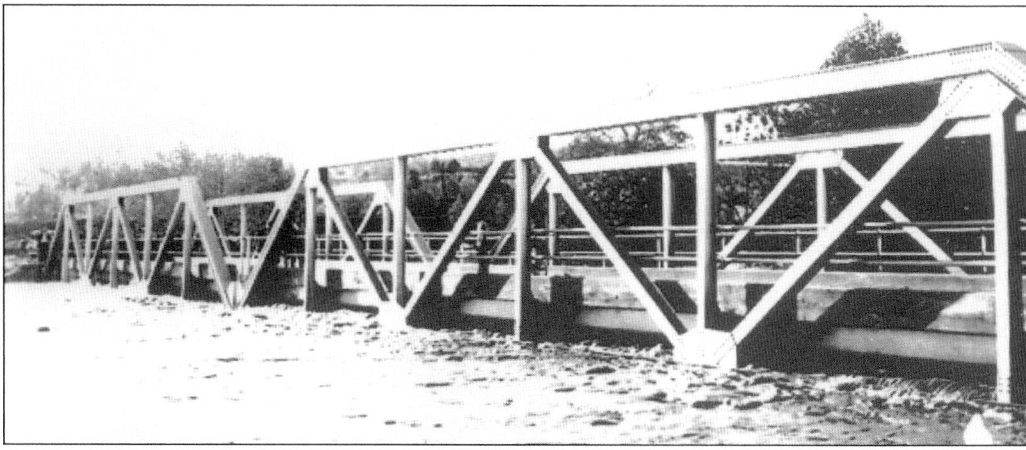

Two images show the flooding Smith River in 1937 and later at the Iron Bridge at Fieldale. Six years earlier, the bridge at this site fell into the river, but no one was hurt. Without the bridge, vehicles had to go to Stanleytown and around to Bassett to make it to Fieldale. Before the construction of the Philpott Dam and Reservoir, the town and mill were at the mercy of the rising water. Power interruptions along with the delay in vehicle and railroad transportation hurt the operation of Marshall Field Company and later Fieldcrest Cannon. (Courtesy of Teddy Compton.)

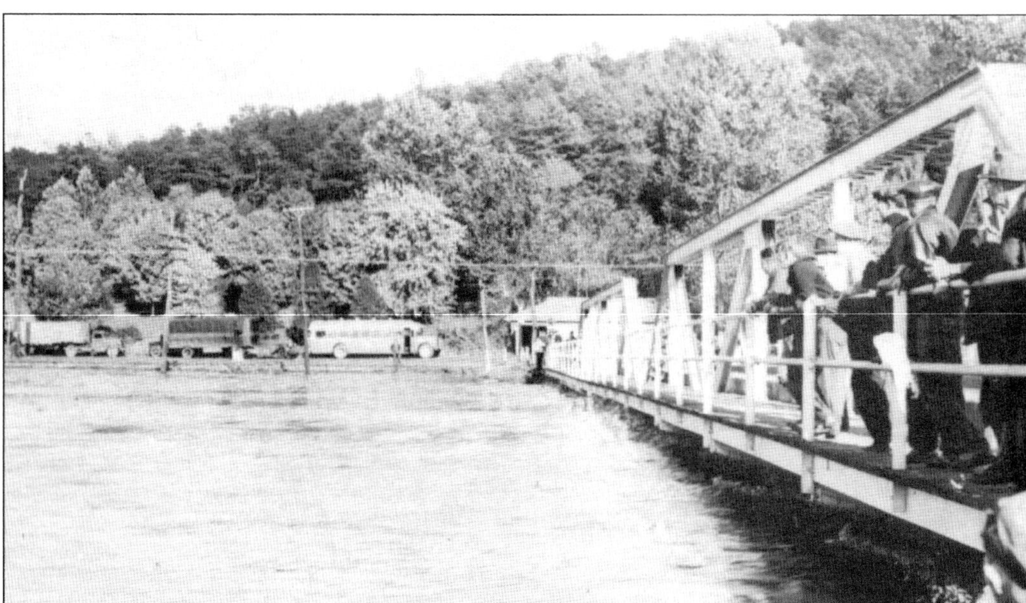

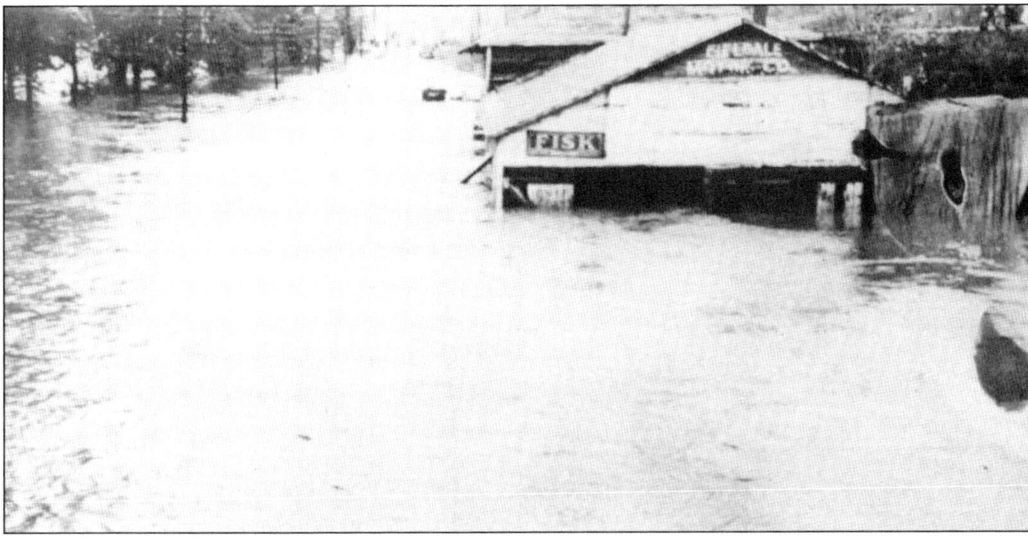

These images show the Arthur Haynes service station, known as the Whippet dealership, south of the River Bridge during the 1937 flood at Fieldale. The normal bed of the Smith River is seen at the top left of this image, giving the reader an idea of the destruction the stream caused during floods. Coy Campbell stands at the Esso gasoline pumps at Haynes Service Station during the 1937 flood. Today Exxon-Mobil continues the brand name for those not old enough to remember Esso, and the Philpott Dam controls the flooding so that neither of the scenes will occur again. (Courtesy of Teddy Compton.)

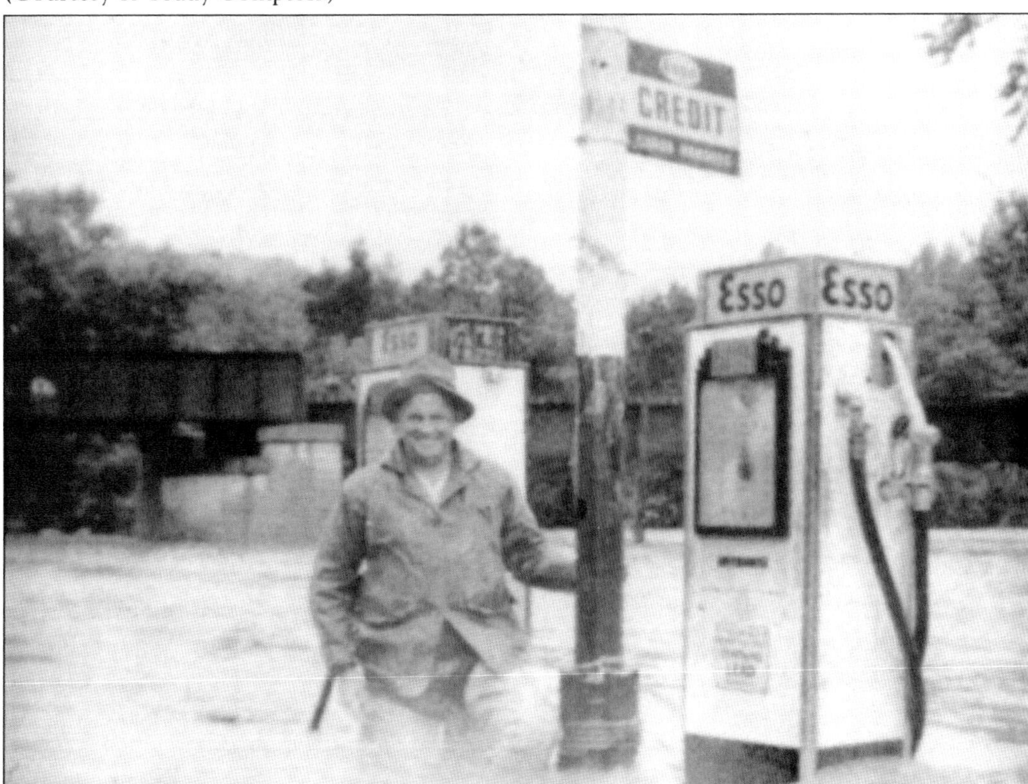

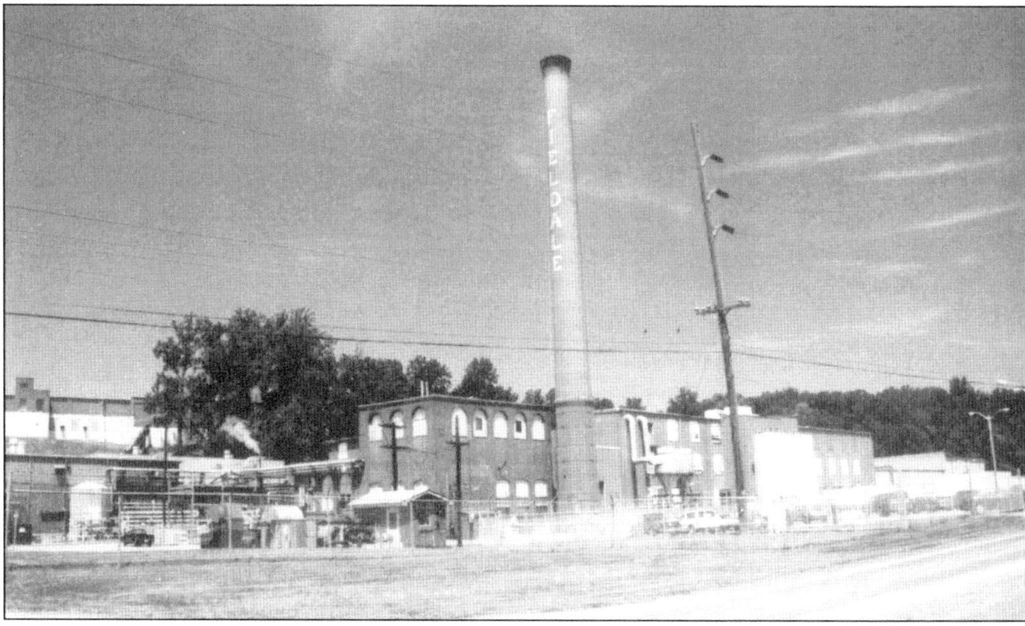

In 1917, Marshall Field Company purchased 1,800 acres and began construction on a plant that eventually took up 4 acres. Production of cloth towels began in 1919. The town of Fieldale takes it name from the family. For the next 80 years, until the plant closed in 2003, the community flourished. Lois Quadrio said of life in the community, "If you grew up in Fieldale you knew everyone. It was like a big family in the mill." Fieldcrest Mills became Fieldcrest Cannon in 1985 and finally Pillowtex, who declared bankruptcy and closed the plant. The weave room in the mill, shown below, was part of a 550-foot-long, 250-foot-wide mill that contained 19,200 spindles and 530 looms that manufactured towels. (Above, courtesy of Teddy Compton; below, courtesy of Anne Copeland.)

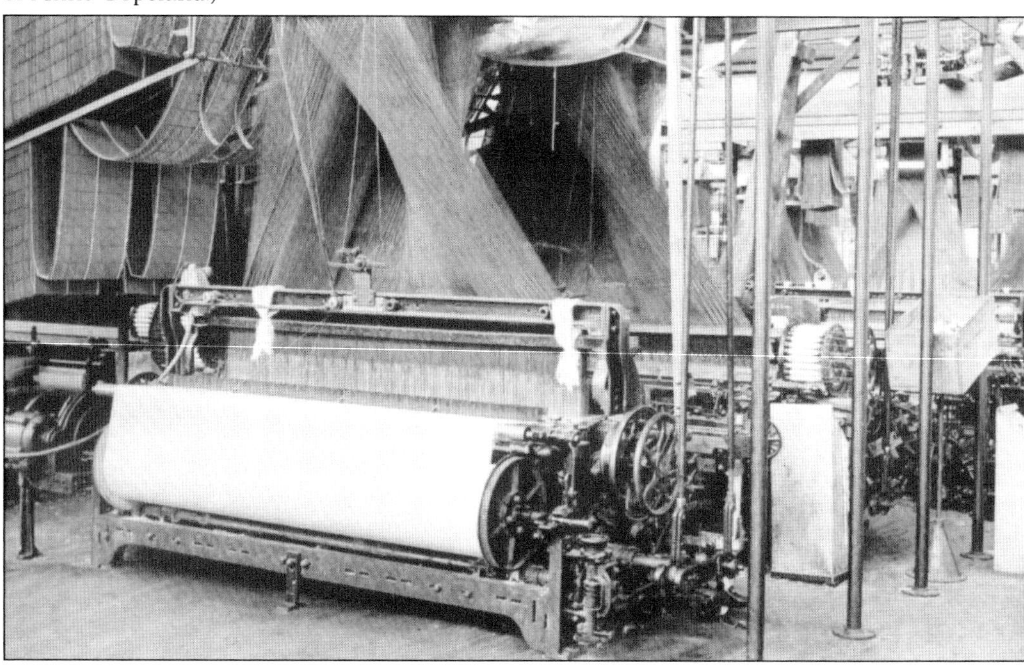

Three

MARTINSVILLE

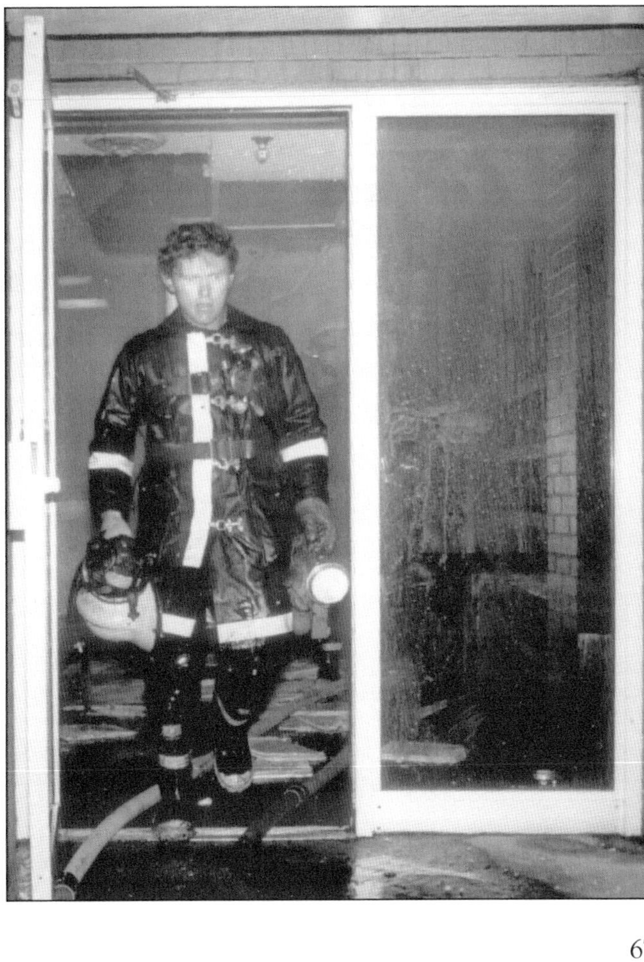

Jerry Brock, chief of the Martinsville Fire Department from 1997 until 2006, is pictured in February 1980 leaving the Pannill Knitting Company fire. Chief Brock, one of 13 men to hold the position of fire chief, shared many of the photographs included in this chapter. Relatives of J. E. B. Stuart started Pannill Knitting, one of the many textile firms that once dominated the area. (Courtesy of the Jerry Brock Collection.)

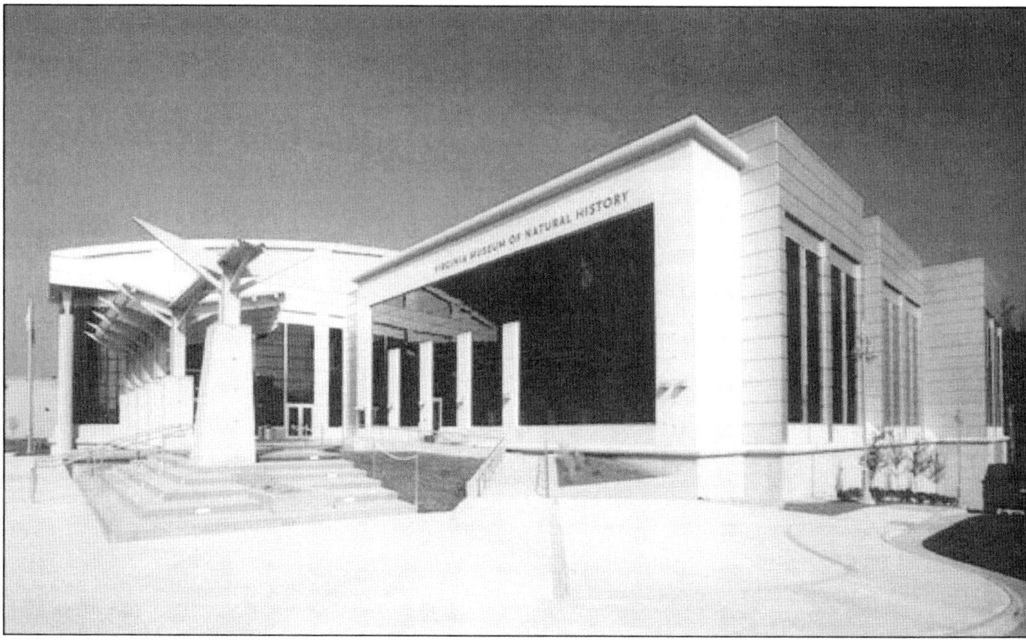

The Virginia Museum of Natural History began in 1984 as the Boaz Foundation. In 2007, the museum moved into a world-class facility in Martinsville after many years in a local school. Affiliated with the Commonwealth of Virginia's Secretary of Natural Resources, this attraction gives the area a new tourism and educational facility. (Courtesy of the Bassett Historical Center.)

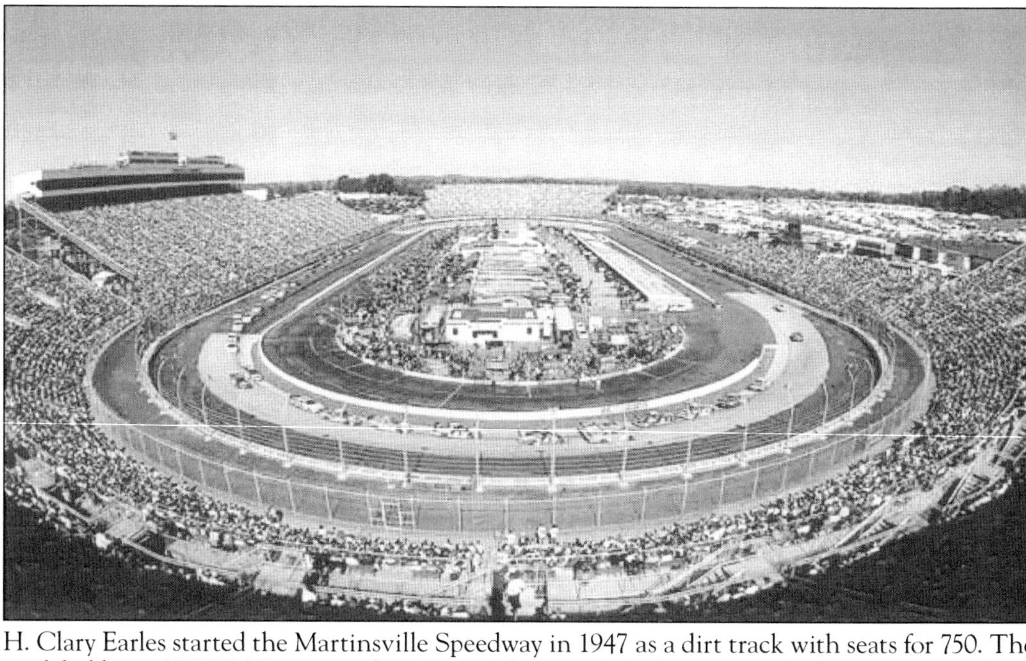

H. Clary Earles started the Martinsville Speedway in 1947 as a dirt track with seats for 750. The track holds two NASCAR races each year, contributing a significant economic impact in the region with over 100,000 attending each race. Richard Petty, "The King," won the most races, with 15 wins at the half-mile track south of Martinsville. (Courtesy of the Bassett Historical Center.)

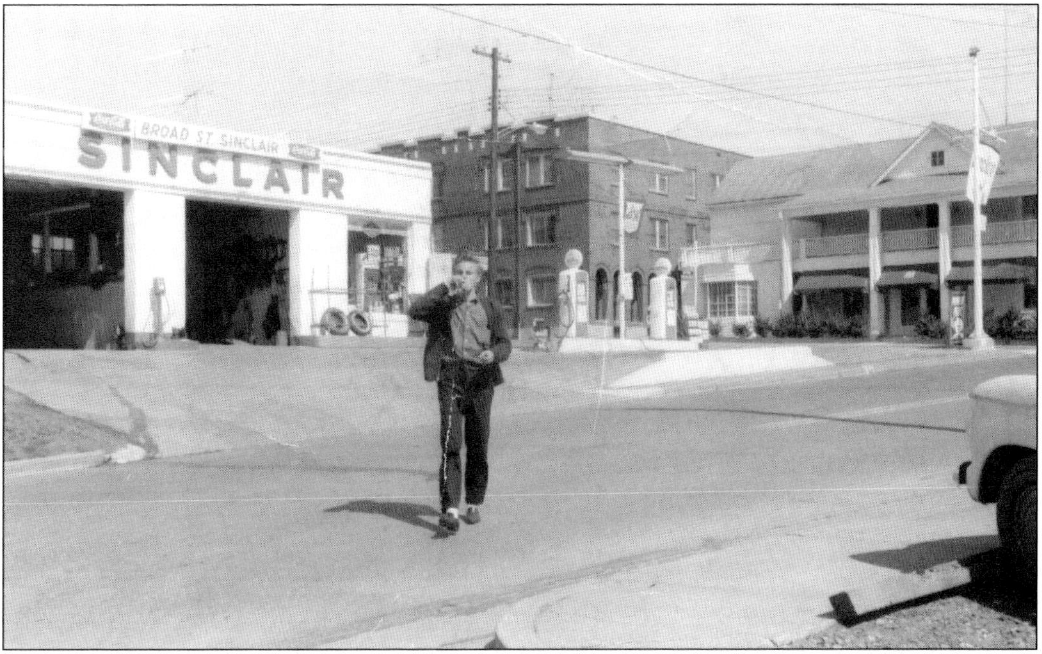

David Minter enjoys a cold Coca-Cola from a Sinclair filling station on Chestnut Street in Martinsville in September 1964 as he strides towards the Broad Street Hotel. The McKee Funeral Home is on the right. Notice the S&H Green Stamps sign and the white socks of a dude enjoying a summer day. (Courtesy of David Minter.)

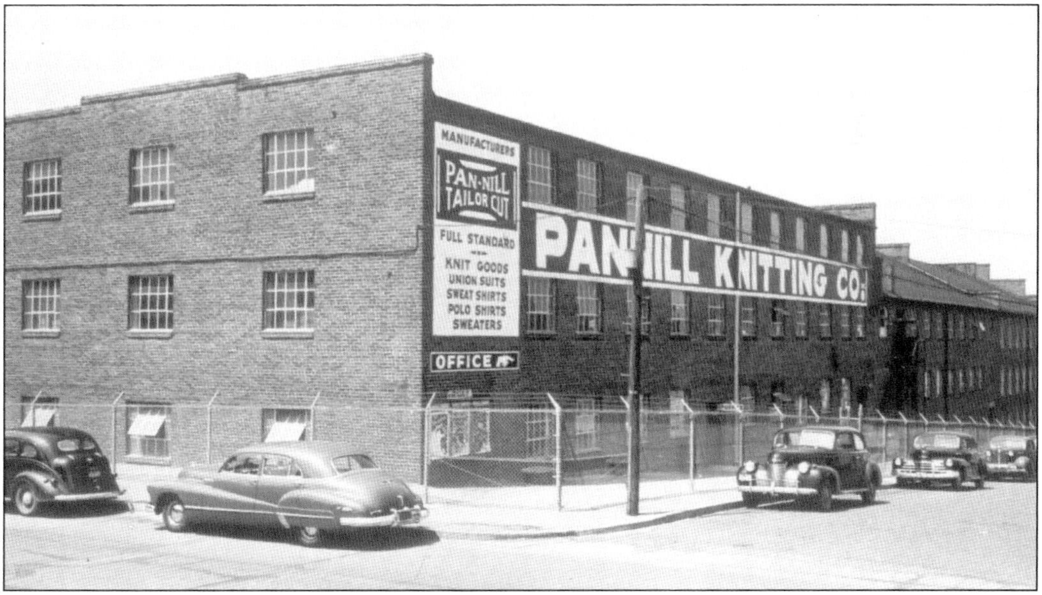

Like the furniture industry, the textile industry became a mainstay of the economy of Henry County, with facilities such as Pannill Knitting Company on Cleveland and Water Streets in Martinsville. The Pannills were descended from William Letcher Pannill, the uncle of Civil War general J. E. B. Stuart of neighboring Patrick County. All were descended from William Letcher, the great-grandfather of Stuart, who died during the American Revolution. (Courtesy of the Jerry Brock Collection.)

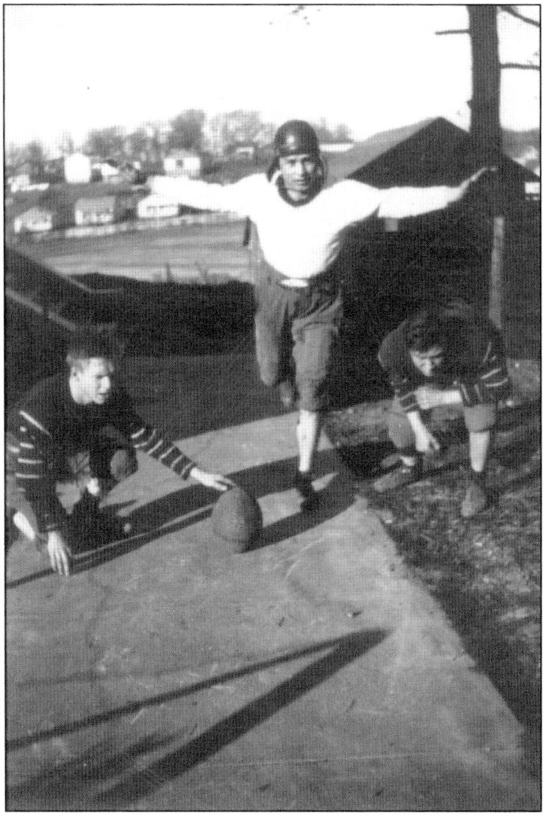

Eugene Copeland, when not kicking footballs at Martinsville High School, worked at Faggs Drugstore. He carpooled from Fieldale to play football. Called "the girls' pet" or the "soda jerker," he graduated in 1929. His interest in girls ended one day when, just as if in a scene from *It's a Wonderful Life*, his future wife, Mary Hurd, walked in. (Courtesy of Anne Copeland.)

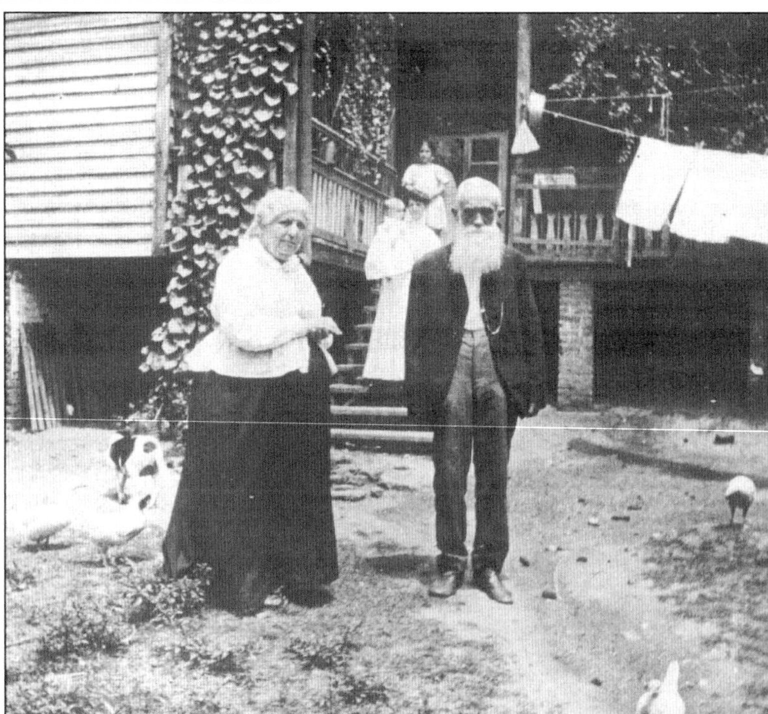

Dr. Henry M. Drewry and his wife, Flora, are pictured with chickens, ducks, dogs, and children at their home on the corner of Church and Cleveland Streets in Martinsville. Drewry-Mason School gets its name partly from the doctor. Notice the laundry drying on the rope and the ivy growing along the side of the house. (Courtesy of John Bing.)

Sonny Wade of Martinsville High School was Virginia College Player of the Year three times, playing at Emory and Henry College from 1966 to 1968. Drafted by the Philadelphia Eagles, Wade chose to play for the Montreal Alloutres of the Canadian Football League, leading them to three championships and earning the same number of Most Valuable Player awards. (Courtesy of the Bassett Historical Center.)

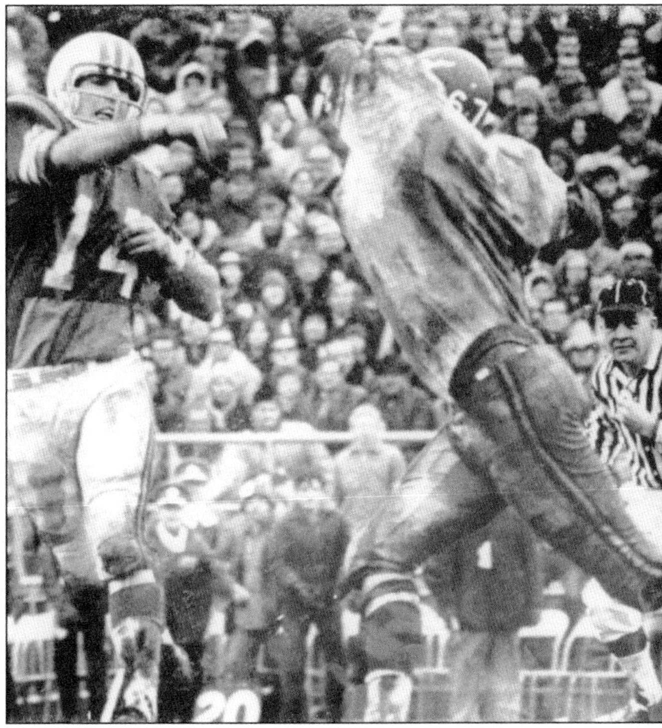

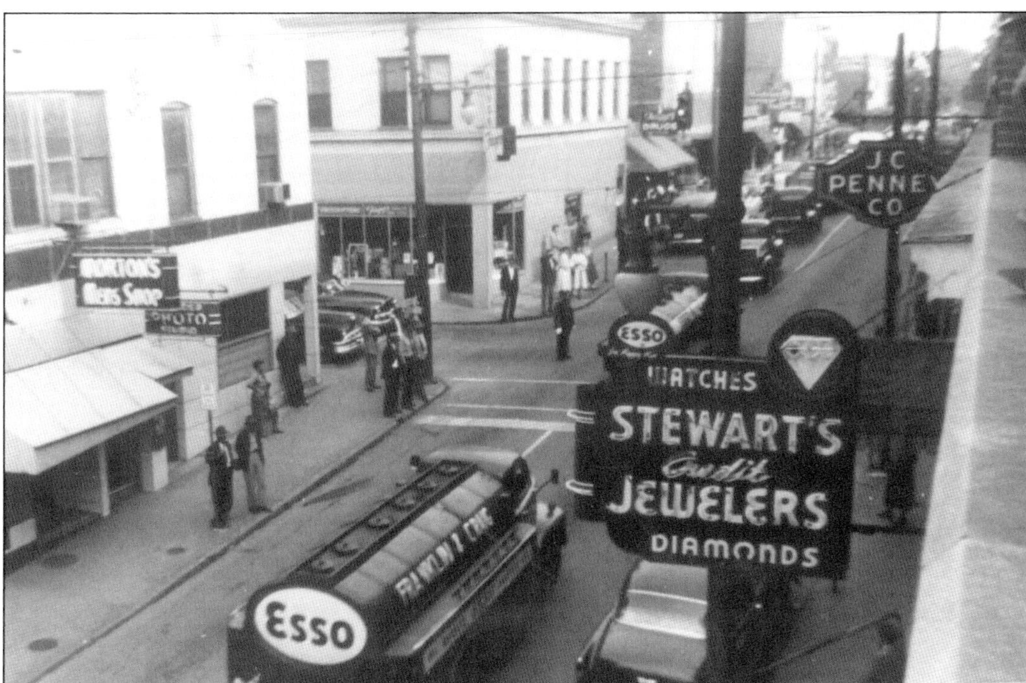

Spectators at the corner of Church and Walnut Streets look east in downtown Martinsville as a parade including Esso gas trucks heads east. Martinsville, named for Joseph Martin, a hero of the American Revolution, is unusual because it is an independent city since 1928 and still the county seat of Henry County. (Courtesy of the Jerry Brock Collection.)

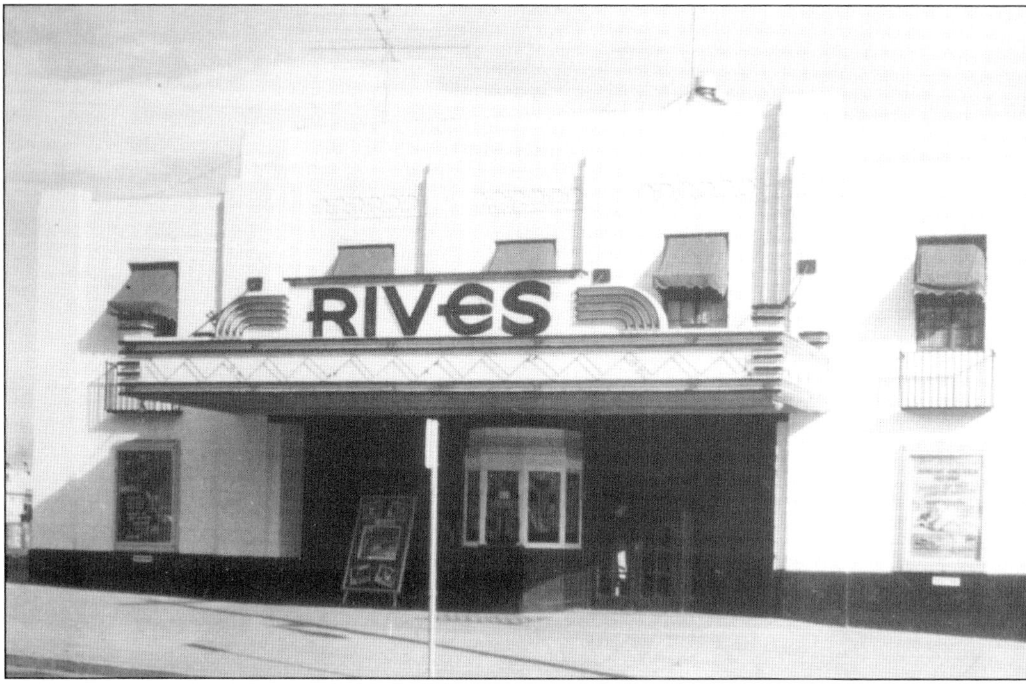

Recently reopened by the Martinsville Uptown Revitalization Association with a grant from the Harvest Foundation, the Rives Theatre on East Church Street shows first-run movies and holds music concerts. With the loss of jobs and industry, these two groups are trying to bring back economic prosperity to the inner city, making sites such as the theater attractive. (Courtesy of the Jerry Brock Collection.)

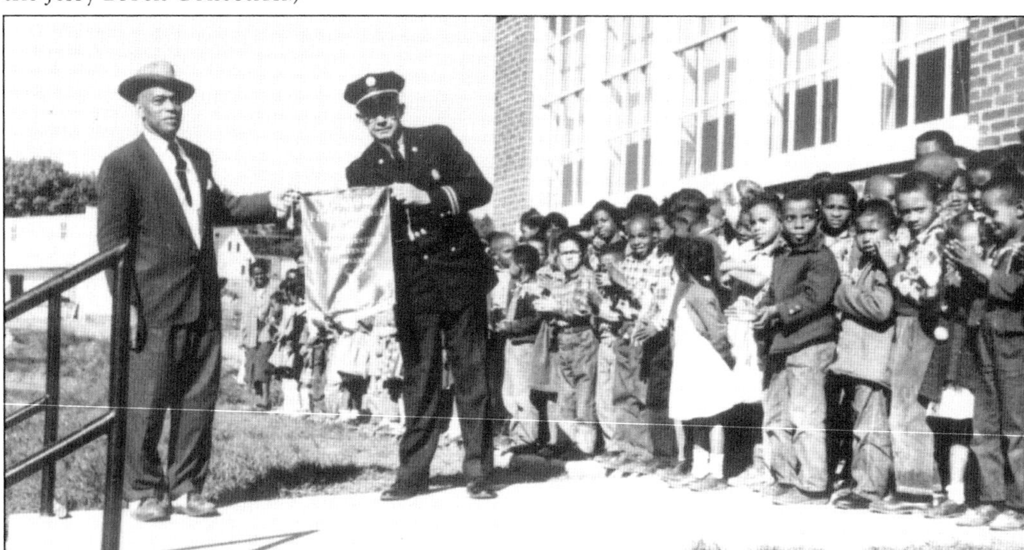

This image of Martinsville fire chief Clay E. Easterly (1956–1968) with educator Rev. R. T. Anderson (left) shows a group of African American students before desegregation of the Virginia public schools. The volunteer fire department, first organized in 1891 with two 500-foot hoses, made a serious effort to educate children about fire safety and prevention. (Courtesy of the Jerry Brock Collection.)

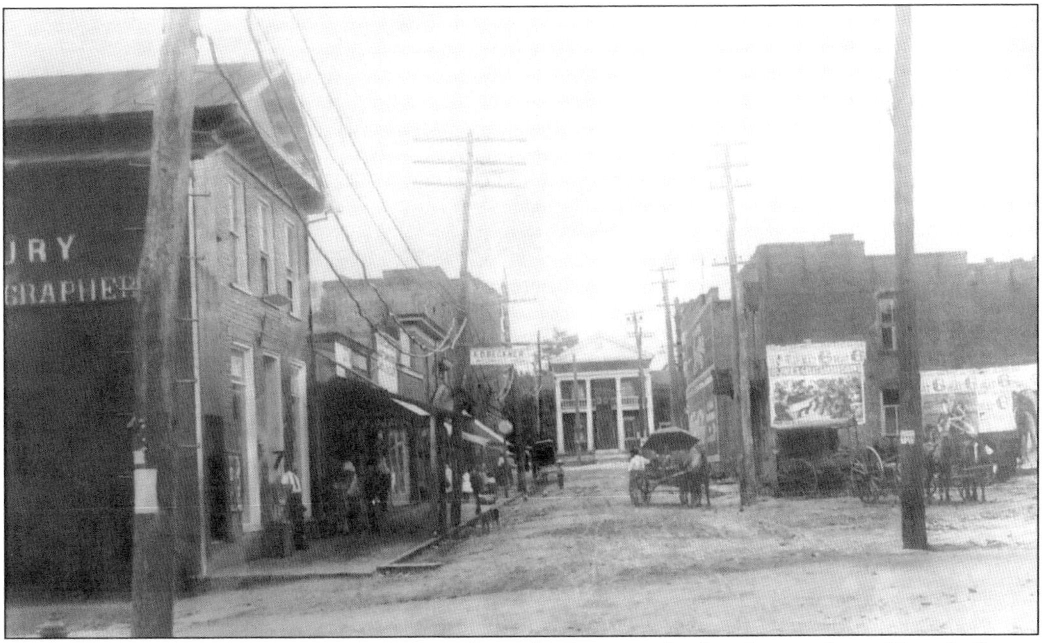

The Henry County Courthouse, shown above looking up Bridge Street from Church Street in 1905 and below from the roof of a nearby building in the 1930s, was the seat of government beginning in 1793. Virginia formed the county in 1777 from Pittsylvania County and named it for the state's first governor, Patrick Henry, who later moved to the area. George Hairston donated the land this structure sits on today. This 1929 structure is the third courthouse on the site. The grounds on the front lawn honor those from Henry County in the armed services. The county government moved to a new facility, abandoning the structure in 1995. At this writing, efforts are underway to stabilize the building and turn it into a museum by the Martinsville Henry County Historical Society. (Courtesy of the Jerry Brock Collection.)

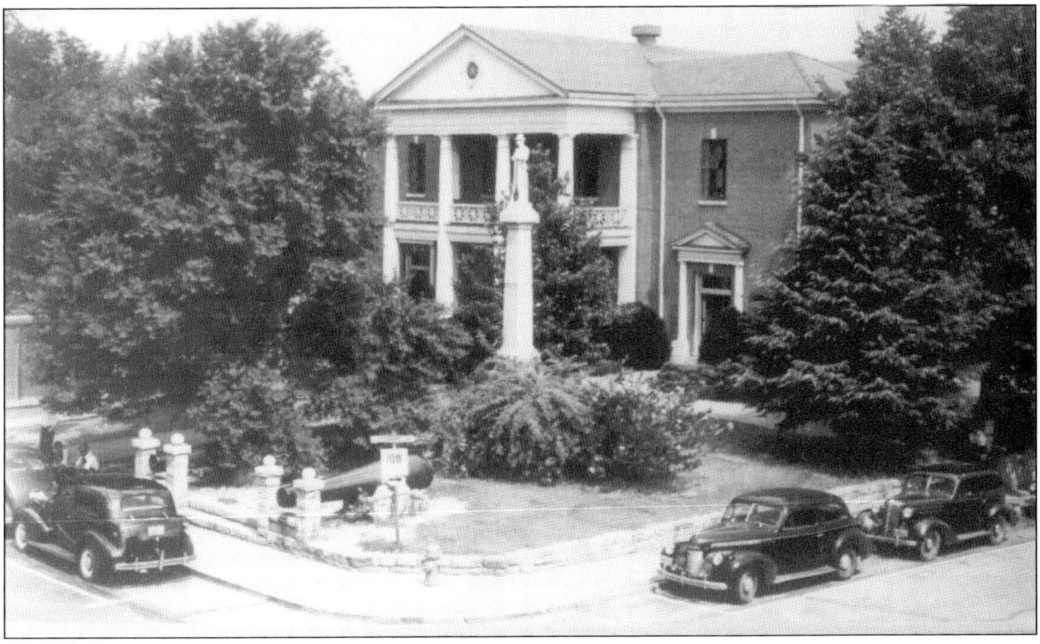

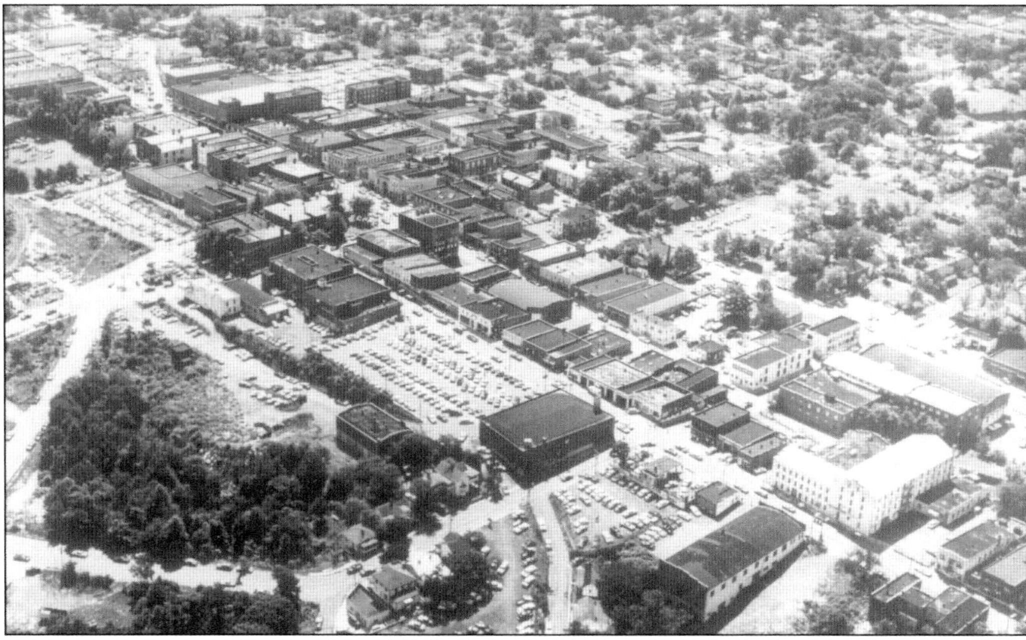

This aerial view of Martinsville during the boom days of the textile and chemical industries shows a crowded and vibrant downtown area. DuPont brought a nylon production facility to the area after World War II, and a resulting boom in textiles occurred, making Martinsville the "Sweatshirt Capital of the World." (Courtesy of the Jerry Brock Collection.)

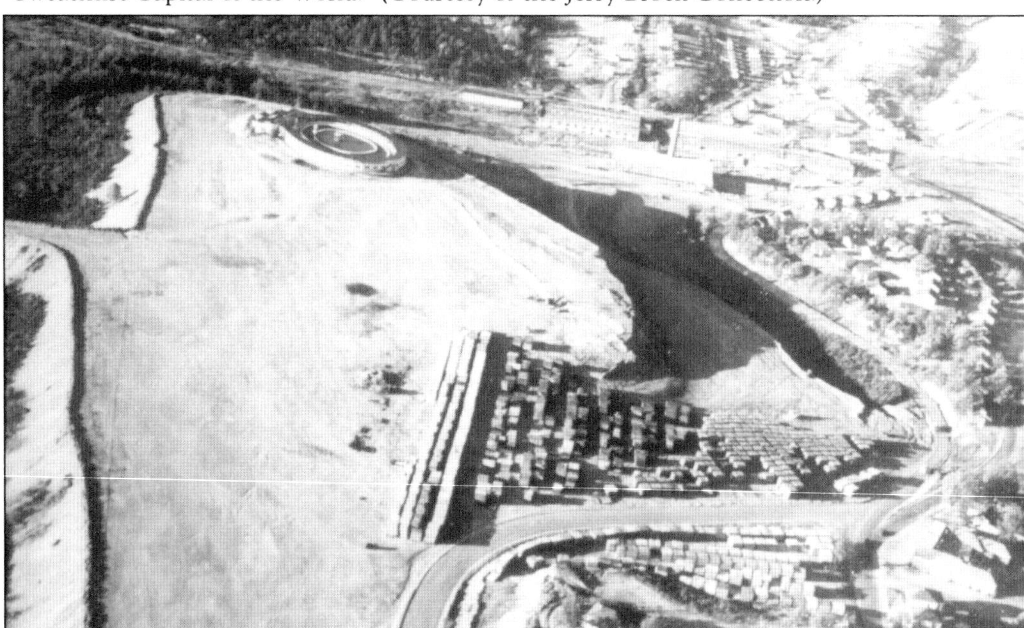

Constructed by Lester Lumber Company as a water source for fire protection, this aerial view shows Liberty Heights Swimming Pool on the left. Notice the lumber stacked at the bottom of the hill on the right. Today this view includes Wal-Mart and Lowe's in area along Jones Creek that was once a battlefield between Union general William J. Palmer and Confederate general James T. Wheeler at the end of the Civil War. (Courtesy of the Jerry Brock Collection.)

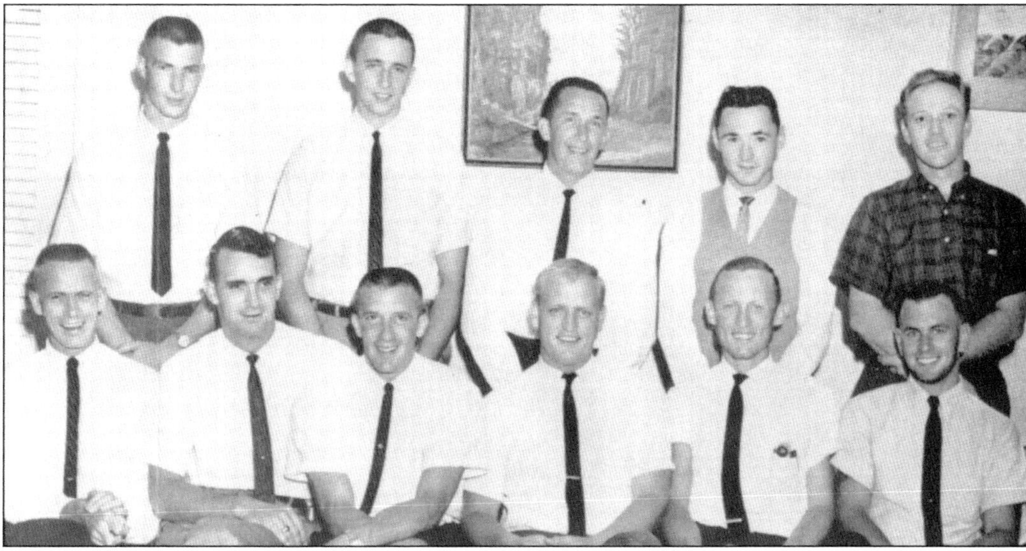

These are the 1966 Industrial Softball Champions of Martinsville from DuPont. From left to right are (first row) John Pulliam, Buford Campbell, Scott White, Jimmy Doyle, Wendell Hubbard, and Dave Ehly; (second row) Jimmy Caldwell, Daryl Grindstaff, Curtis Tilley, Roger Scott, and Teddy Compton. DuPont won championships in baseball, basketball, and bowling. (Courtesy of Teddy Compton.)

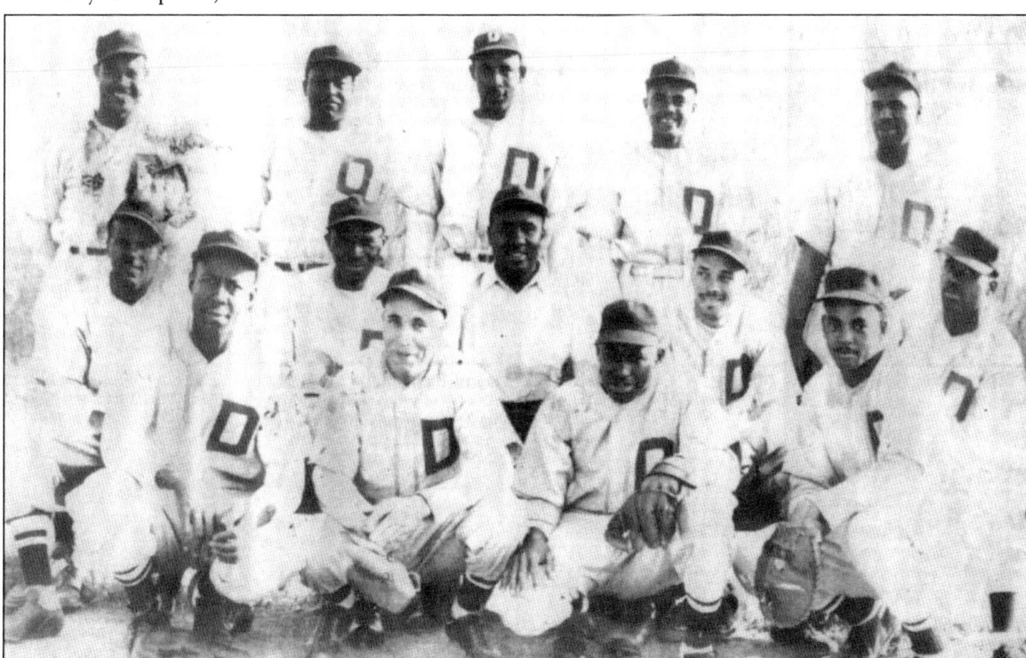

Before the days of integration, DuPont sponsored separate teams for their African American employees. This baseball team from the 1950s included, from left to right, George Reed, James Naylon, Steve Wingfield, and Robert Spencer on the front row. The second row included Johnny Burnette, Russell Wingfield, James Draper, George Strickland, and James Redd. The third row includes James Ellis, Joe Taylor, Lee Patterson, Llewellyn Moyer, and John Hylton. (Courtesy of Teddy Compton.)

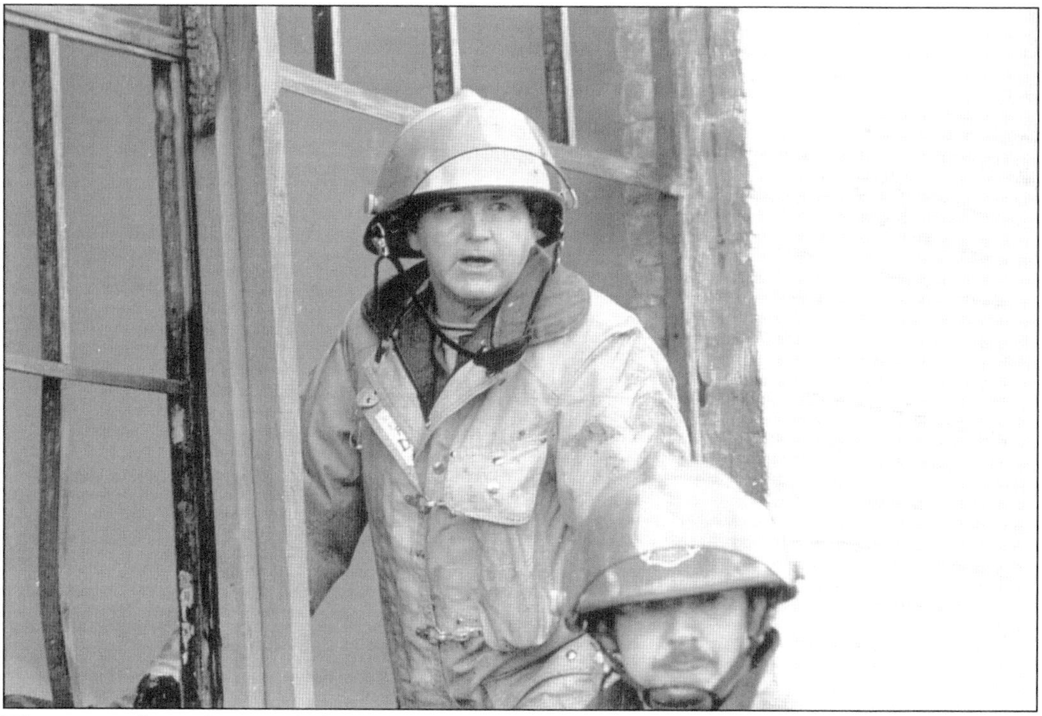

This image shows fire marshal Frank L. Draper Jr. in November 1980 as he enters the Specialty Packing Company fire. Beginning in 1949, the fire marshal trained the volunteer firefighters and educated the public with fire prevention programs. The volunteers received the same training as the paid firefighters. (Courtesy of the Jerry Brock Collection.)

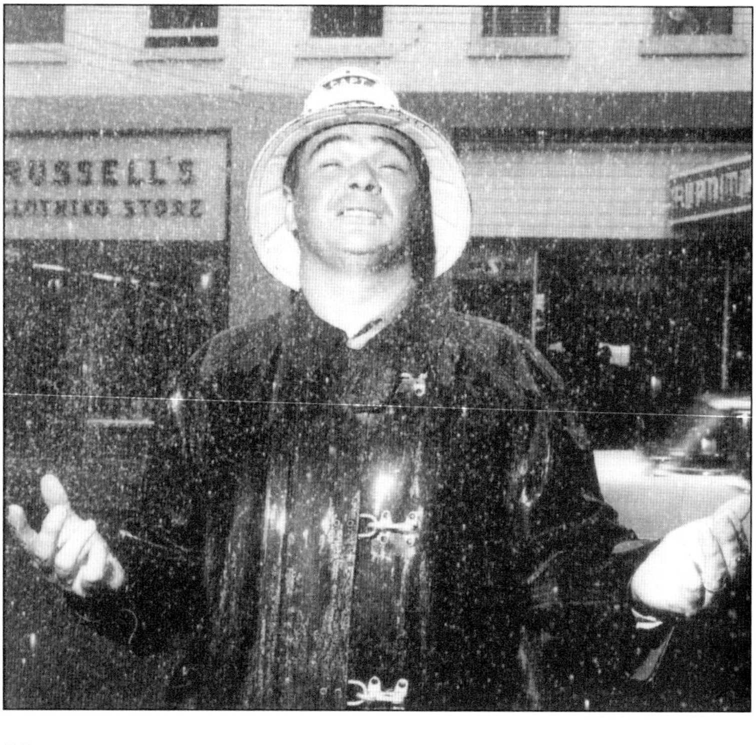

This image is of J. Lloyd Gregory, Martinsville fire chief from 1968 until 1988, as the water from a firefight falls down on him in downtown Martinsville. Presently, the fire department operates two stations with 30 full-time personnel, 13 part-time, 27 volunteer firefighters, and an 18-member honor guard. (Courtesy of the Jerry Brock Collection.)

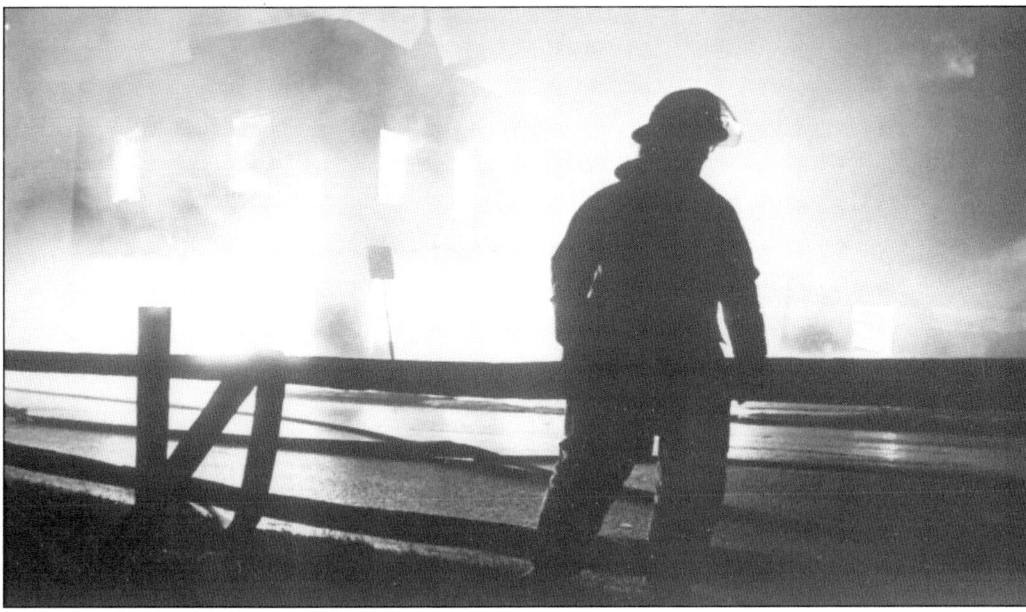

This haunting image comes from the L. and F. Repair fire on Chestnut Street. From Samuel Morgan in 1891 to Kenneth Draper beginning in 2007, 13 men have served as chief of the Martinsville Fire Department, including J. D. Aaron, P. S. Ford, J. H. Pharis, J. R. Henley, James E. Minter, Clay E. Easterly, J. Lloyd Gregory, W. Lewis Reeves, Jerry Brock, and Clarence Monday. (Courtesy of the Jerry Brock Collection.)

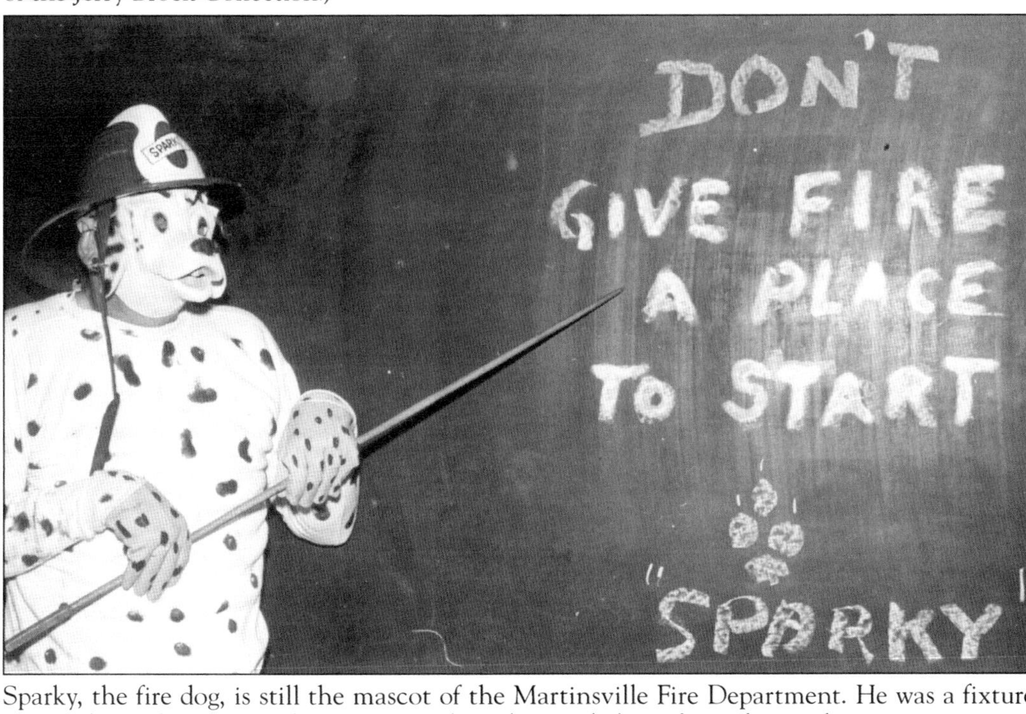

Sparky, the fire dog, is still the mascot of the Martinsville Fire Department. He was a fixture in parades and events in the area, spreading the word about fire safety and prevention started by the fire marshal. One of the events is putting together bicycles for the Salvation Army each Christmas. (Courtesy of the Jerry Brock Collection.)

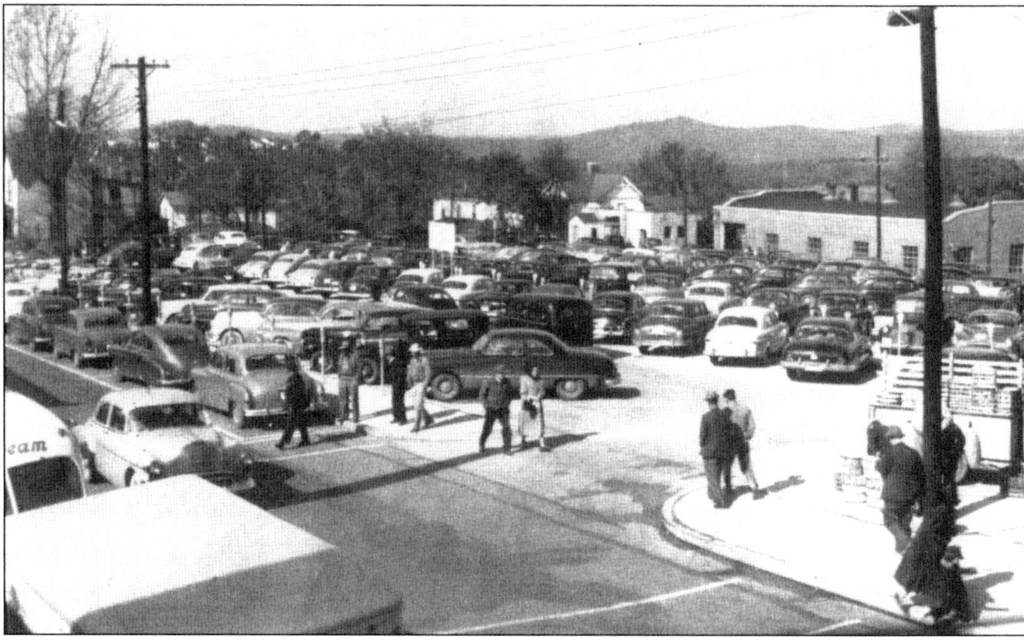

This image of the parking lot on Fayette Street in downtown Martinsville, with the City Maintenance Garage in the background, reflects the vibrant downtown area after World War II. Collaborating with the Virginia Foundation for the Humanities, a grassroots effort called the Fayette Area Historical Initiative today includes an African American History Museum. (Courtesy of Teddy Compton.)

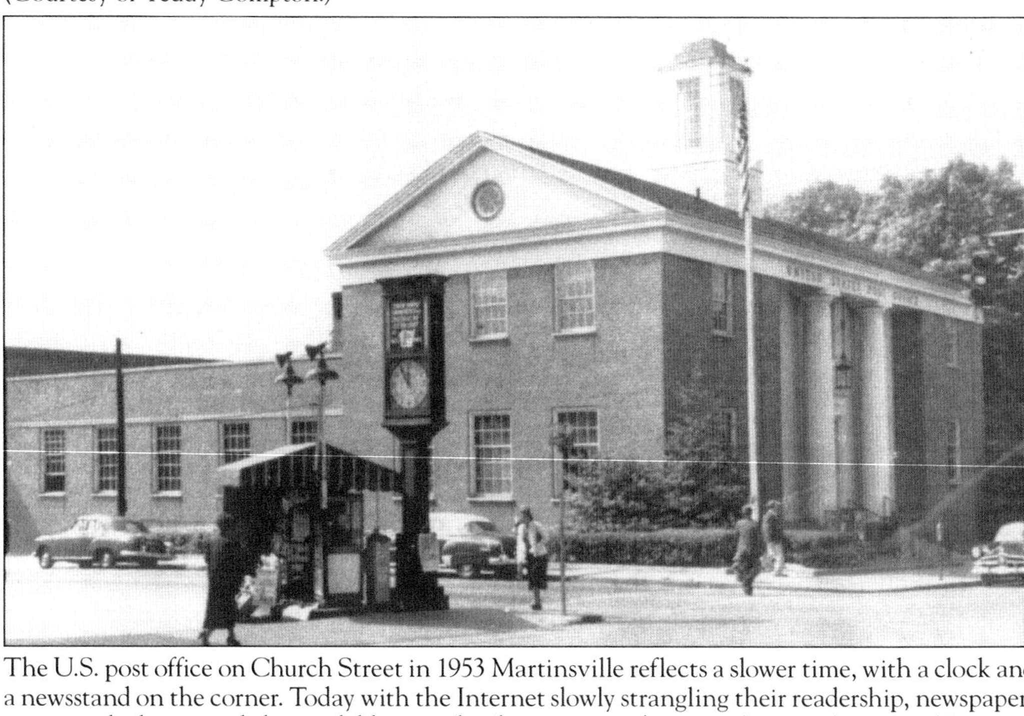

The U.S. post office on Church Street in 1953 Martinsville reflects a slower time, with a clock and a newsstand on the corner. Today with the Internet slowly strangling their readership, newspapers may soon be history, while email, blogs, and websites pose a threat to the postal service. (Courtesy of Teddy Compton.)

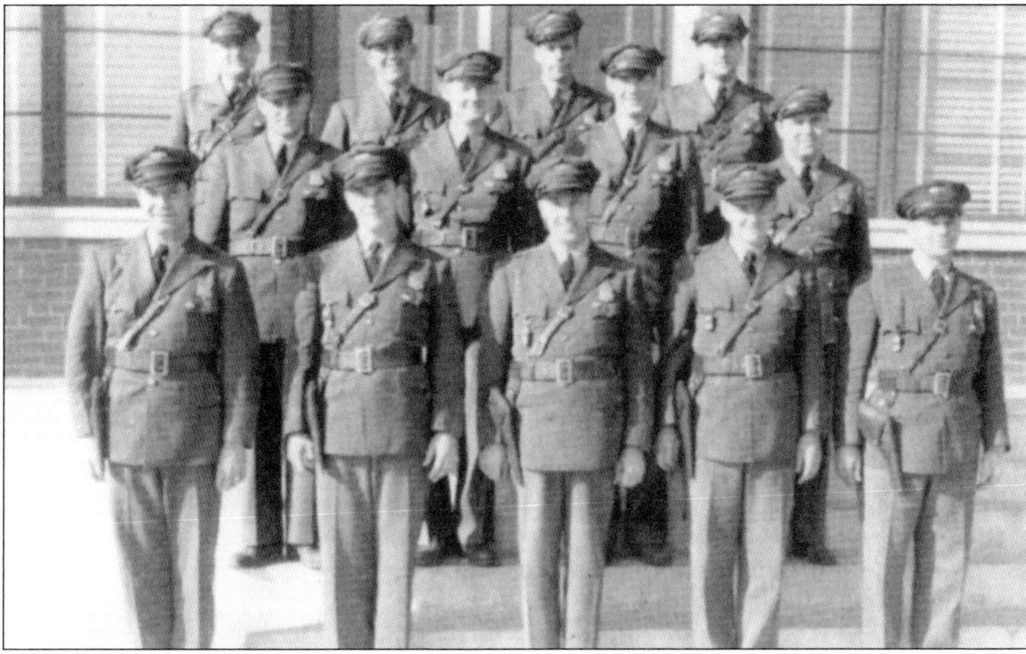

The DuPont Guard Force was security for the Martinsville nylon manufacturing facility. E. I. du Pont de Nemours and Company came from France to manufacture gunpowder in 1802 along Brandywine Creek in Delaware. By the time it came to Henry County, nylon was the commodity, and its importance made Martinsville a strategic bombing target during the cold war. (Courtesy of Teddy Compton.)

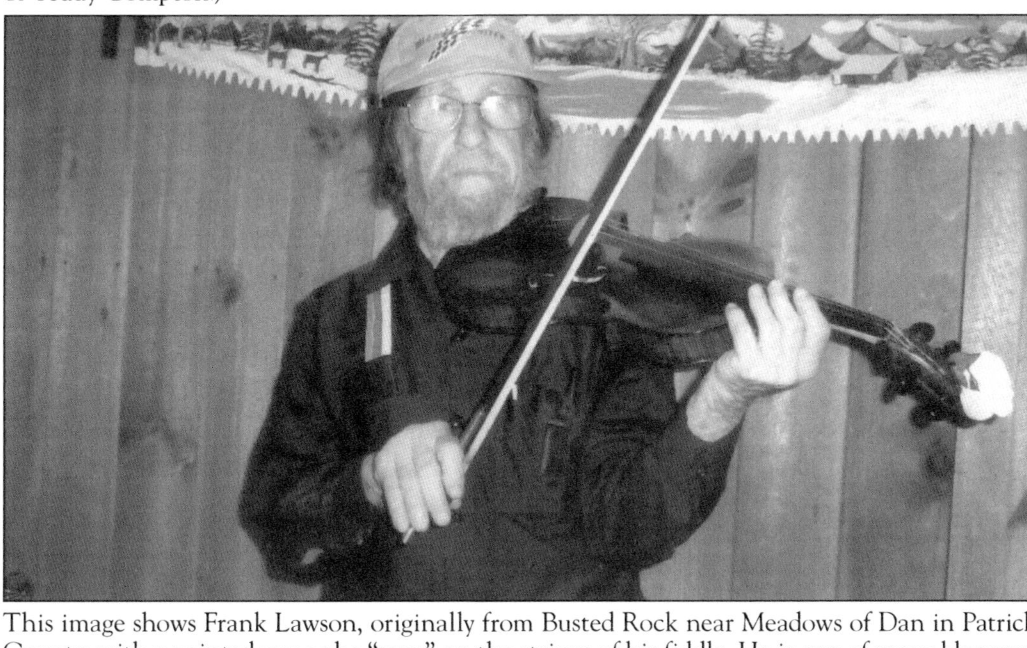

This image shows Frank Lawson, originally from Busted Rock near Meadows of Dan in Patrick County, with a painted saw as he "saws" on the strings of his fiddle. He is one of many bluegrass musicians who live in Henry County. A resurgence in this music has occurred over the last few years, and Virginia promotes it with the Crooked Road Music Heritage Trail, which sadly does not include Henry County. (Courtesy of Teddy Compton.)

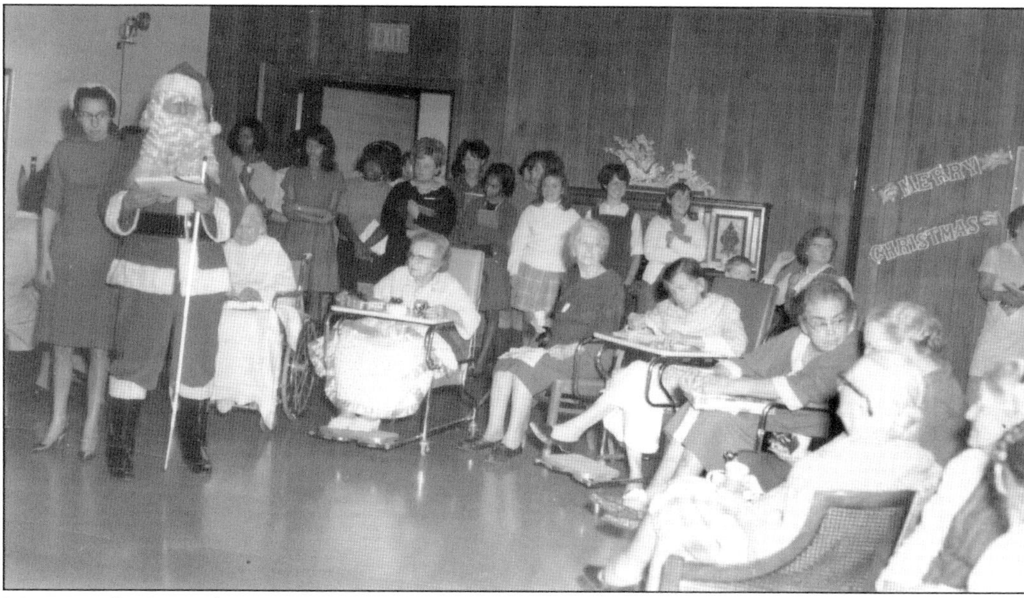

Martinsville Convalescent Center was the first nursing home in Henry County, as this image of a Christmas party shows. Today modern facilities, such as King's Grant on the land once owned by the Hairston family, continue to provide a good quality of life for the elderly through nursing and retirement care. (Courtesy of Deborah Hodges.)

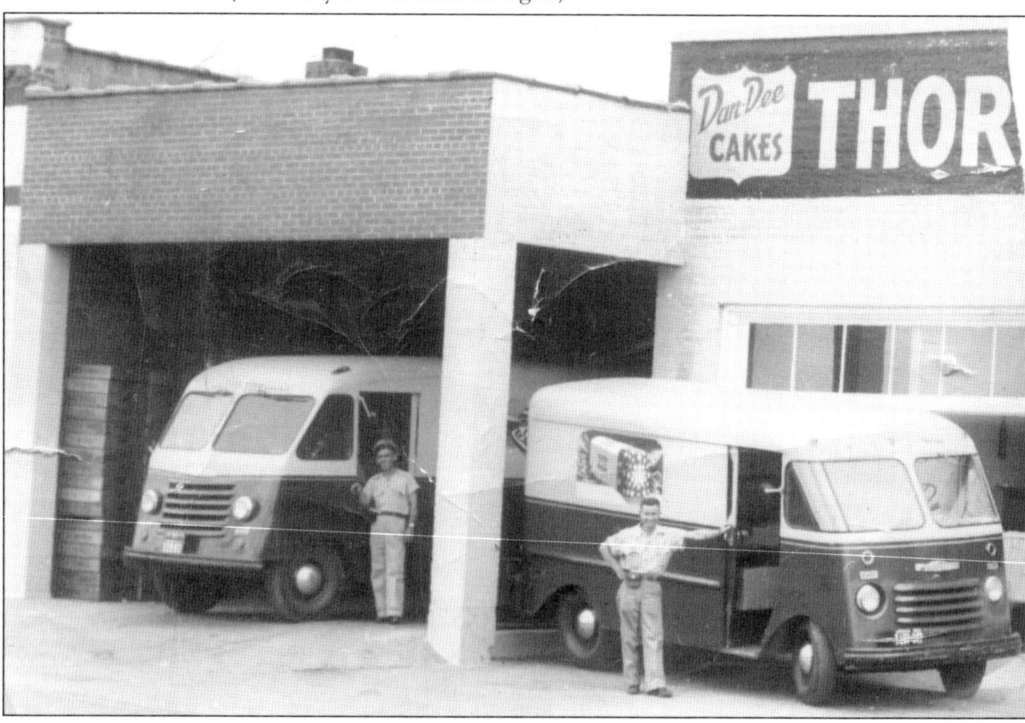

Thornton's Bakery, at the corner of Moss and Fayette Streets, was a fixture in Henry County, delivering bread and cakes in its two trucks. In 2007, forty-two acres of the Fayette Street Historic District and 13 surrounding streets became part of the Virginia Landmarks Register. Read more about it at www.aaheritageva.org. (Courtesy of Deborah Hodges.)

Jesse Frith works with T29 nylon on the second floor of the DuPont plant in Martinsville. For safety purposes, he wears safety glasses, long sleeves, and no jewelry. The DuPont website says, "Nylon was the world's first true synthetic textile fiber. It now is found in hundreds of applications from carpets to clothing to luggage to automobile parts." Beginning in 1941, when the company began operations, until 1998, when nylon manufacturing ceased, DuPont was an important part of the Henry County economy. Today the name DuPont returns twice a year on the NASCAR racecar of Jeff Gordon (24) at the Martinsville Speedway. (Courtesy of Joan Frith.)

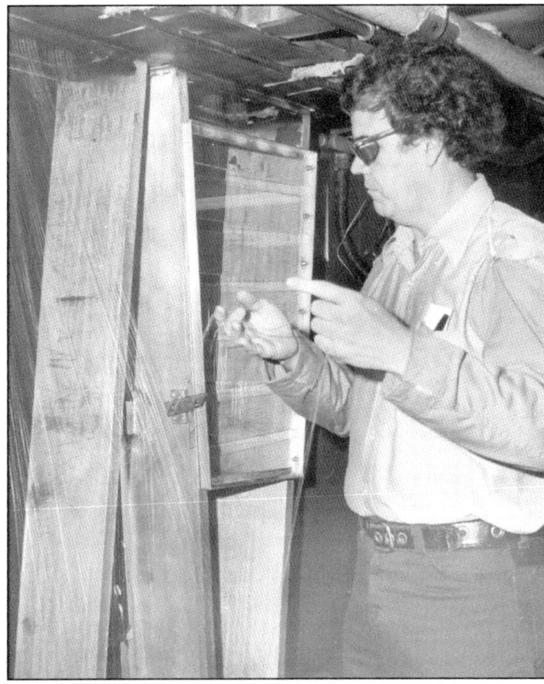

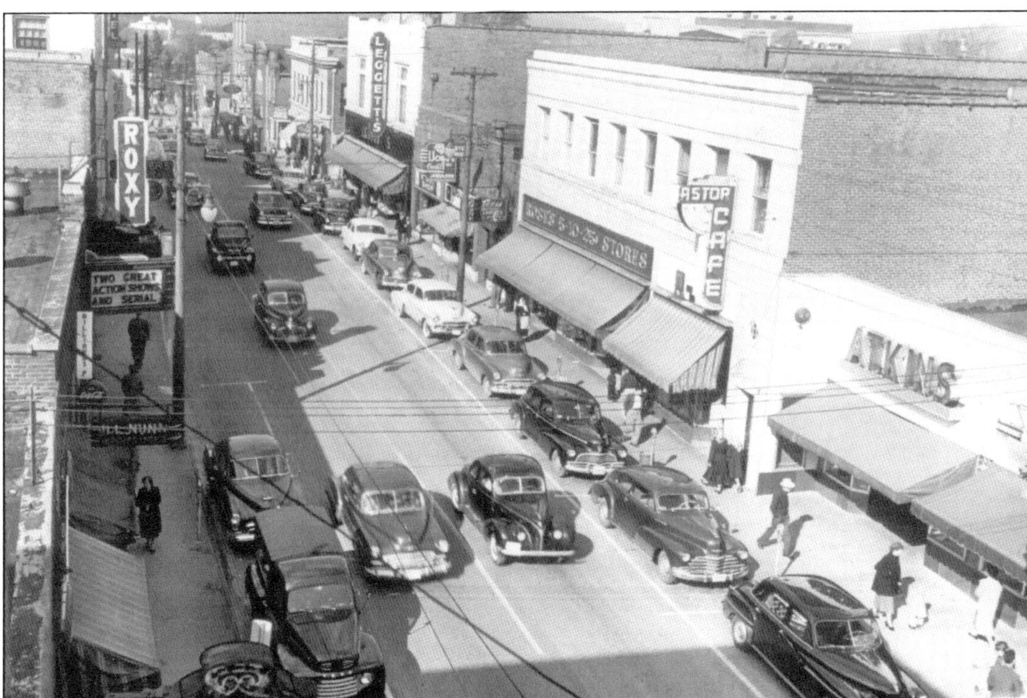

This view of Church Street from 1953 looking west shows one-way traffic as people make their way around. Before the days of strip malls, all-in-one stores, megaplex theaters, and fast food, people shopped at specialized stores and lunched at the local café, catching a movie while shopping downtown and knowing the lost art of parallel parking. (Courtesy of the Jerry Brock Collection.)

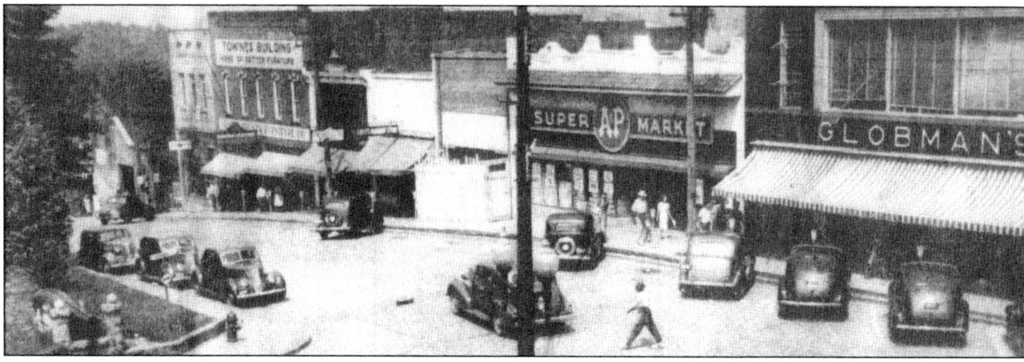

This 1941 image of the courthouse square in downtown Martinsville shows Globman's department store, the A&P supermarket, and the Townes Building, the "Home of Better Furniture." A cannon on the left shows the location of the Henry County Courthouse. The Globman family was part of a vibrant Jewish community in town. (Courtesy of Harold Smith.)

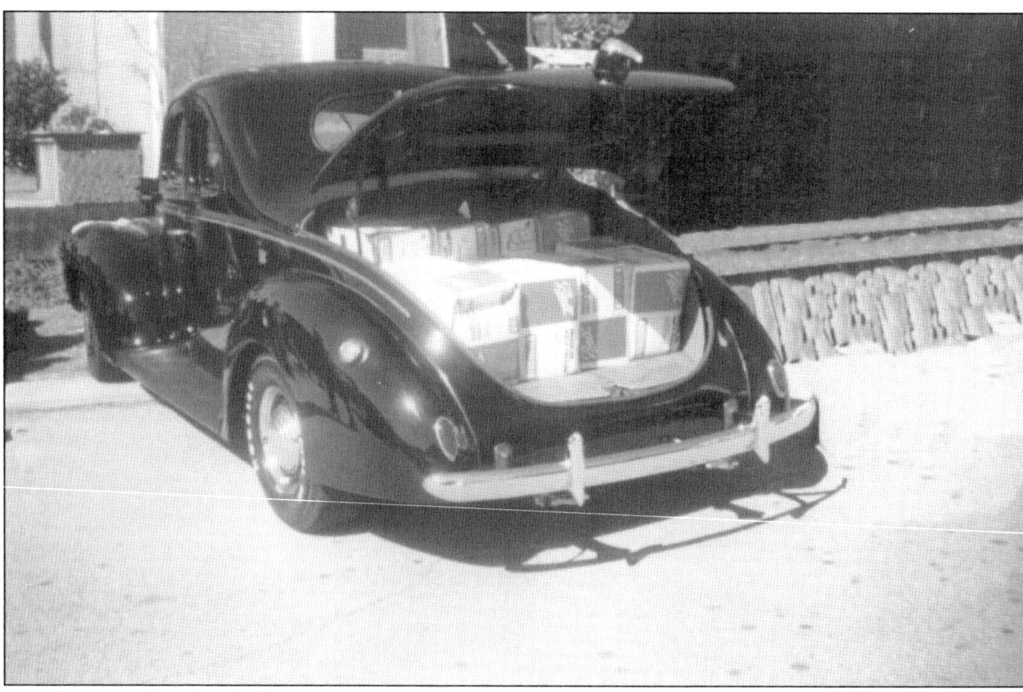

This 1939 Ford Coupe is "loaded for business"—the business of delivering illicit liquor tax free, or "bootlegging." The term originates from hiding a flask of illegal alcohol in a boot covered by a pant leg. Modern car racing and many of the early drivers of NASCAR got their start running moonshine by the light of the moon. (Courtesy of Harold Smith.)

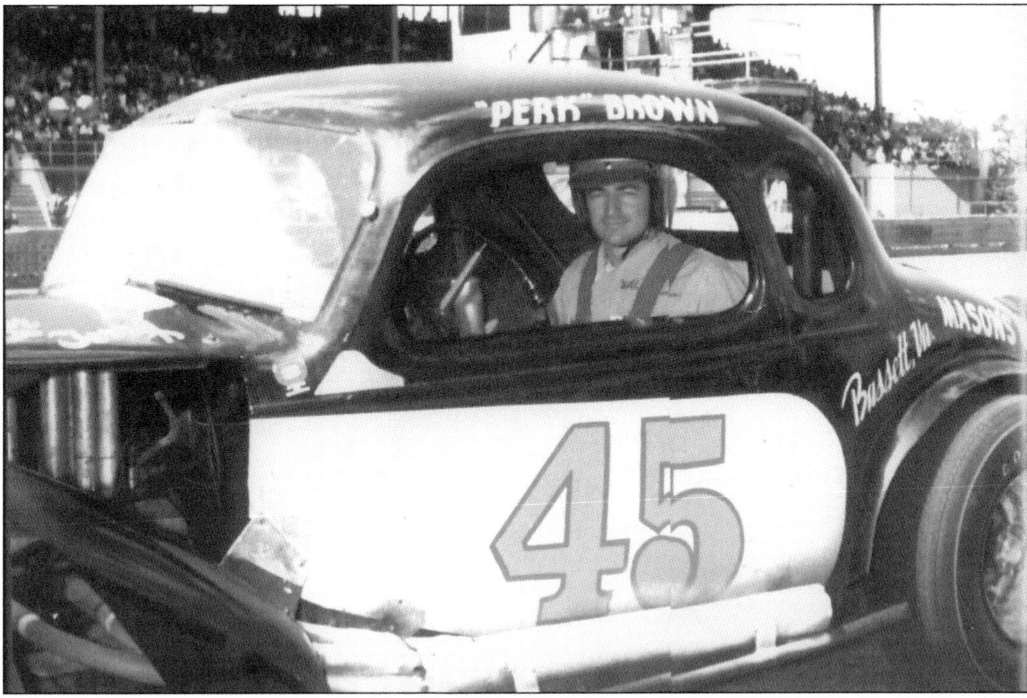

Bobby Allison is pictured in the car owned by Bassett's own "Perk" Brown at the Martinsville Speedway in the 1950s. Martinsville was one of the first paved racetracks. Many local drivers and NASCAR drivers enjoyed running at the racetrack in other classes of cars, as they still do at Oak Level and other dirt tracks in the area. (Courtesy of Harold Smith.)

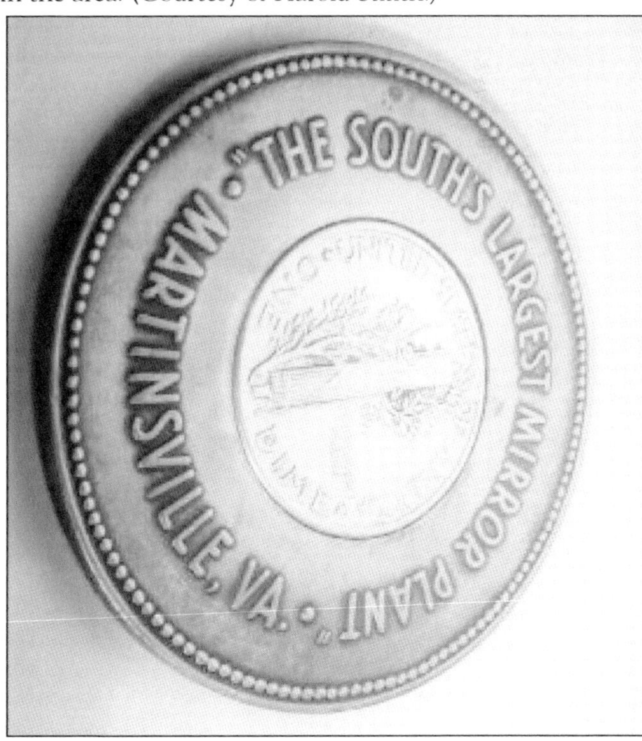

This image shows that Martinsville once had "The South's Largest Mirror Plant." The 1939 token is from the Virginia Mirror Company. Founded in 1913, the company operates today a 176,000-foot plant in Martinsville and 110,000-foot facility in Ridgeway in southern Henry County. While textiles and chemicals have left, the glass and mirror business remains. (Courtesy of Douglas Stegall.)

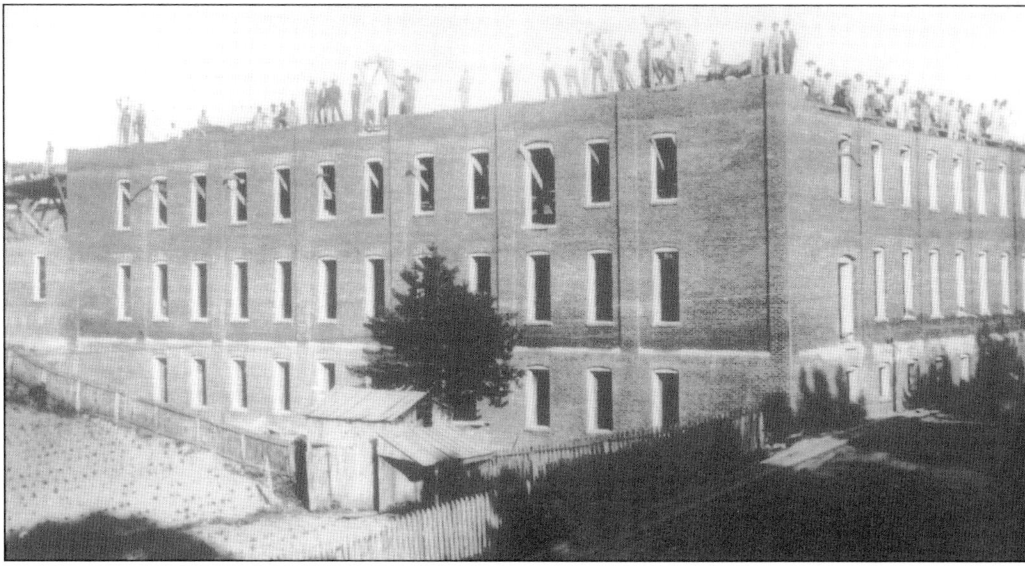

This image shows the Rucker-Witten Tobacco Factory under construction near Liberty Fair Mall. Later sold to R. J. Reynolds Tobacco for storage, it became the Martinsville Cotton Mill, Sale Knitting, and Tultex facility. Now unoccupied, it reflects the tobacco and textile industries that once dominated the area's economy. (Courtesy of the Jerry Brock Collection.)

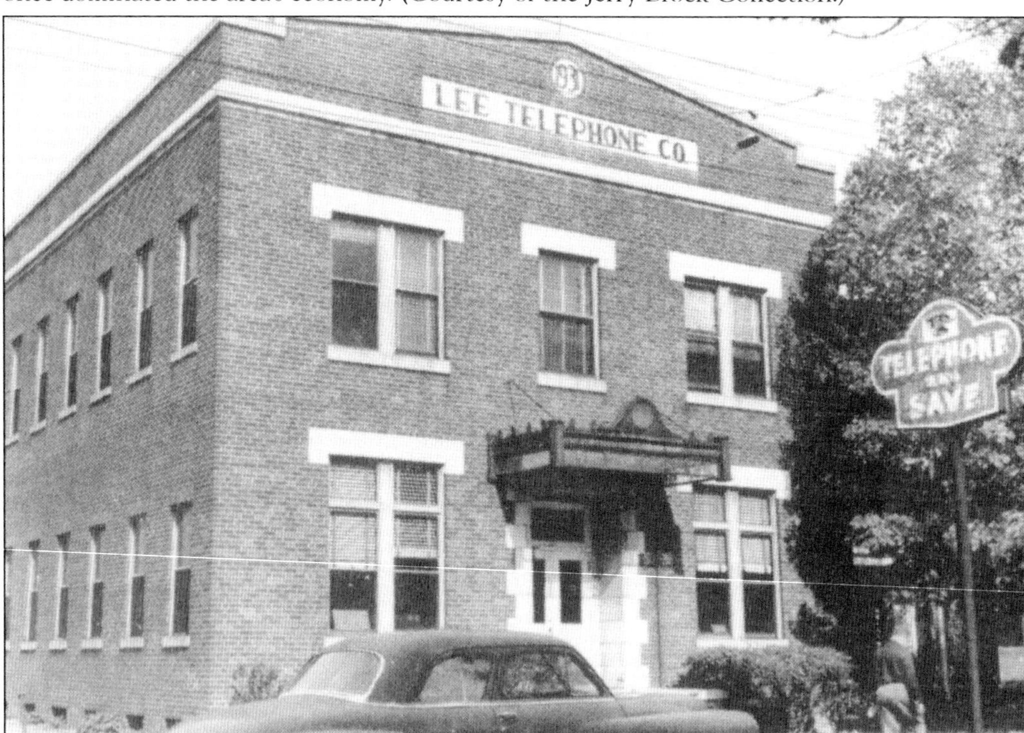

This image of the Lee Telephone Company Building on Church Street in Martinsville reflects a time when local entrepreneurs started utilities. Work began each Monday with a Bible school and church service for all employees, except the operators who kept the switchboard. Today Embarq owns the building and the telephone service. (Courtesy of Teddy Compton.)

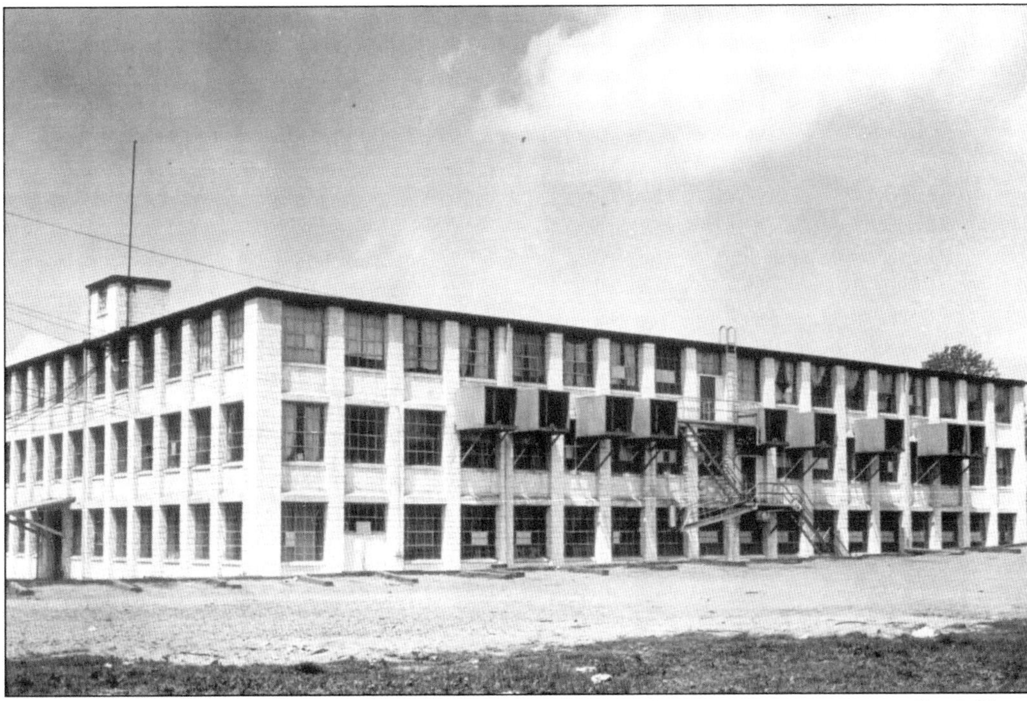

This image is of Jobbers Pants Factory on Fayette and Market Streets in Martinsville. Jobbers, founded in 1933, was one of many textile manufacturing companies that drove the region's economy. Bassett-Walker, Pannill Knitting, Sale, and Tultex were some of the manufacturers in Henry County that produced mainly sweatpants and cotton T-shirts. Today most of these factories stand empty. The loss of jobs and economic base is making the region rethink economic development. (Courtesy of the Jerry Brock Collection.)

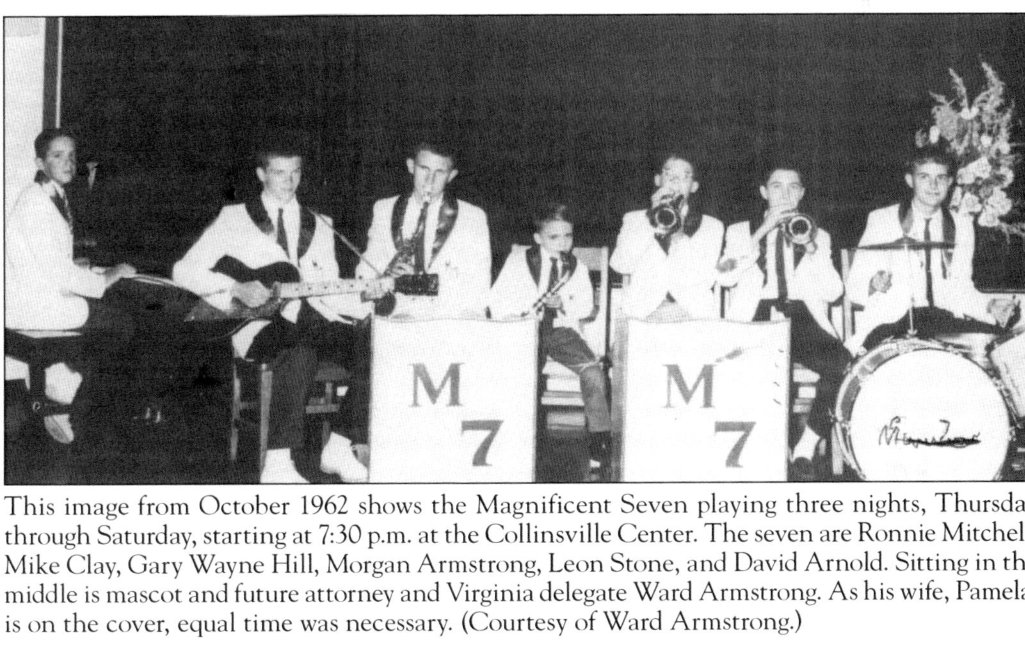

This image from October 1962 shows the Magnificent Seven playing three nights, Thursday through Saturday, starting at 7:30 p.m. at the Collinsville Center. The seven are Ronnie Mitchell, Mike Clay, Gary Wayne Hill, Morgan Armstrong, Leon Stone, and David Arnold. Sitting in the middle is mascot and future attorney and Virginia delegate Ward Armstrong. As his wife, Pamela, is on the cover, equal time was necessary. (Courtesy of Ward Armstrong.)

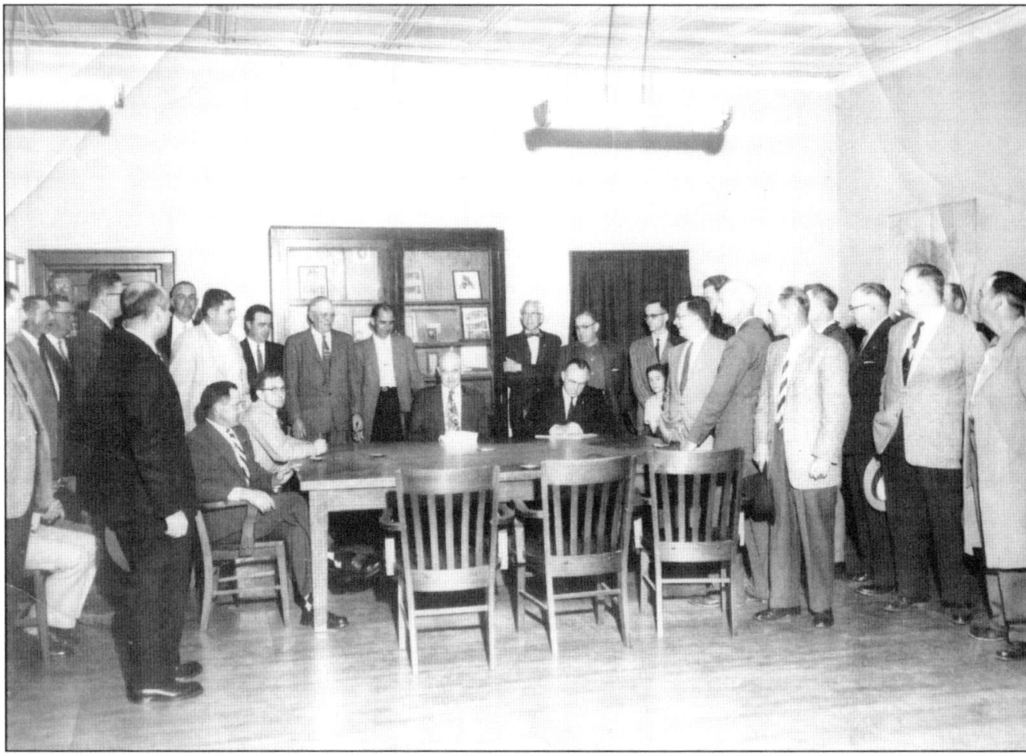

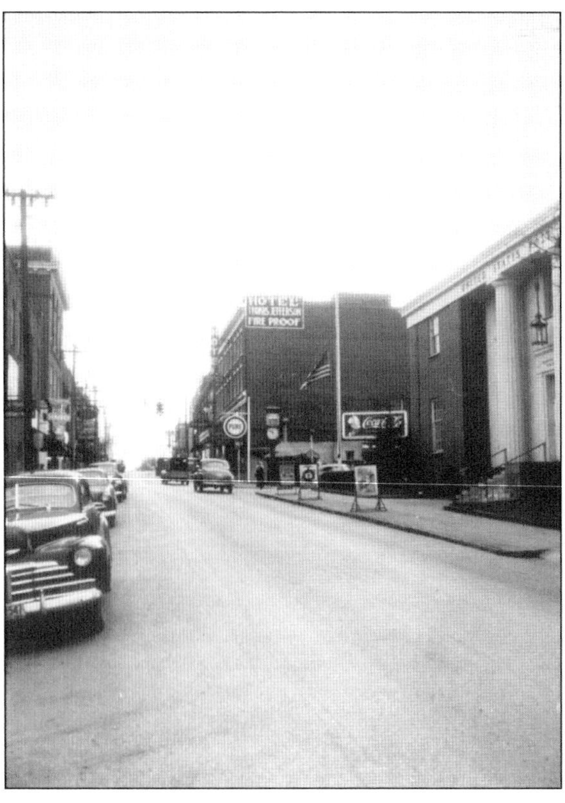

This Henry County Democratic Party meeting in Martinsville includes among others, from left to right, Gold Prillaman, Arthur Horsely, S. E. Moran, John Philpott, Lafayette Prillaman, J. L. Racey, James Franklin, Stover Terry, Clyde Fentress, Branch K. Rives, and J. W. Vipperman. Seated at the left of the table wearing a pair of argyle socks is Lowell Young. (Courtesy of Vickie Stone Helmstutler.)

Two-way traffic traverses Church Street in this 1951 image; the U.S. Post Office on the right has flags at half-staff, and Eagles's Coffee Shop is on the left. Looking east towards the Thomas Jefferson Hotel beside a Pure filling station, the Henry County Courthouse is one block to the left. (Courtesy of the Jerry Brock Collection.)

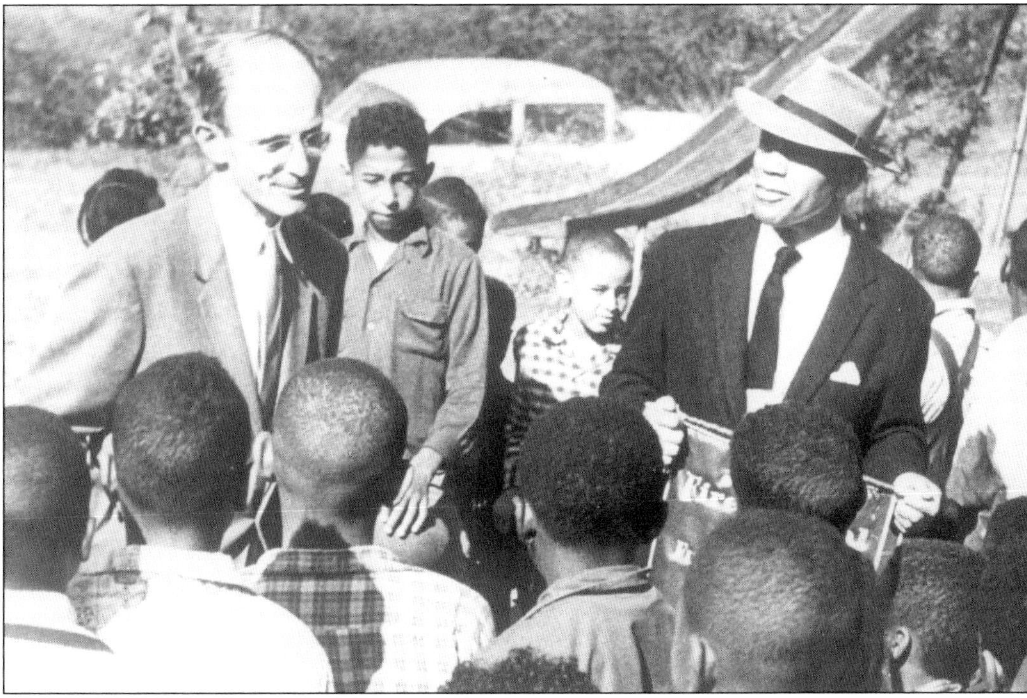

This 1956 image shows Julian Hurst, the first city manager of Martinsville, who later went to Roanoke, Virginia, and principal R. T. Anderson of East Martinsville School. With schools still segregated and two year after the 1954 Brown Supreme Court decision, this group came together as part of the fire safety program of the Martinsville Fire Department. (Courtesy of the Jerry Brock Collection.)

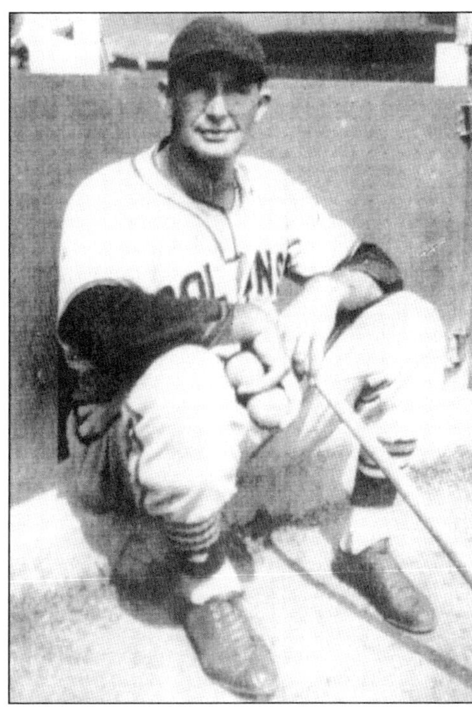

Baseball player Bill Curlee played on DuPont and Martinsville teams. Almost forgotten now was the Bi-State League, formed in 1934, that included 10 teams from Virginia and 8 from North Carolina, including the Fieldale Virginians, who played until 1942. The Bassett Furnituremakers won the title four times, including three in a row from 1936 to 1938. (Courtesy of Teddy Compton.)

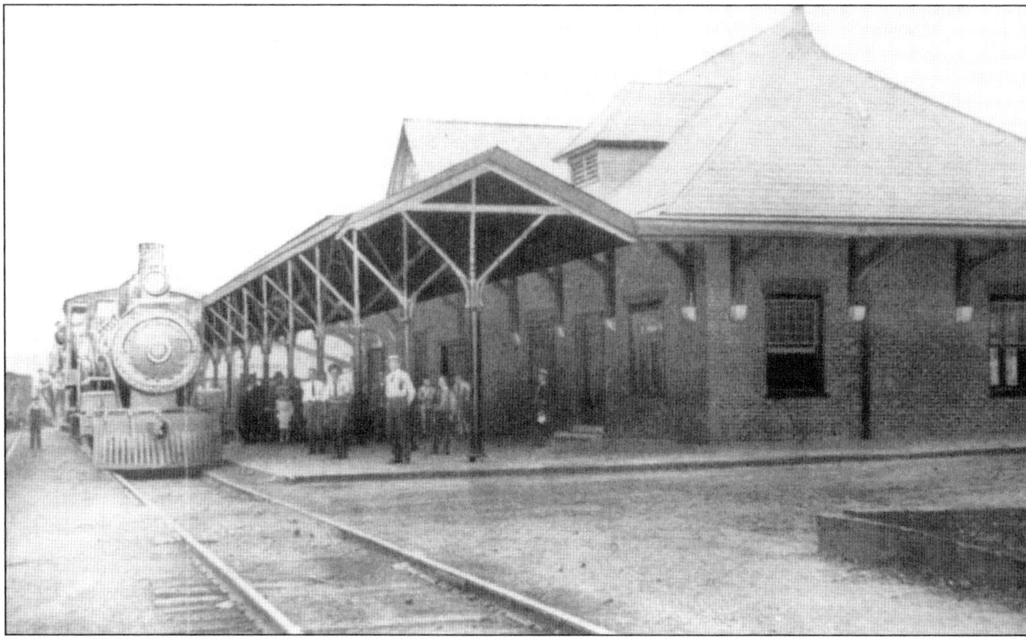

This image shows The Norfolk and Western Railroad Station on Broad Street in Martinsville around 1910. This railroad came in 1892, and the Danville and Western, the "Dick and Willie," came to the city in 1881. Railroads brought the telegraph, electricity, and the telephone following the route of the tracks along with passengers, mail, and freight service. (Courtesy of Kenney Kirkman.)

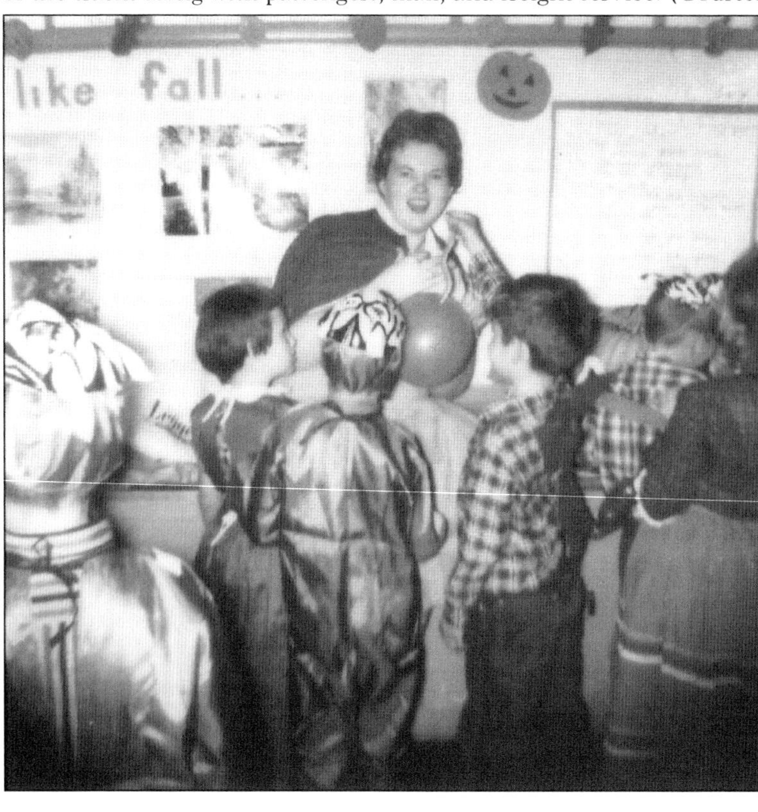

This c. 1963 image shows Clearview Elementary School teacher Beverly Lipford Yeager in Martinsville. The city operates a school system separate from Henry County that includes Clearview Early Educational Center, Patrick Henry and Albert Harris Elementary Schools, Martinsville Middle School, and Martinsville High School. Albert Harris was an African American Methodist minister who started a school for black children. (Courtesy of Beverly Yeager.)

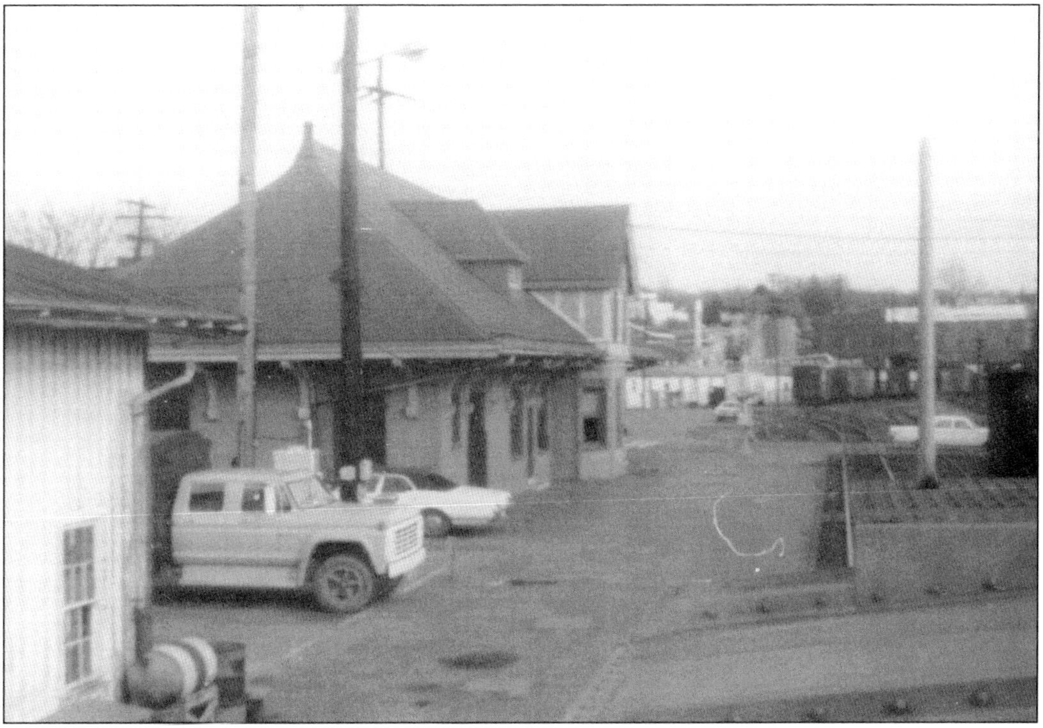

This image taken from the caboose of a northbound freight train by Kenney Kirkman on the Norfolk and Western Railroad in 1976 shows the Broad Street Station at Martinsville. The manufacturing plant of American Furniture is in the background. Fire destroyed the factory in 1995 and the railroad station in 1978. (Courtesy of Kenney Kirkman.)

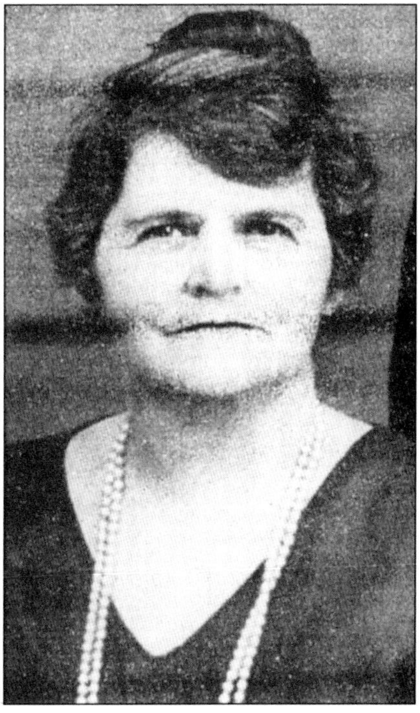

Cassie Gravely, who died in 1967 at age 93, wrote the official salute to the Virginia flag, which read, "I salute the flag of Virginia, with reverence and patriotic devotion to the 'Mother of States and Statesmen' which it presents—the 'Old Dominion' where liberty and independence were born." Gov. Thomas Stanley of Henry County signed the salute into law in 1954. (Courtesy of the Bassett Historical Center.)

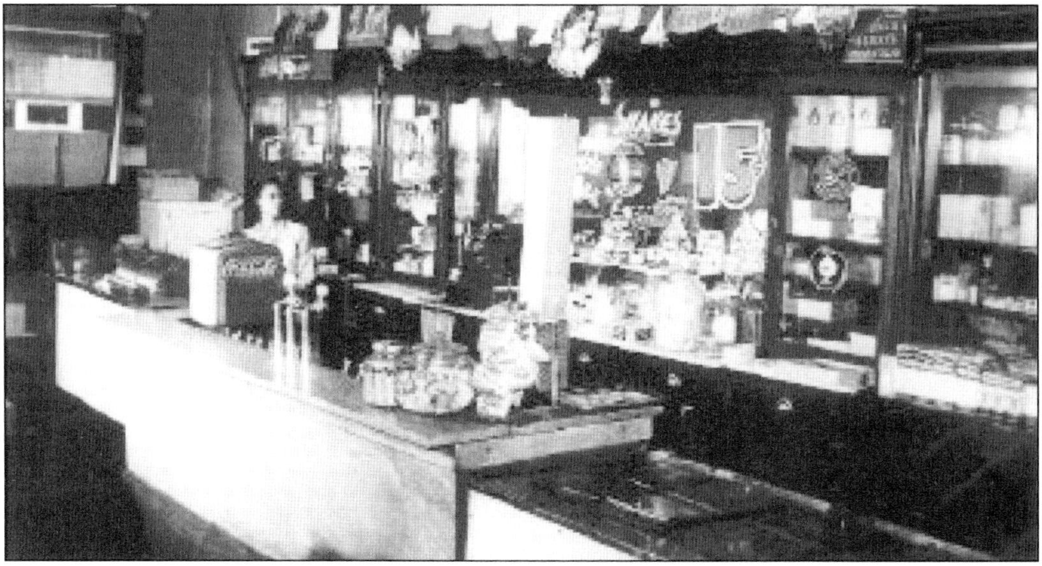

Dr. Dana Owen Baldwin (1881–1972), who served in World War I, moved to Martinsville in 1910 as the first African American physician and set off a business expansion called the Baldwin Block. He is credited with businesses such as brick company, pool hall, dance hall, and café. His pharmacy, shown in this image, was the centerpiece of the block described as a shopping center today. (Courtesy of the Bassett Historical Center.)

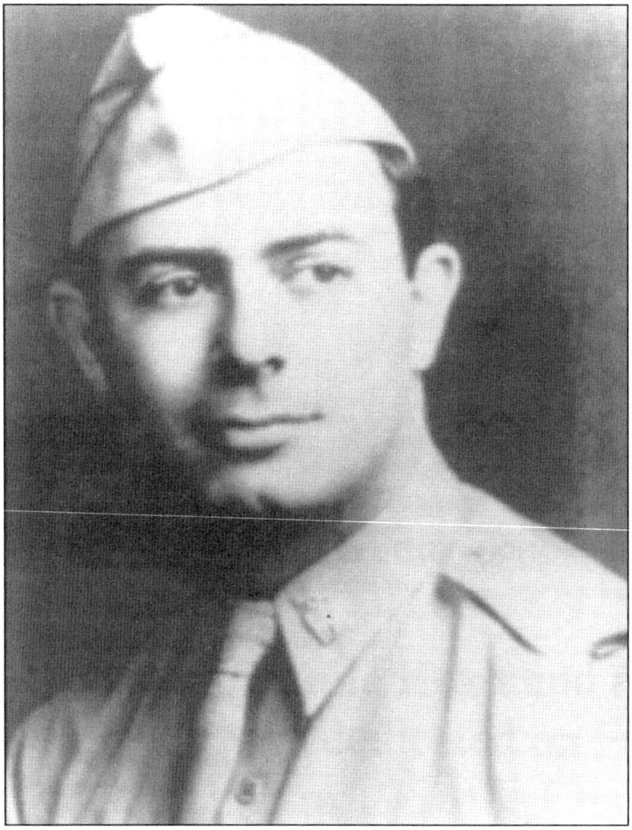

Alexander D. Goode (1911–1943) was the son of a Jewish rabbi who lived for a time in Martinsville. He gave his life with three other chaplains in the U.S. Army when the USAT *Dorchester* sank during World War II. Grace Baptist Church in Philadelphia honors the chaplains with a stained-glass window dedicated in 1951 by President Truman. (Courtesy of the Bassett Historical Center.)

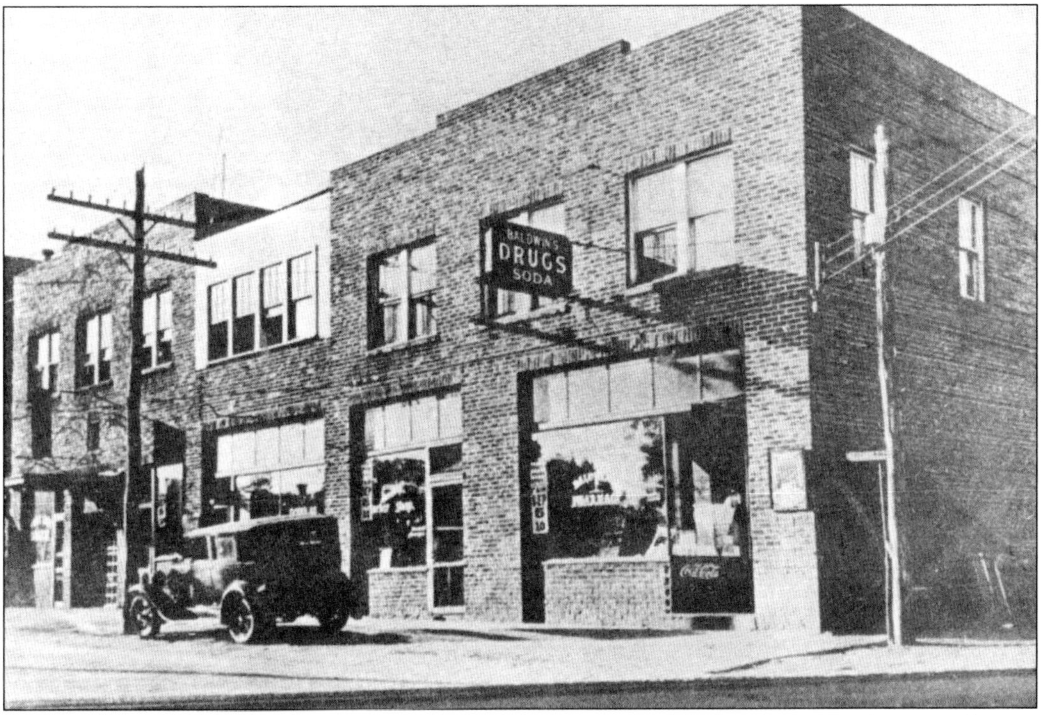

The Baldwin Business Center or the "Baldwin Block" was an African American business district along Fayette Street. Dr. D. O. Baldwin's home is on the right, with Jobbers Pants Factory on the far left. Baldwin and his family started the Black Fiddler's Conventions, Agricultural Fairs, and June German Ball, recently revived by the Fayette Historical Initiative. (Courtesy of the Bassett Historical Center.)

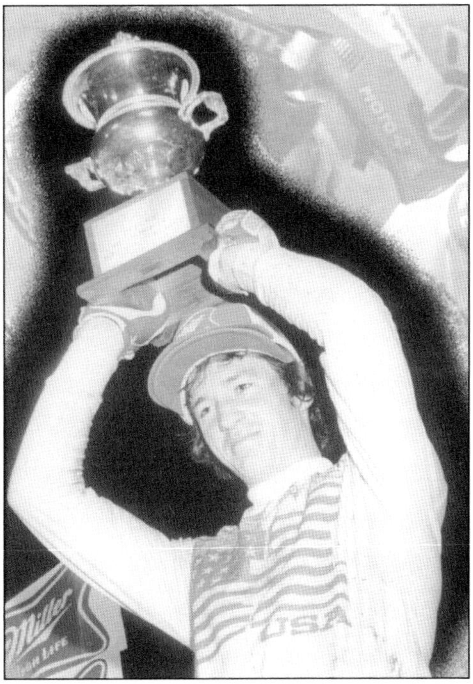

David Bailey, a graduate of the Carlisle School in Henry County, was a 10-time world and 10-time national motocross champion. Paralyzed from the waist down in 1987, Bailey works as an ESPN commentator on motorcycle racing and speaks for the Full Circle Foundation, which works to find assistance for those with and to find a cure for spinal cord injuries. (Courtesy of the Bassett Historical Center.)

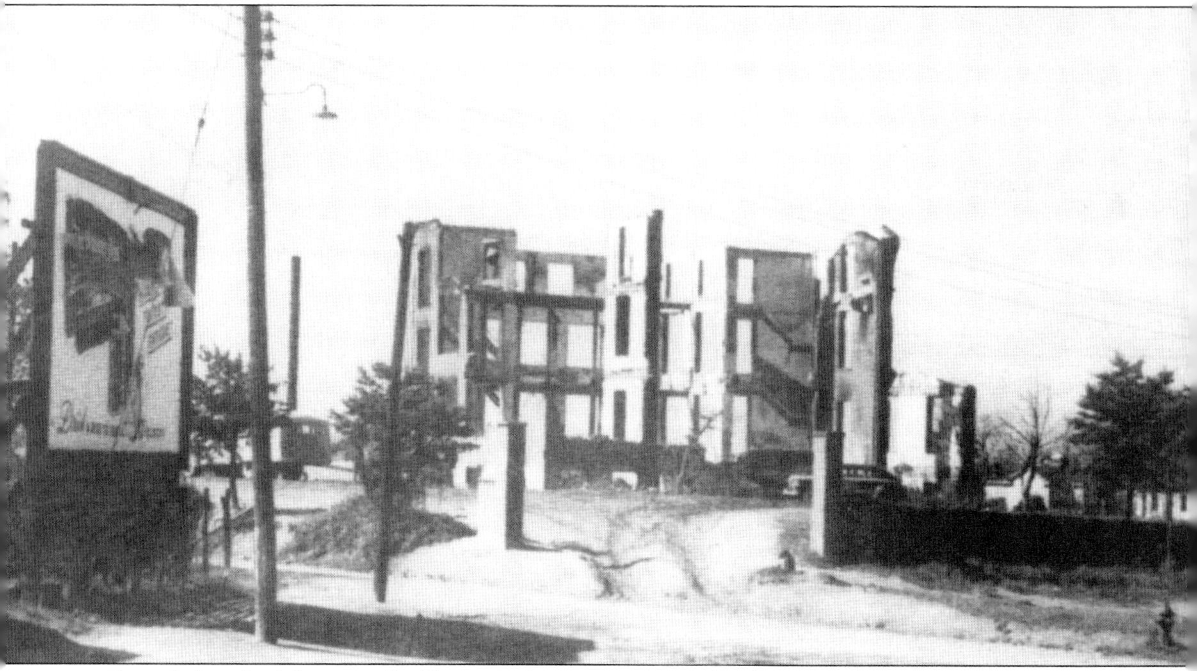

Founded as the Martinsville Christian Institute in 1900 by the Fayette Street Christian Church, the Henry County Training School's 18-room Smith Hall rose in 1906. Before it burned in 1940s, the school provided education to African American students. From 1948 until integration, Albert Harris High School continued this work. (Courtesy of Teddy Compton.)

Four

Henry County

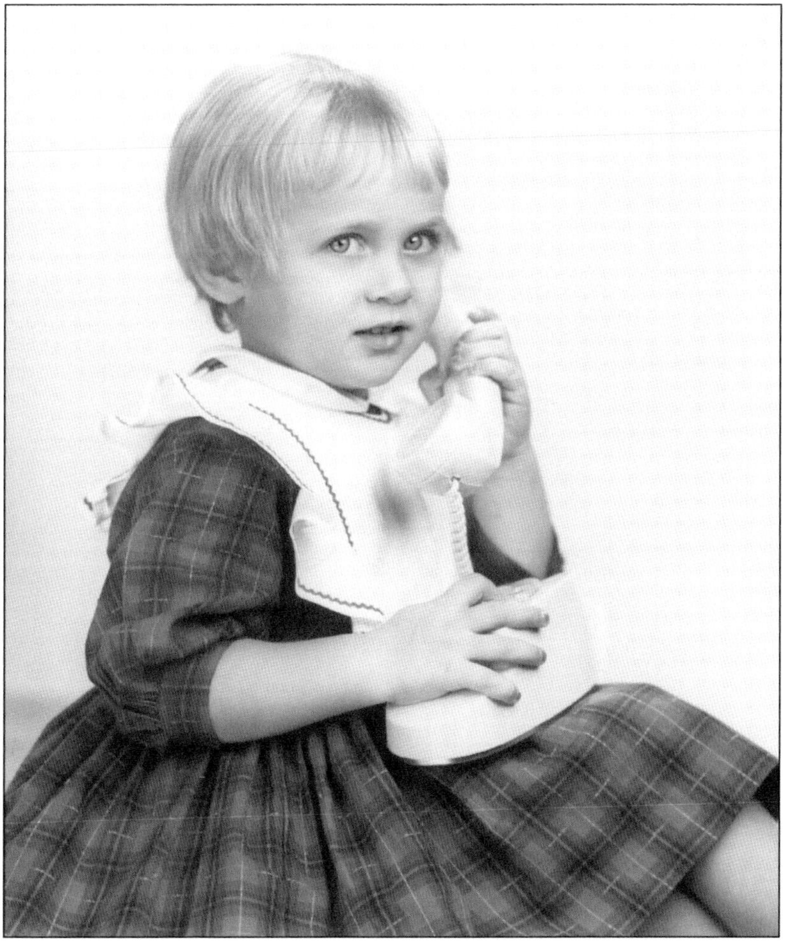

Young Cynthia Hubbard of Collinsville talks on the phone. The daughter of Wendell R. and Madeline Shelton Hubbard married "Her Beloved," Mark Headen, and had sons Devon, Dustin, and Gavin. She sat nearby as the author scanned the images for this book at the Bassett Historical Center. One of her duties is answering the phone. (Courtesy of Cynthia Headen.)

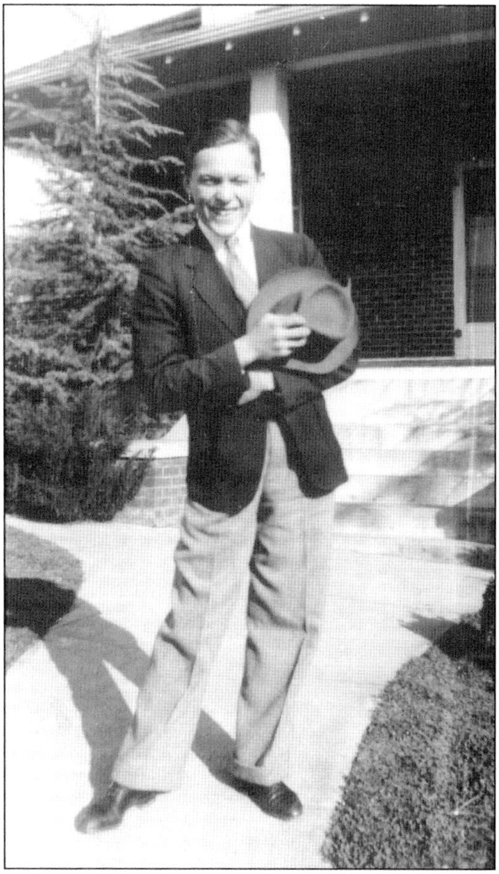

Albert Lee Philpott, born in this house in the northwestern part of Henry County, attended the University of Richmond, receiving a bachelor's degree and a law degree. The son of John Elkanah and Mary Gertrude Prillaman Philpott, he married Katherine Addison. He practiced law before becoming commonwealth attorney of Henry County. In 1957, he went to the Virginia House of Delegates, becoming speaker of that body from 1980 until his death in 1991. His influence brought Patrick Henry Community College and the Virginia Museum of Natural History to the area, and Highway 58 is now the A. L. Philpott Highway. (Above, courtesy of the Bassett Historical Center; below, courtesy of Douglas Stegall.)

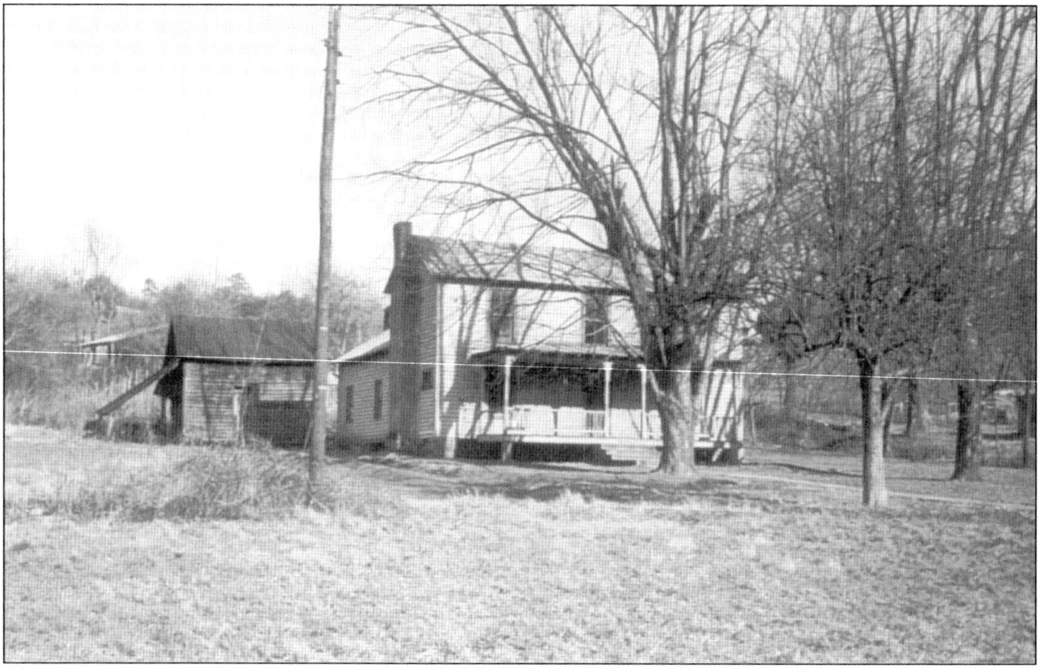

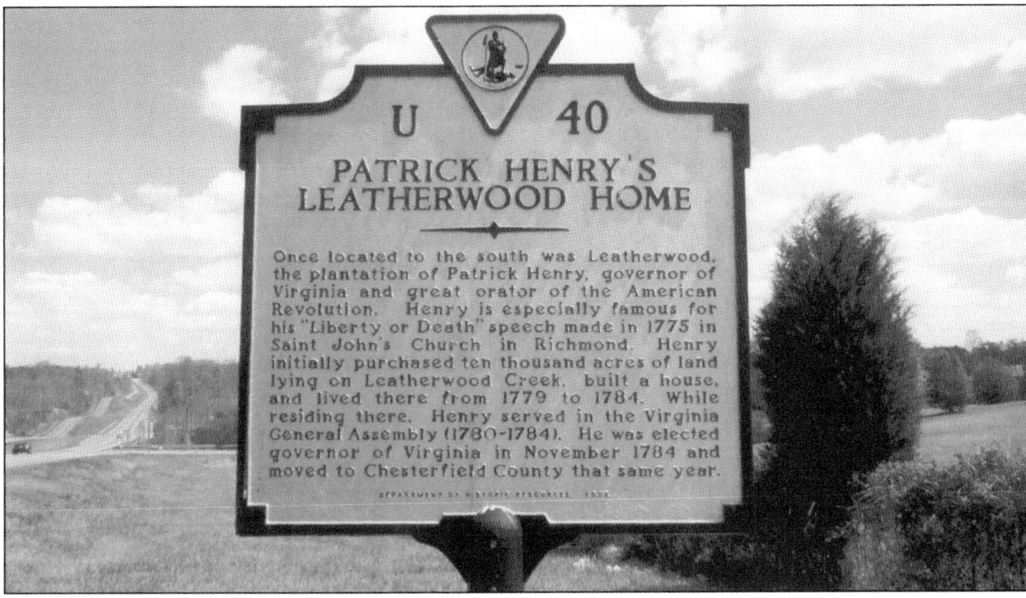

Patrick Henry's name adorns all Virginia maps today, as two counties side by side bear it. The man who proclaimed, "Give me liberty, or give me death" lived in the Leatherwood section of Henry County during the latter stages of the American Revolution and beyond after serving as Virginia's first governor. He died in 1799 at Red Hill, Virginia. (Courtesy of the Bassett Historical Center.)

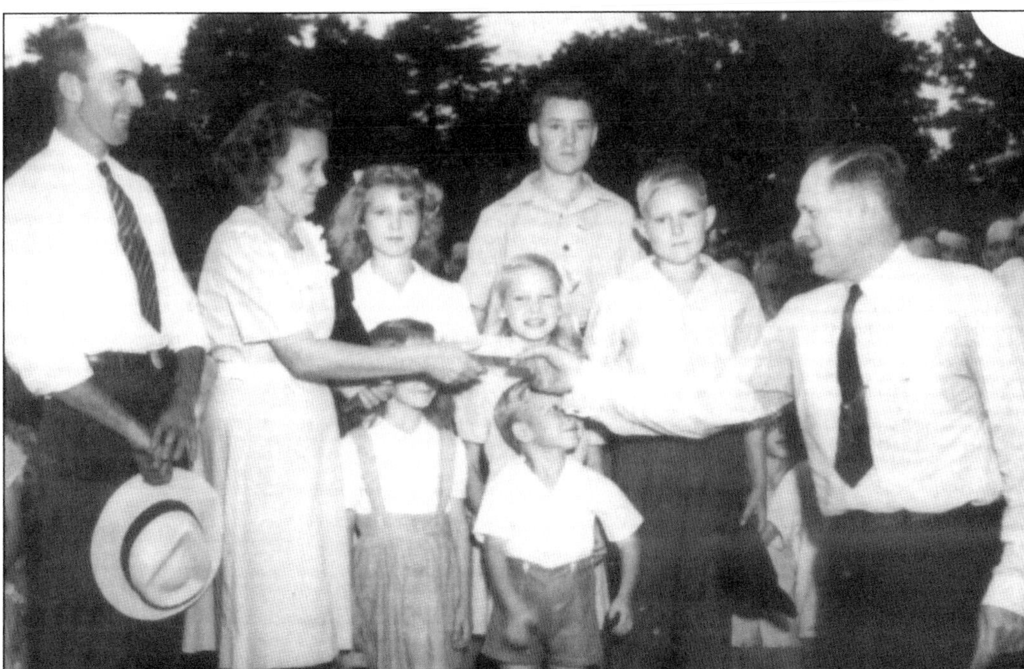

The Belvie Young family, pictured in August 1946 at the Stanley Furniture Company picnic, received an award for the largest family from Pres. Thomas B. Stanley, governor of Virginia from 1954 until 1958. Pictured are Belvie, Vickey, Lois, Bobby, Allen, Louise, Erma, and Bill Young. Bill worked for the Miss America pageant, judging it twice himself. (Courtesy of Bill Young.)

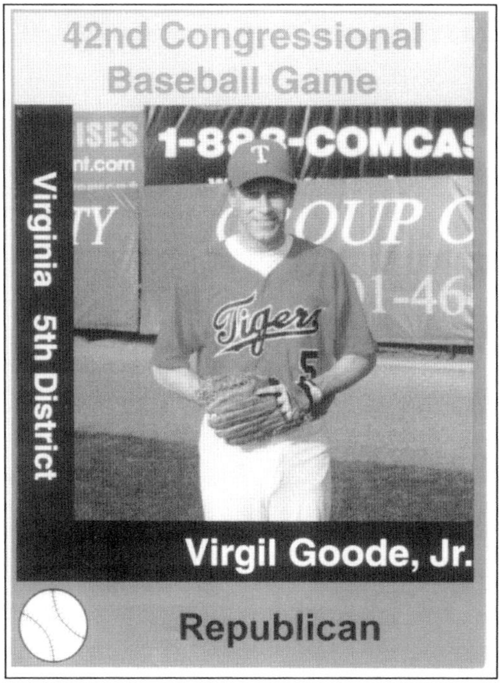

A strong supporter of the Bassett Historical Center, Virgil H. Goode represented Henry County in the Virginia Senate and then as congressman from the Fifth District in the U.S. House of Representatives beginning in 1997. He switched from the Democratic to the Republican Party. Goode has played in several Congressional baseball games. (Courtesy of Virgil Goode.)

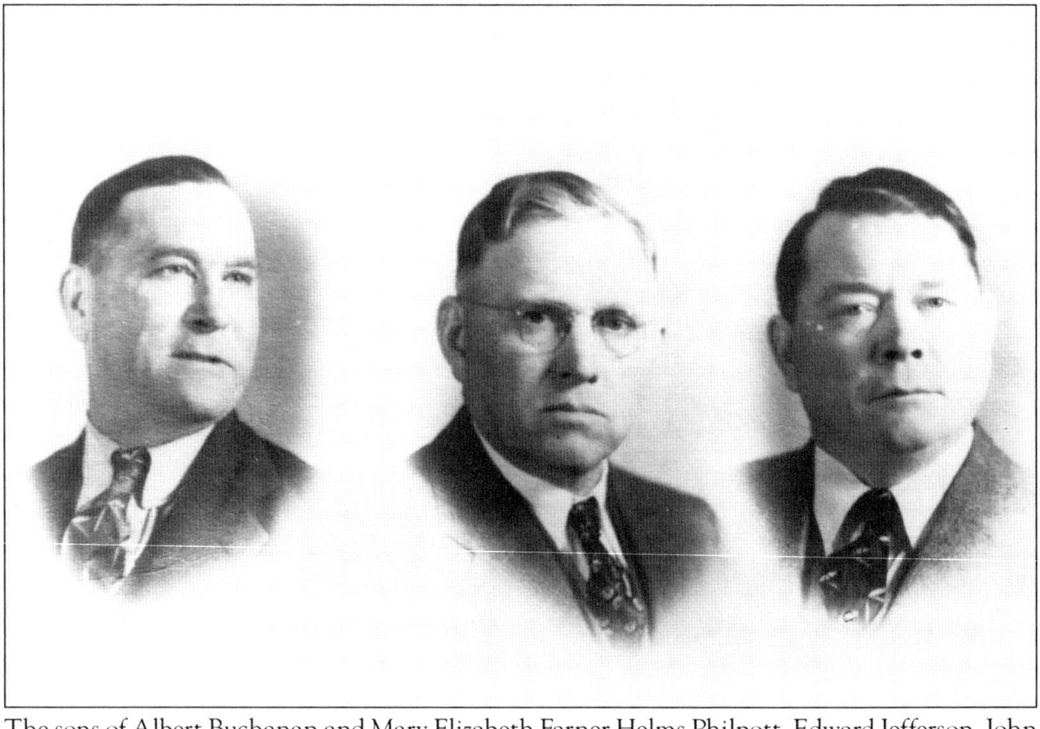

The sons of Albert Buchanan and Mary Elizabeth Farner Helms Philpott, Edward Jefferson, John Elkanah, and Charles Thomas Philpott, had four sisters. Their father and his brothers began the community of Philpott in northwestern Henry County. Today the dam and reservoir on the Smith River bear the family name. John was the father of A. L. Philpott. (Courtesy of the Bassett Historical Center.)

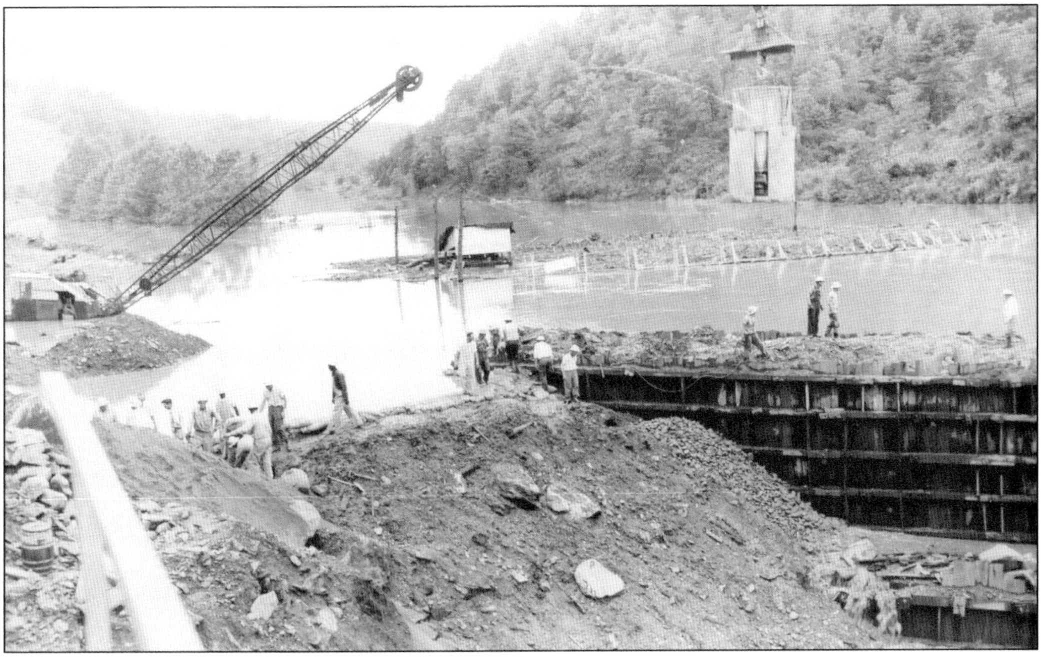

Construction on the Philpott Dam along the Smith River began in 1948, with operations generating hydroelectric power starting in 1953. With a shoreline of 100 miles covering 2,800 acres, the lake behind the dam provides recreational opportunities on the Philpottt Reservoir and Fairystone State Park in Patrick County. The dam stopped the flooding of communities such as Bassett and Fieldale downstream. William Byrd, on his survey of the Virginia and North Carolina boundary line in 1728, first named the Smith River, a tributary of the Dan River, the Irwin River. Today the Smith River flows passively behind the Bassett Historical Center. (Courtesy of the Bassett Historical Center.)

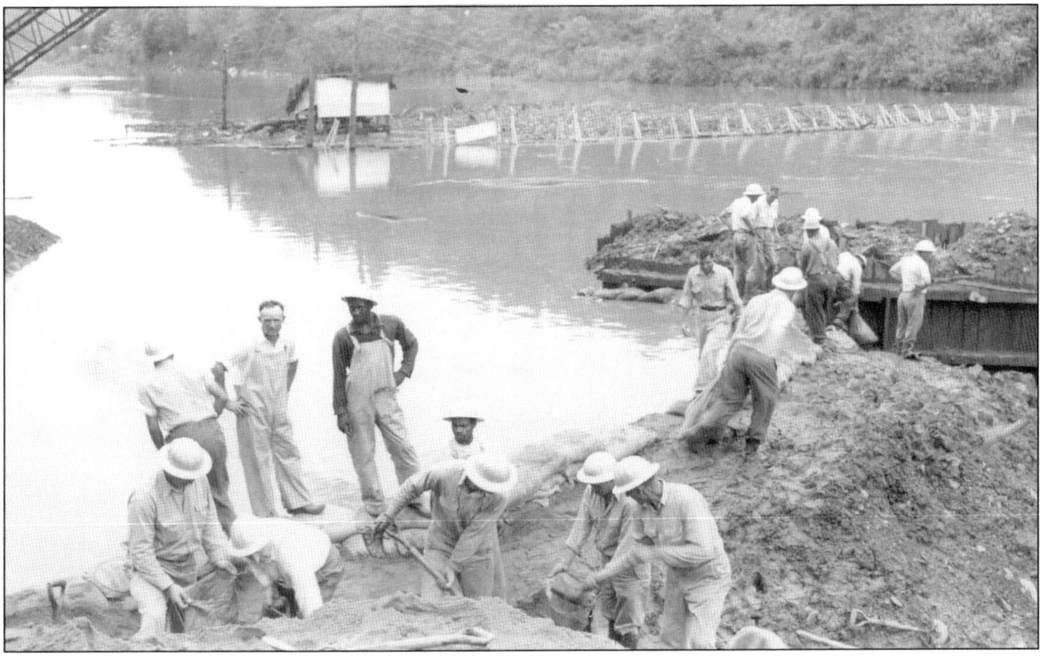

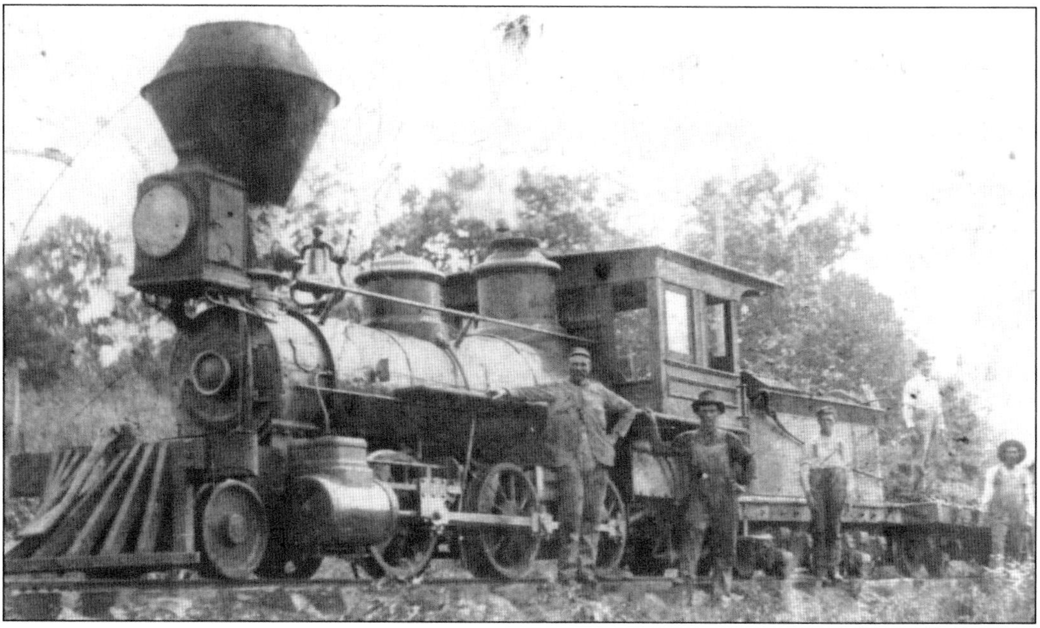

Known initially as the Danville and New River Railroad and later the Danville and Western Railroad, this railway is in the hearts of the local people as the "Dick and Willie" Railroad. With tracks spanning the region from Danville to Stuart, Virginia, the railroad first came to Henry County in 1881. These images show Engine No. 1 in the early days of the railroad and Engine No. 23 around 1925–1930. This railroad was a vital part of the industrial growth that occurred with Marshall Field Company at Fieldale and the textile and furniture business throughout Henry County. Parts of this rail system are now walking trails, while other sections still carry trains as part of the Norfolk Southern Railroad. (Courtesy of Kenney Kirkman.)

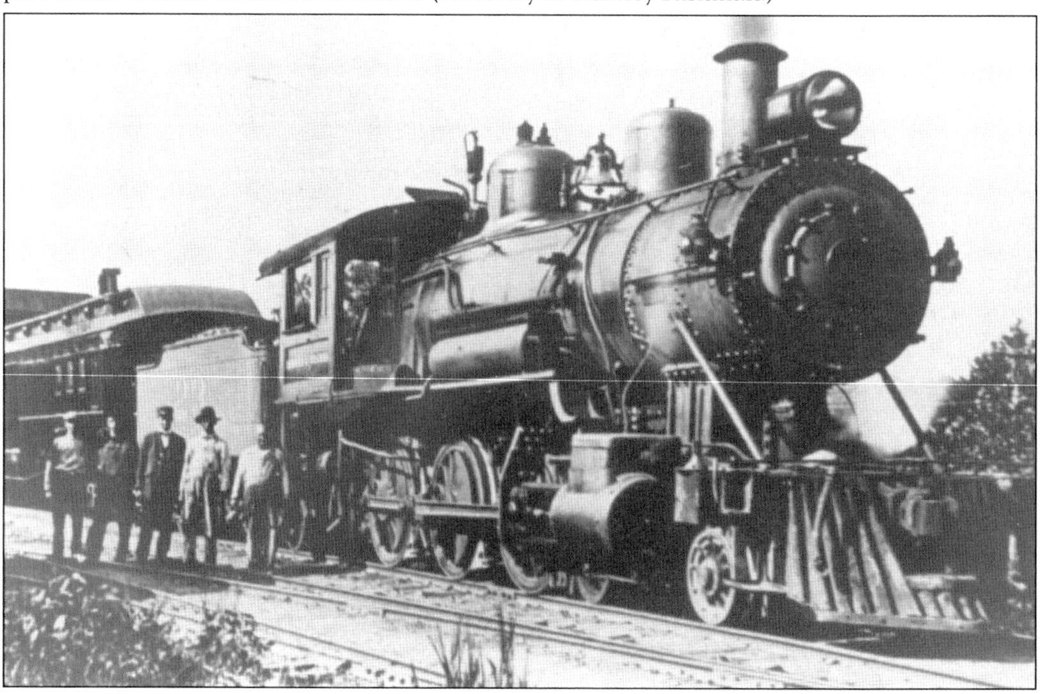

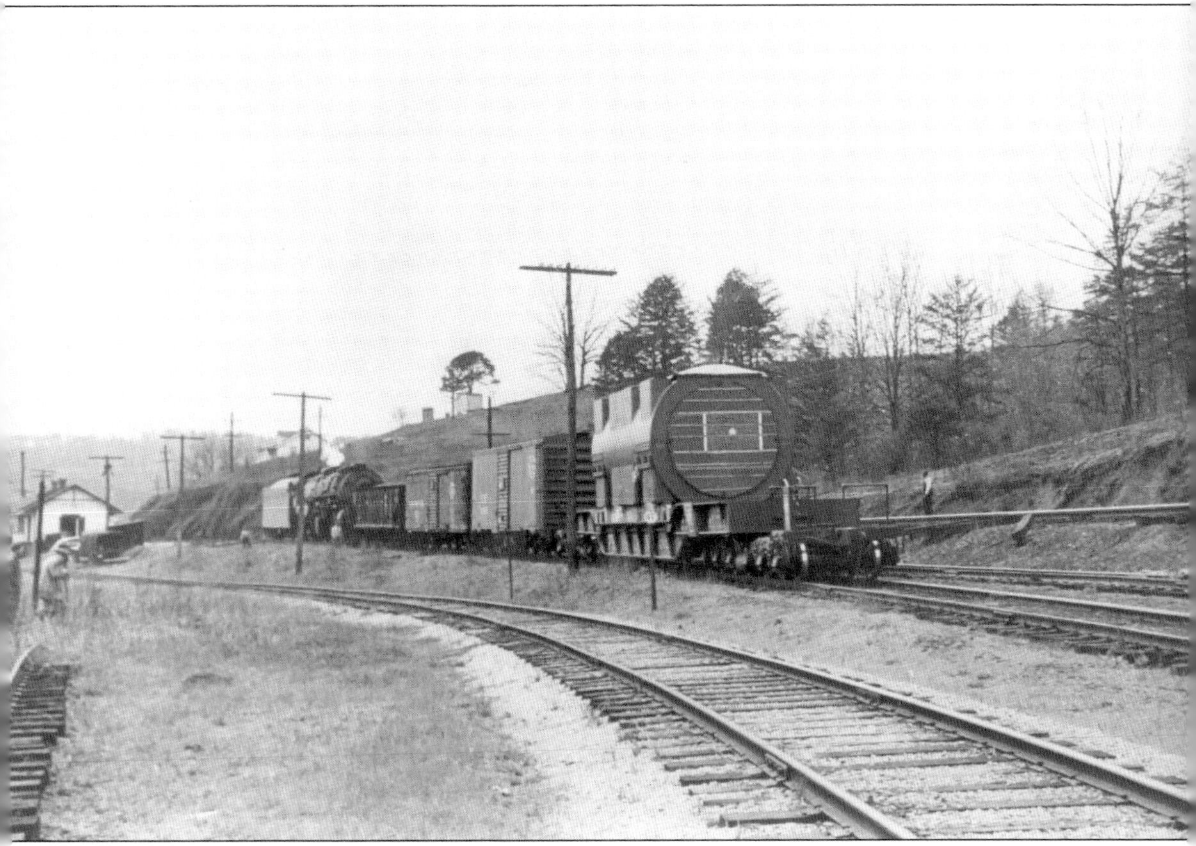

A transformer bound for the Duke Power Power Plant in Eden, North Carolina, sits on the Norfolk and Western Railroad at the Koehler Station in Henry County. This c. 1950 image shows a transfer to the Danville and Western Railroad waiting to occur. As the two rail systems diverged at Koehler, Virginia, transfers at sidings like this were commonplace. (Courtesy of Kenney Kirkman.)

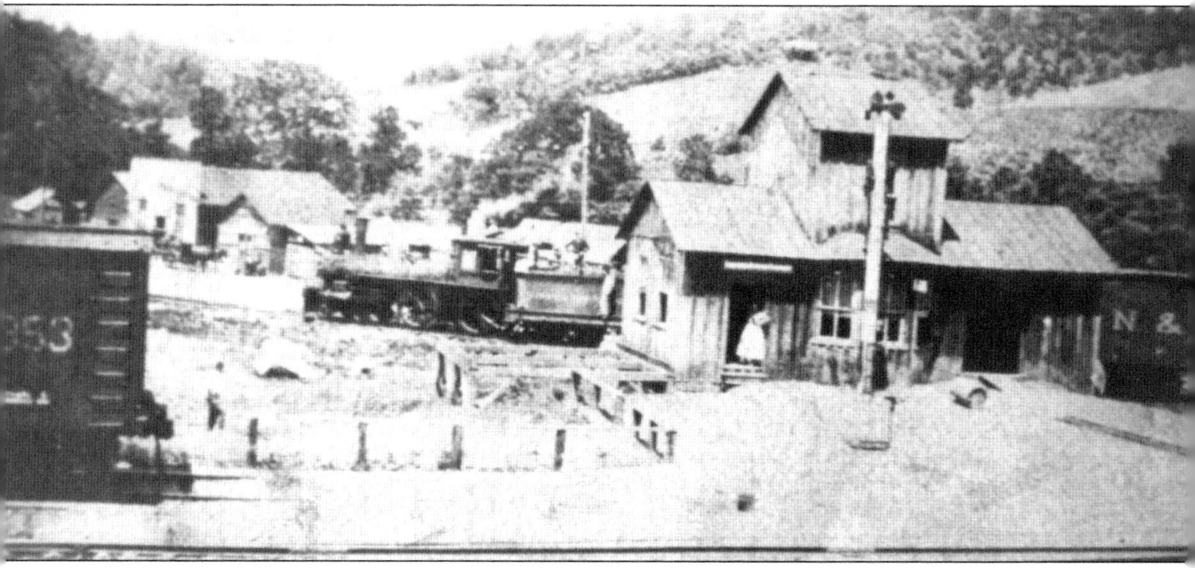

A train heads up the Fayerdale Railroad on its way from the Philpott Station around 1920. This standard-gauge track went up the Smith River to present-day Fairy Stone State Park but is now under the waters of Philpott Lake. In the foreground are the tracks of the standard-gauge Norfolk and Western. (Courtesy of Kenney Kirkman.)

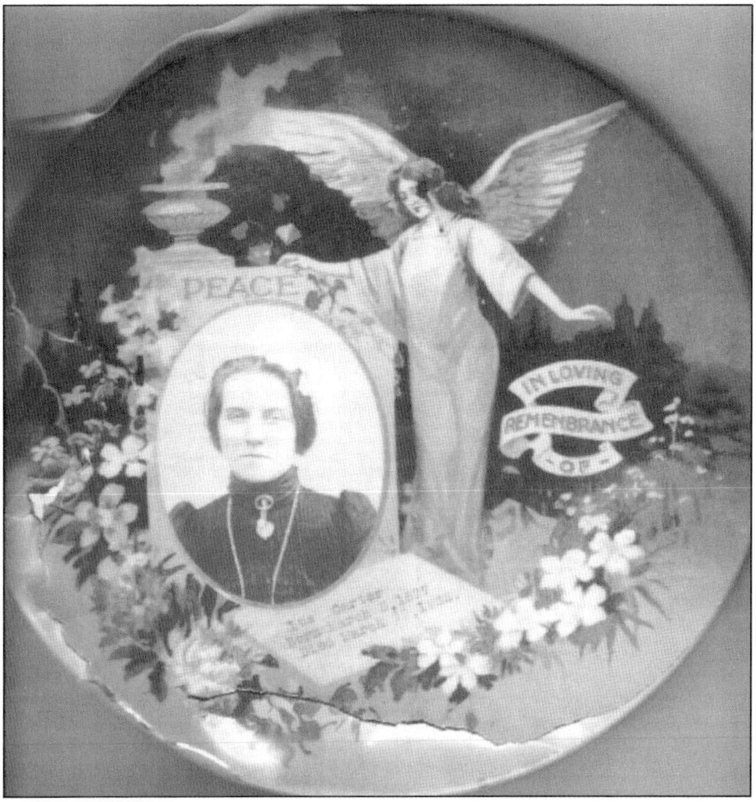

This display from the funeral of Ida Carter (March 3, 1877–March 12, 1932) came to the author from several relatives, including Avis Carter Turner, the granddaughter of Ida Carter. The death of a loved one often was cause for families to come together to share food and memories, and with the size of some families, these became major events. (Courtesy of Rebecca Dyer.)

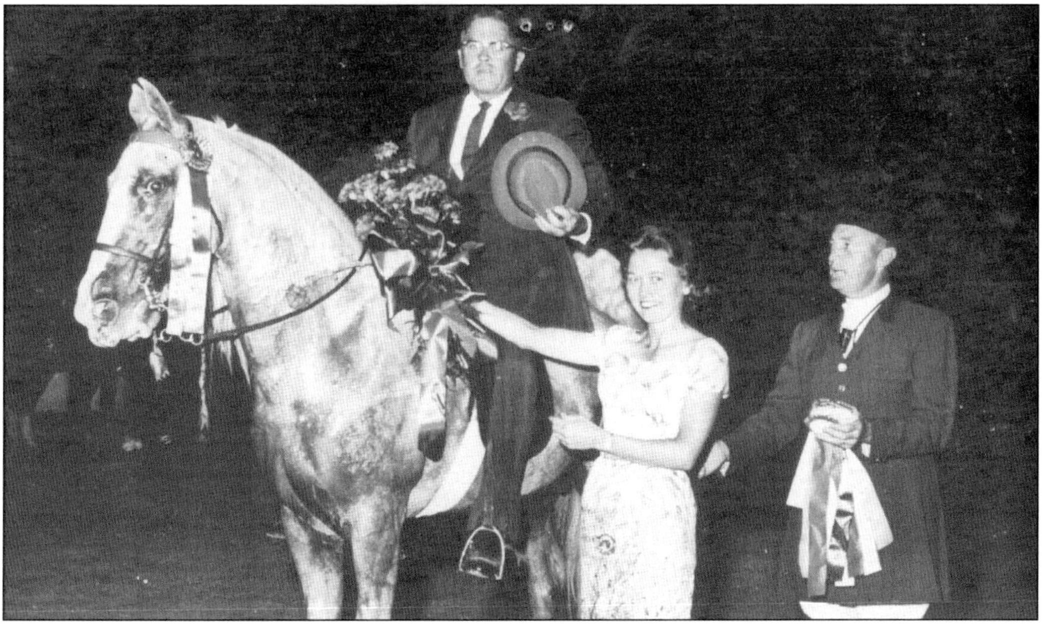

Grey Sun was a champion on the local and state level. Stanley W. Bowles rides his champion horse with Adlynn Philpott Wilson and an unidentified horse show official around 1962. Grey Sun was a Tennessee Walker shown at the state show in Charlotte, North Carolina, at which he and Bowles were victorious. (Courtesy of David Bowles.)

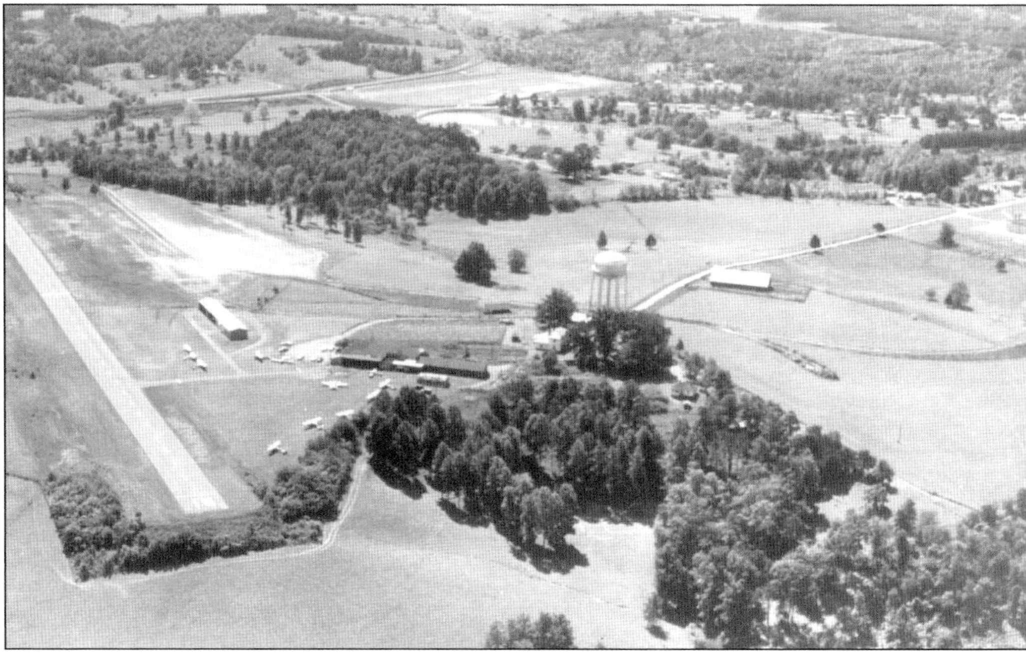

Today visitors fly into Henry County at the Blue Ridge Airport in the eastern section, near Spencer, for races at the Martinsville Speedway. Another airport, shown in this image, was along Highway 220 South near the Martinsville Industrial Park. It is now the Stone Container near Ridgeway. (Courtesy of the Jerry Brock Collection.)

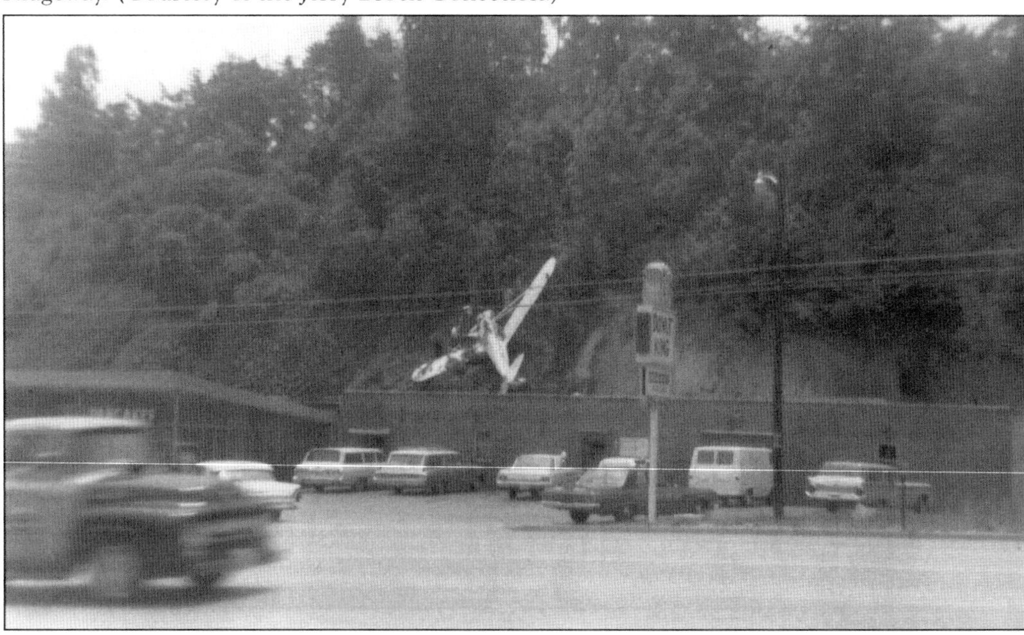

Not everyone flying into Henry County had a smooth landing, as this 1965 plane crash next door to the Dutch Inn motel and behind the bowling lanes in Collinsville proves. The Dutch Inn, with a large windmill on its facade, welcomes visitors and hosts many local events. Just down the street is the Collinsville Branch of the Blue Ridge Regional Library, which holds History Day the third Sunday of February, May, August, and November. (Courtesy of Teddy Compton.)

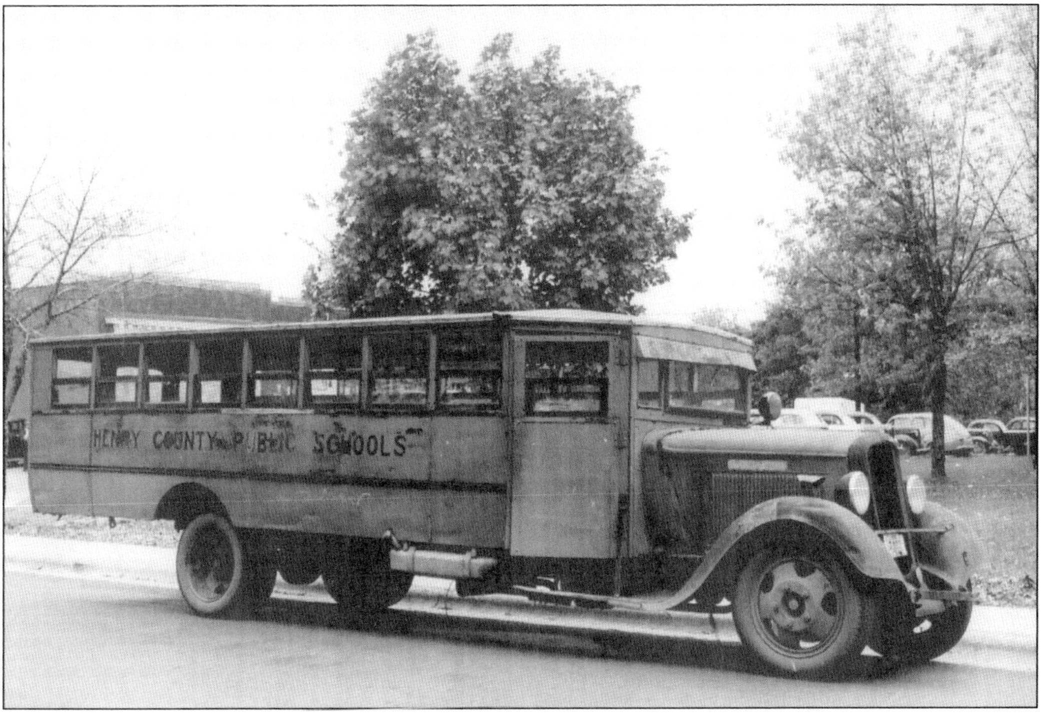

This image of a Henry County school bus parked in Fieldale gives an opportunity to discuss schools. Henry County operates Bassett and Magna Vista High Schools; Fieldale-Collinsville and Laurel Park Middle Schools; and Axton, Carver, Campbell Court, Collinsville, Irisburg, John Redd, Mount Olivet, Rich Acres, Ridgeway, Sanville, and Stanleytown Elementary Schools. (Courtesy of Teddy Compton.)

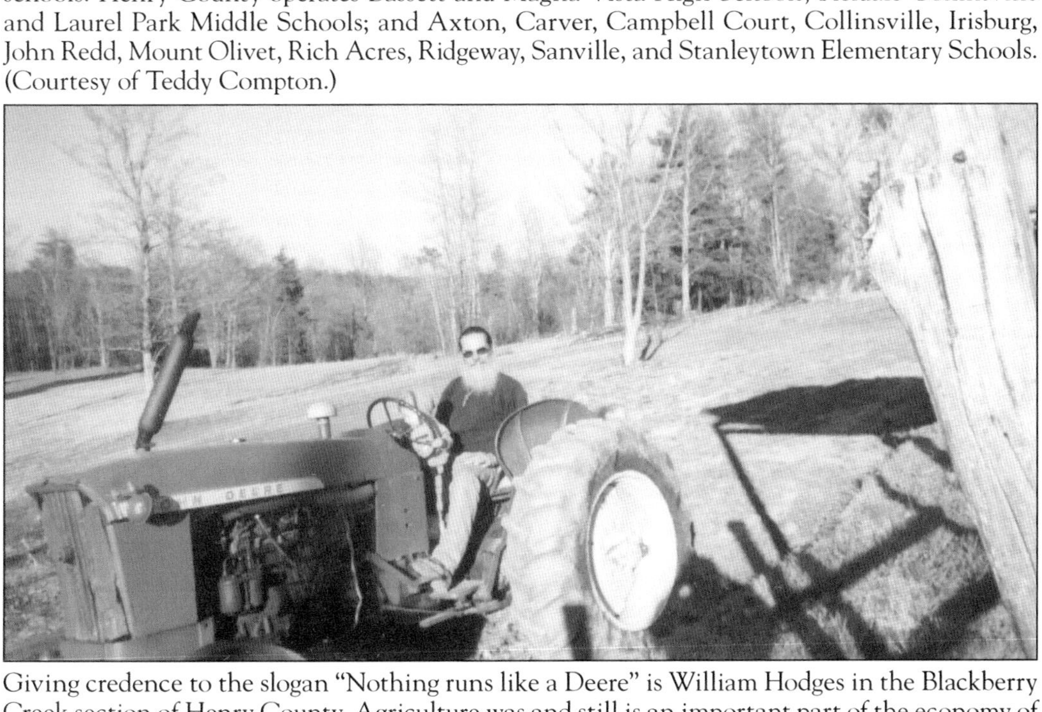

Giving credence to the slogan "Nothing runs like a Deere" is William Hodges in the Blackberry Creek section of Henry County. Agriculture was and still is an important part of the economy of the region. Tobacco farming and manufacturing once was a major force in the Piedmont section of Virginia and North Carolina. (Courtesy of Deborah Hodges.)

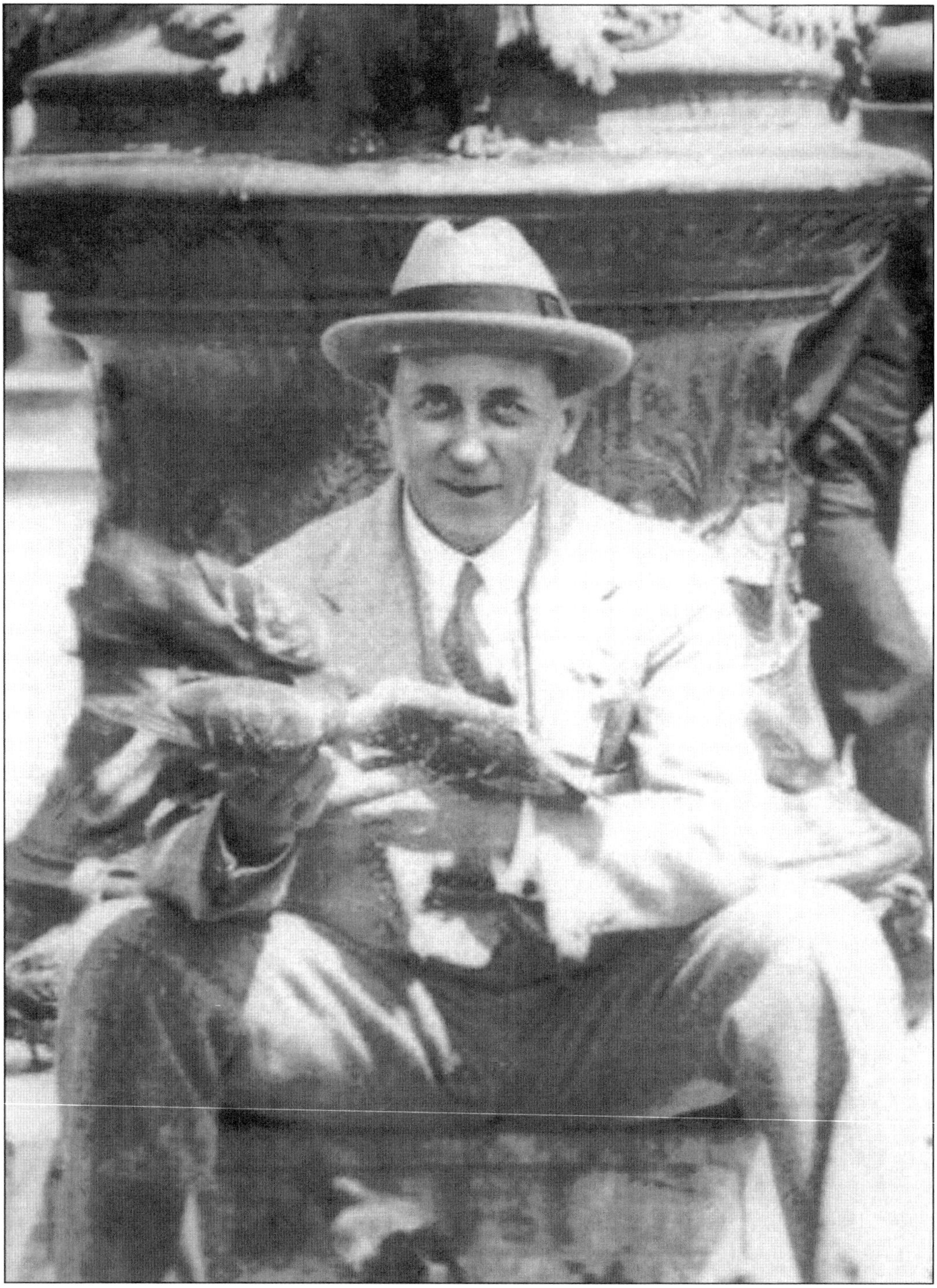

Dr. Morton E. Hundley, who practiced medicine in Ridgeway and Martinsville, is feeding the pigeons, possibly in Europe. He attended the Medical College of Virginia and Johns Hopkins Medical School. He died of a heart attack on January 2, 1928, in Switzerland on his third honeymoon. He started the Lucy Lester Hospital on Church Street in Martinsville. (Courtesy of Sam Eanes.)

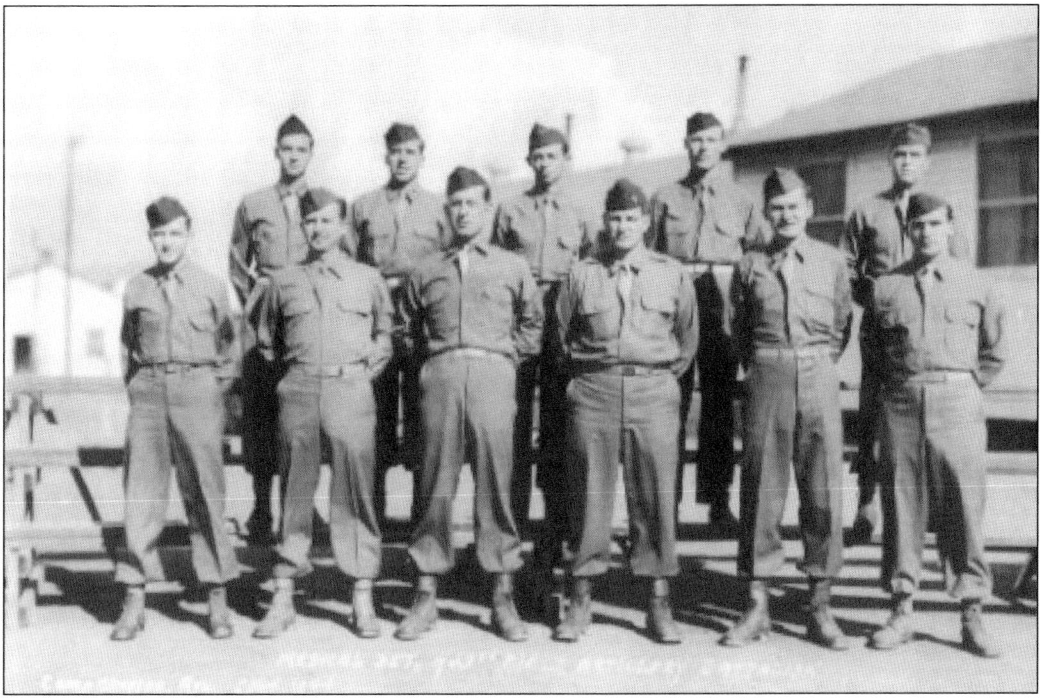

Garland Atlas Carter is at far left in the second row in this photograph from November 6, 1944. A medical DET (detachment), he served with men from California, Pennsylvania, New Jersey, Vermont, and New Hampshire in the 743rd Field Artillery Battalion at Camp Chappel, Arkansas, during World War II. (Courtesy of Rebecca Dyer.)

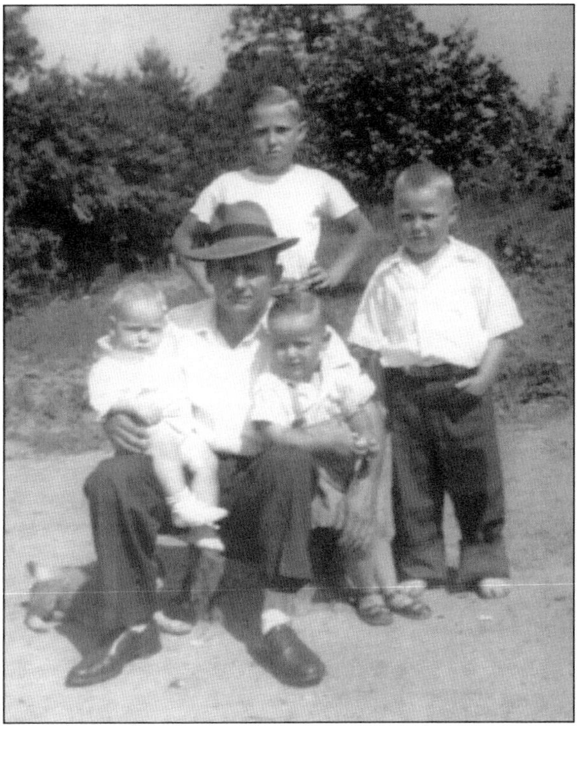

Floyd Glenn Eanes (1912–1984) is pictured around 1951 with his sons in the Redwood section of Franklin County. From left to right are (first row) Larry Lee Eanes, Floyd Jr., Lewis Allen; (second row) Samuel Elbert (who works at the Bassett Historical Center) and Glyn. Floyd Sr. served in World War II and delivered the mail but spent most of his life as an auto mechanic. The family moved to the Barrow's Mill section of Henry County in 1954. (Courtesy of Sam Eanes.)

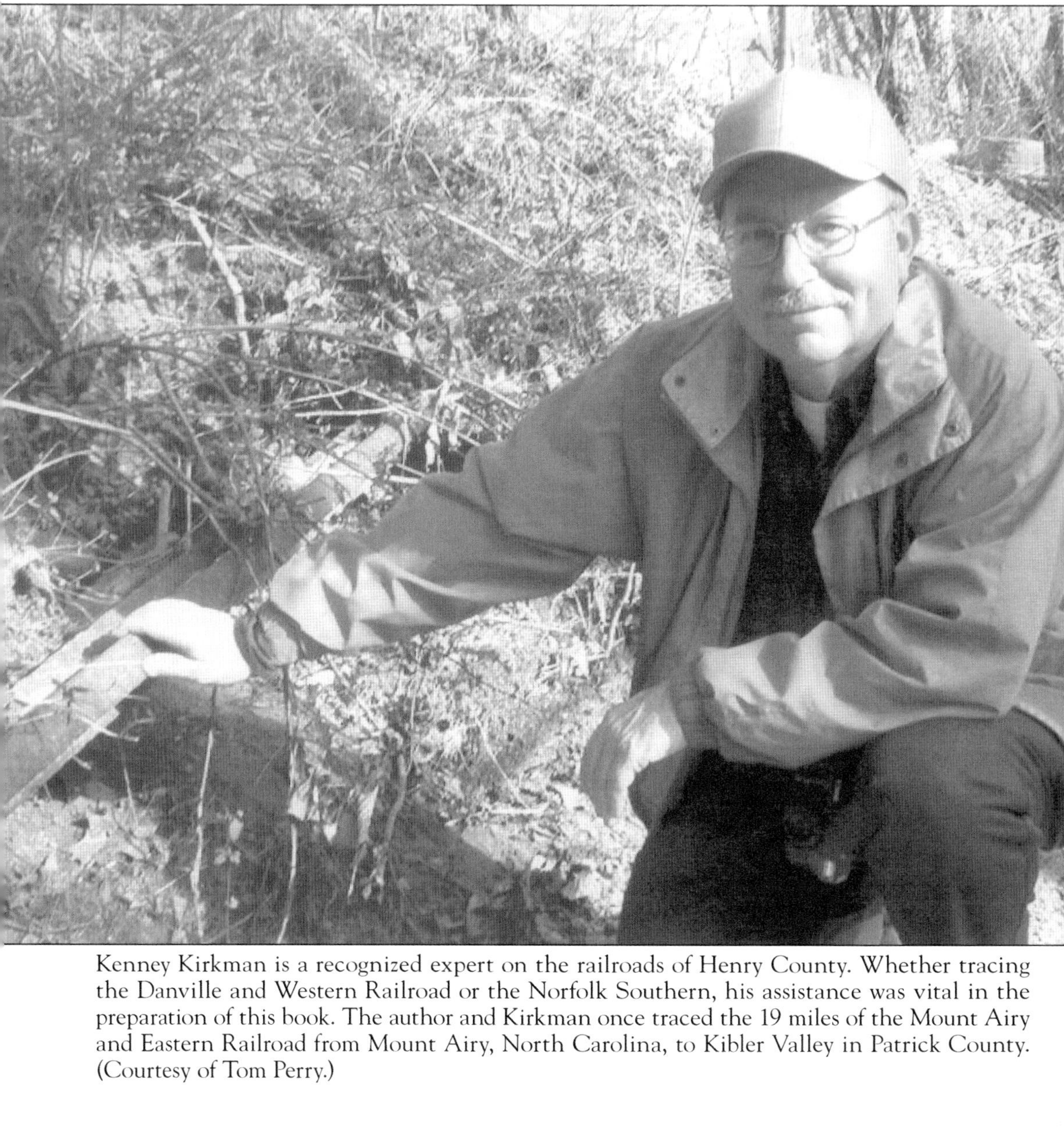

Kenney Kirkman is a recognized expert on the railroads of Henry County. Whether tracing the Danville and Western Railroad or the Norfolk Southern, his assistance was vital in the preparation of this book. The author and Kirkman once traced the 19 miles of the Mount Airy and Eastern Railroad from Mount Airy, North Carolina, to Kibler Valley in Patrick County. (Courtesy of Tom Perry.)

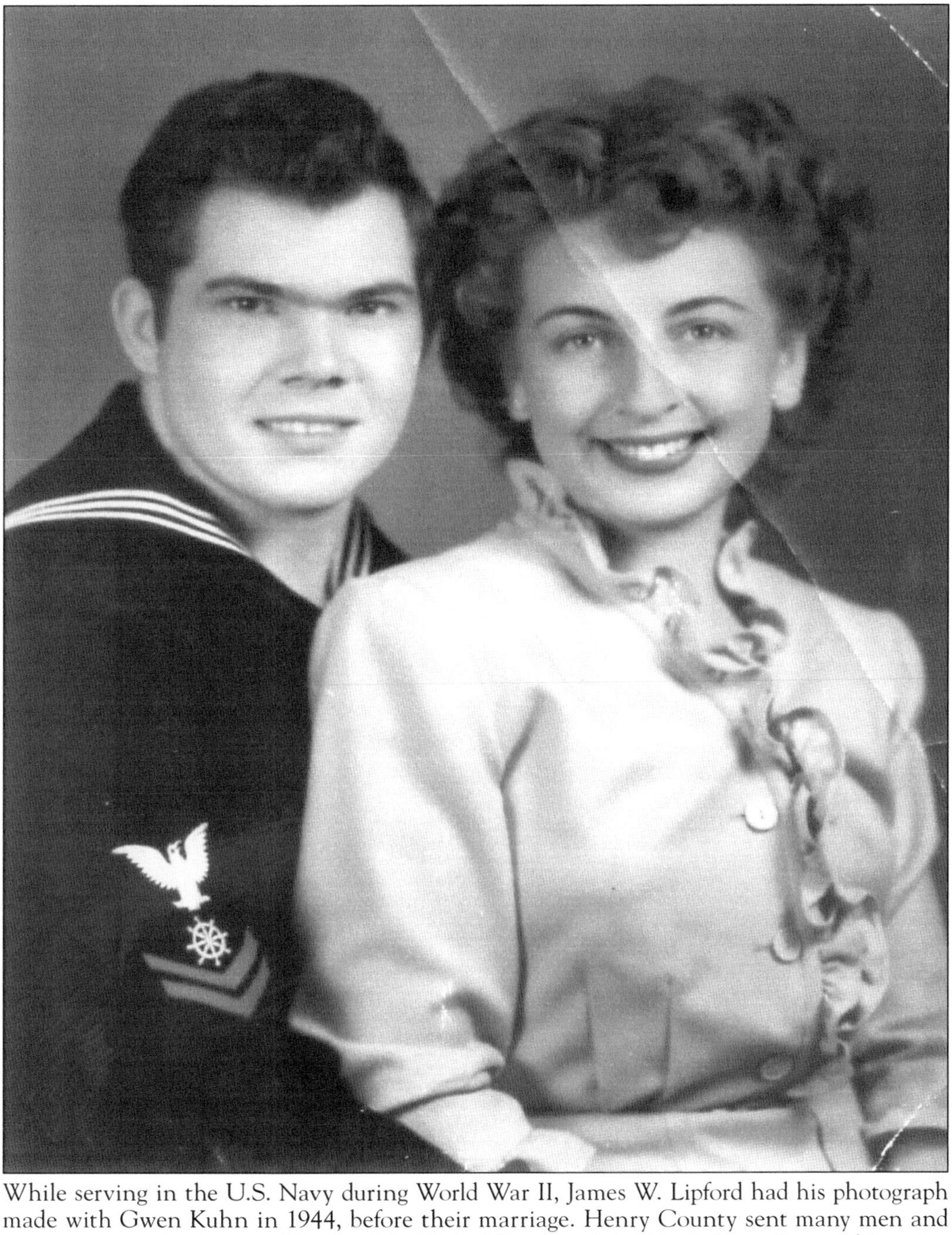

While serving in the U.S. Navy during World War II, James W. Lipford had his photograph made with Gwen Kuhn in 1944, before their marriage. Henry County sent many men and women to serve in the armed forces of the United States and the Confederate States of America from the American Revolution through the present wars in Iraq and Afghanistan. (Courtesy of Beverly Yeager.)

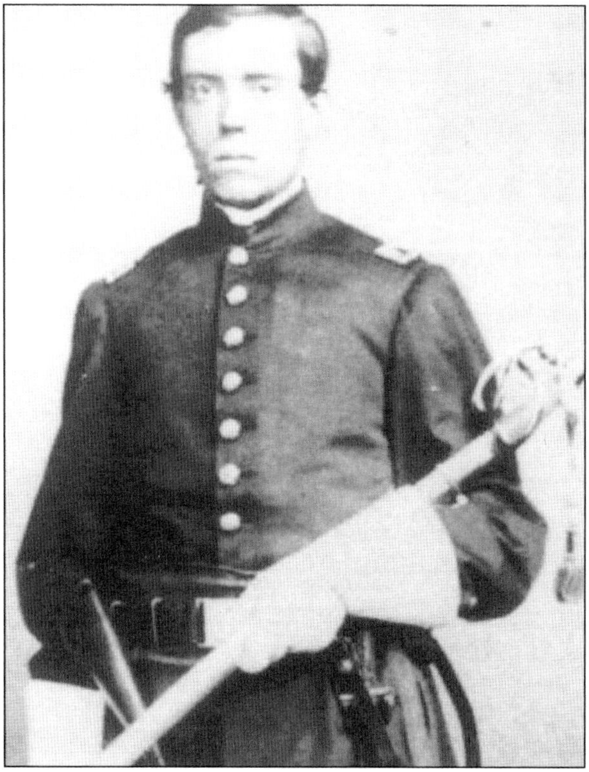

Bvt. Brig. Gen. William Jackson Palmer came through Henry County in April 1865 as part of George Stoneman's raid at the end of the War Between the States. Stoneman did not enter the county, as he was further west in Patrick County. Palmer, who after the war went to Colorado to build a railroad business, received the Medal of Honor for his service in the Civil War. (Courtesy of Tom Perry.)

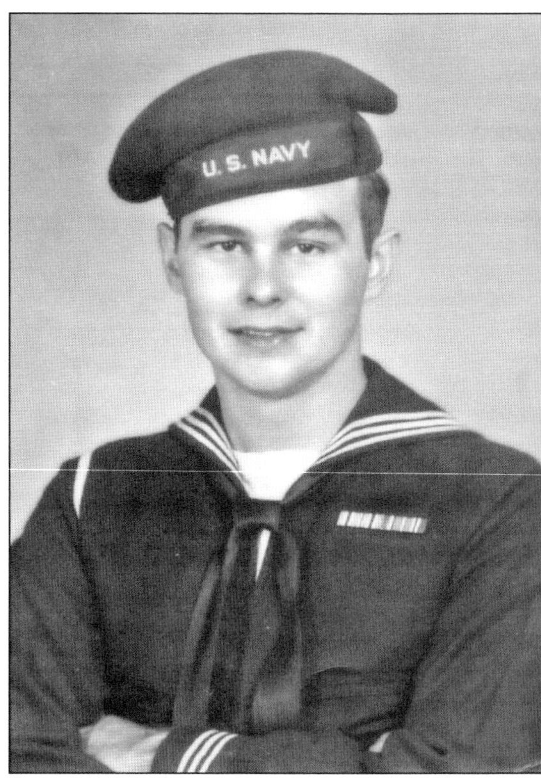

Another navy man from Henry County in World War II was Norris Smith. The Bassett Historical Center is interviewing service members as part of the Veterans History Project of the Library of Congress to preserve the memories of those who served. The library sends one copy of the interviews on DVD to Washington, D.C., and one copy remains at the library. (Courtesy of Beverly Yeager.)

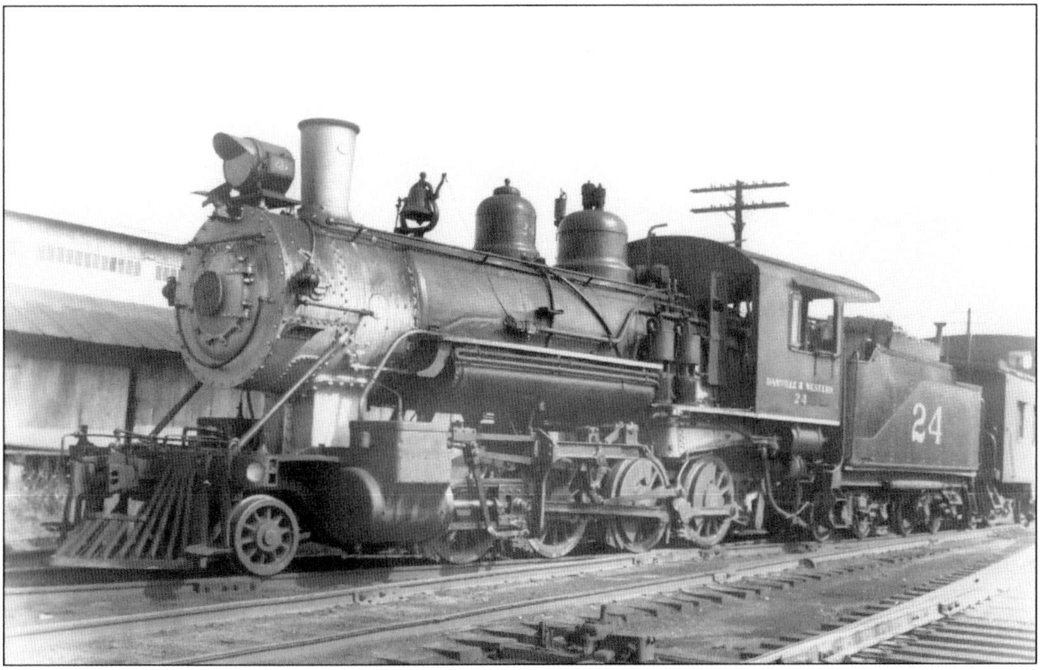

Steam engine No. 24 of the Danville and New River Railroad, later the Danville and Western, is photographed on June 12, 1939. Chartered in 1873 by the Commonwealth of Virginia, the railroad reached Martinsville in 1882. Financial problems kept the railroad from reaching the New River. Note the caboose on the right attached to the locomotive tender. (Courtesy of Kenney Kirkman.)

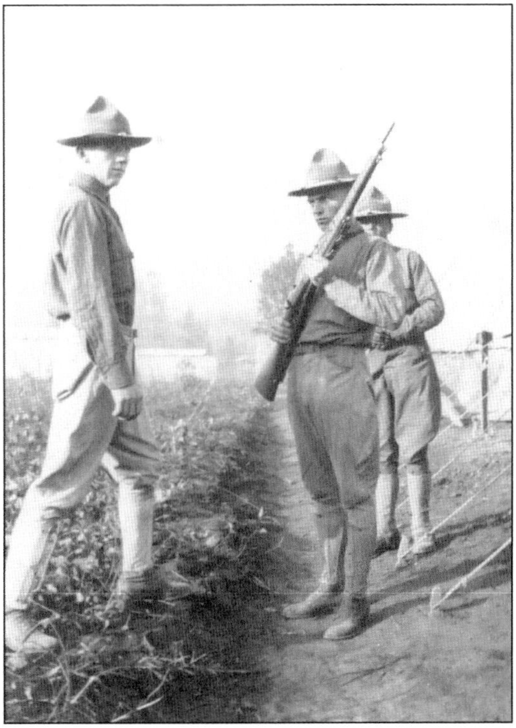

Holding his rifle during World War I is doughboy M. E. Helms. Helms returned to open a shoe store in Bassett and carry the mail. We should remember the service of these men as we approach the 100th anniversary of the "war to end all wars." The Bassett Historical Center contains an entire room focusing on the wars fought by this country. (Courtesy of Rachel Koontz.)

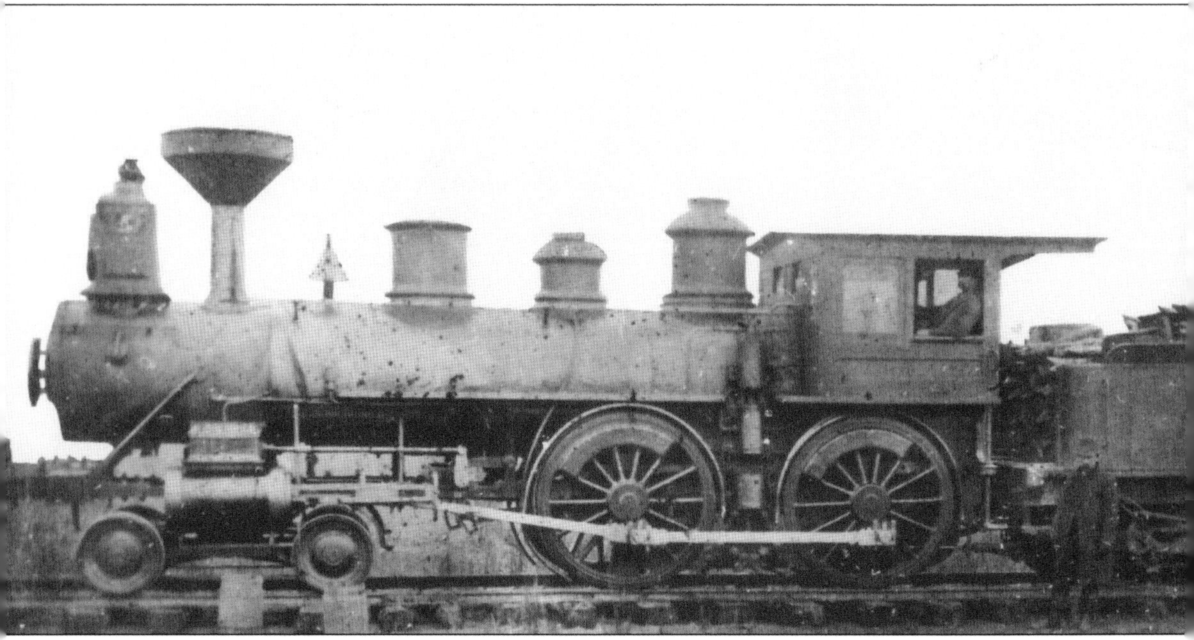

Steam locomotive No. 1 of the Roanoke and Southern Railway, pictured in 1888, pulled the first passenger train from Winston-Salem, North Carolina, to Roanoke, Virginia, four years later, in 1892. This railroad became the Norfolk and Western Railroad and later the Norfolk and Southern, which still operates through Henry County. (Courtesy of Kenney Kirkman.)

Mary Magdalene Payne, the daughter of Alfred and Bessie Jones Payne of Pulaski County, Virginia, poses at the house of her neighbors, S. B. and Mary Spears, in Koehler around 1955. Koehler, located along Highway 57 on the Smith River, is near Fieldale. Mary married John Payne, the son of Reuben and Cora Graham Payne of Wythe County, Virginia. (Courtesy of Ronnie Payne.)

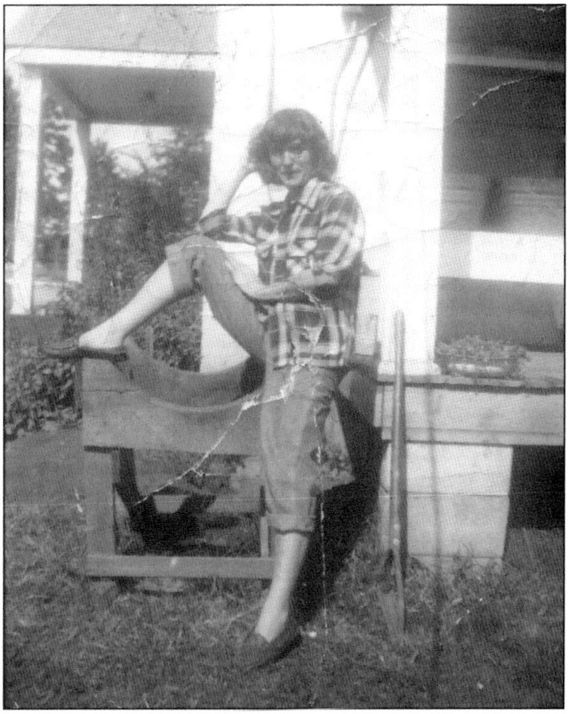

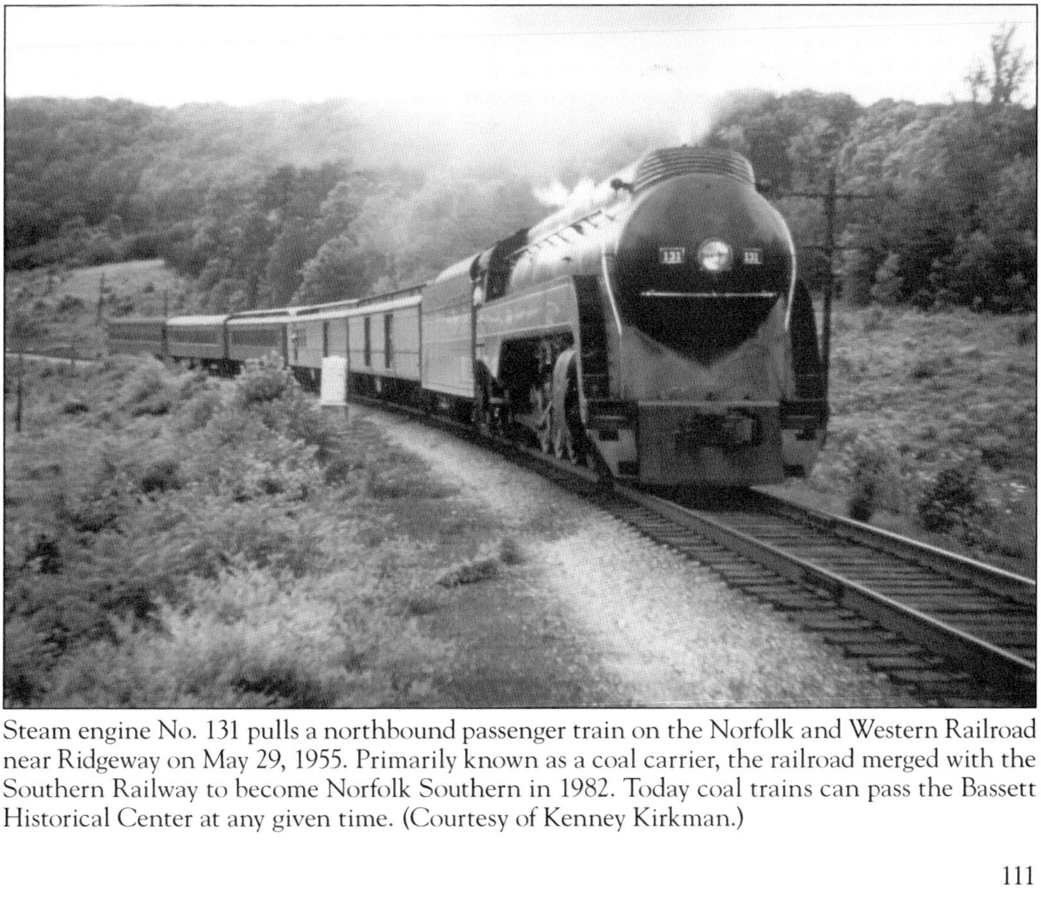

Steam engine No. 131 pulls a northbound passenger train on the Norfolk and Western Railroad near Ridgeway on May 29, 1955. Primarily known as a coal carrier, the railroad merged with the Southern Railway to become Norfolk Southern in 1982. Today coal trains can pass the Bassett Historical Center at any given time. (Courtesy of Kenney Kirkman.)

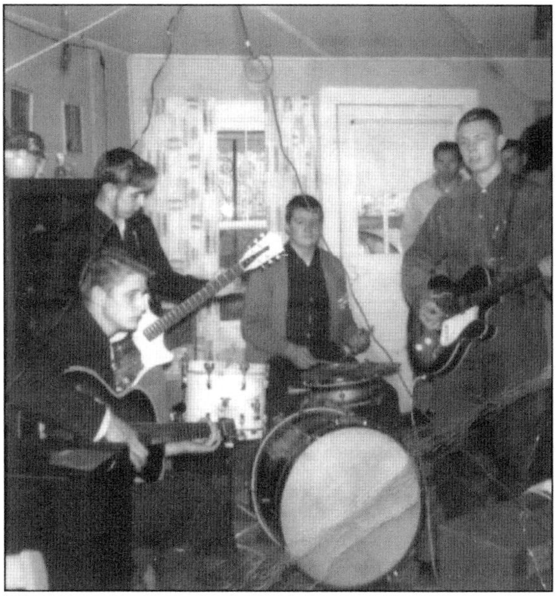

Inspired by the Beatles one month after they appeared on the Ed Sullivan Show, the Furys rehearsed in the Tilley House in Koehler, Virginia. Reed and Buster Tilley, Ronnie Payne, and Mike Spears practice in March 1964. While they never made it to New York, the band reflects a time before the turbulence of the 1960s reached Henry County. (Courtesy of Ronnie Payne and Mike Spears.)

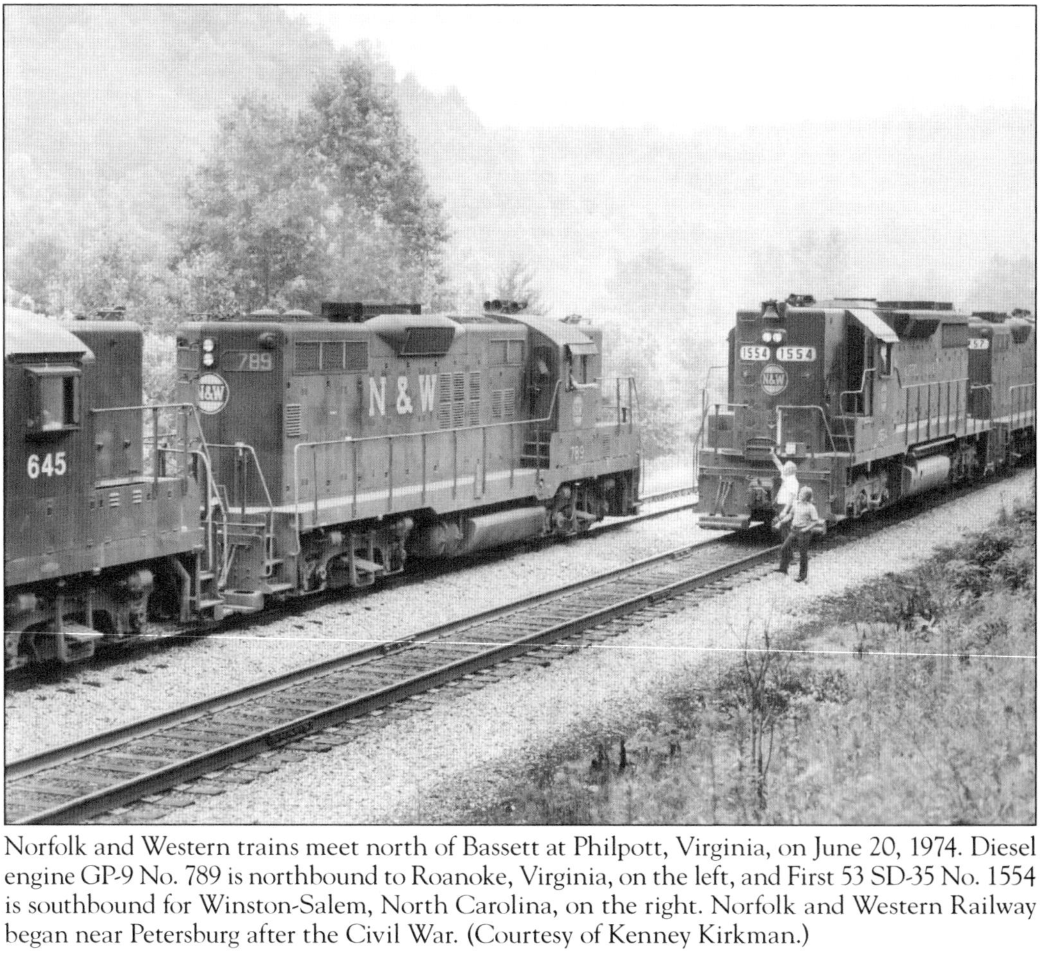

Norfolk and Western trains meet north of Bassett at Philpott, Virginia, on June 20, 1974. Diesel engine GP-9 No. 789 is northbound to Roanoke, Virginia, on the left, and First 53 SD-35 No. 1554 is southbound for Winston-Salem, North Carolina, on the right. Norfolk and Western Railway began near Petersburg after the Civil War. (Courtesy of Kenney Kirkman.)

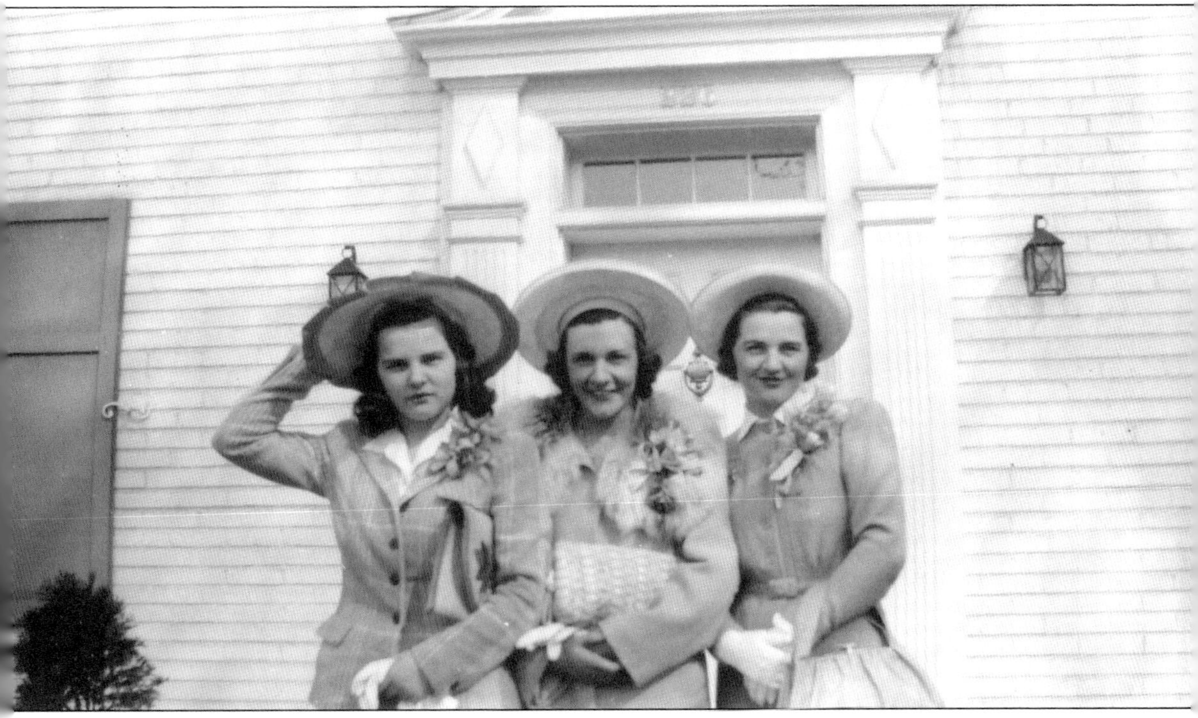

Dressed in their Sunday finest are, from left to right, Virginia Windle, Warren Gardner, and Geneva Chappell, the daughters of Samuel Lucius and Nora Taylor Stone. Virginia is the author of *Some Stone Stats* and *The Way It Was in Henry County and Martinsville, Virginia*, detailing the history of Henry County. Her collection resides today in the Bassett Historical Center. (Courtesy of the Bassett Historical Collection.)

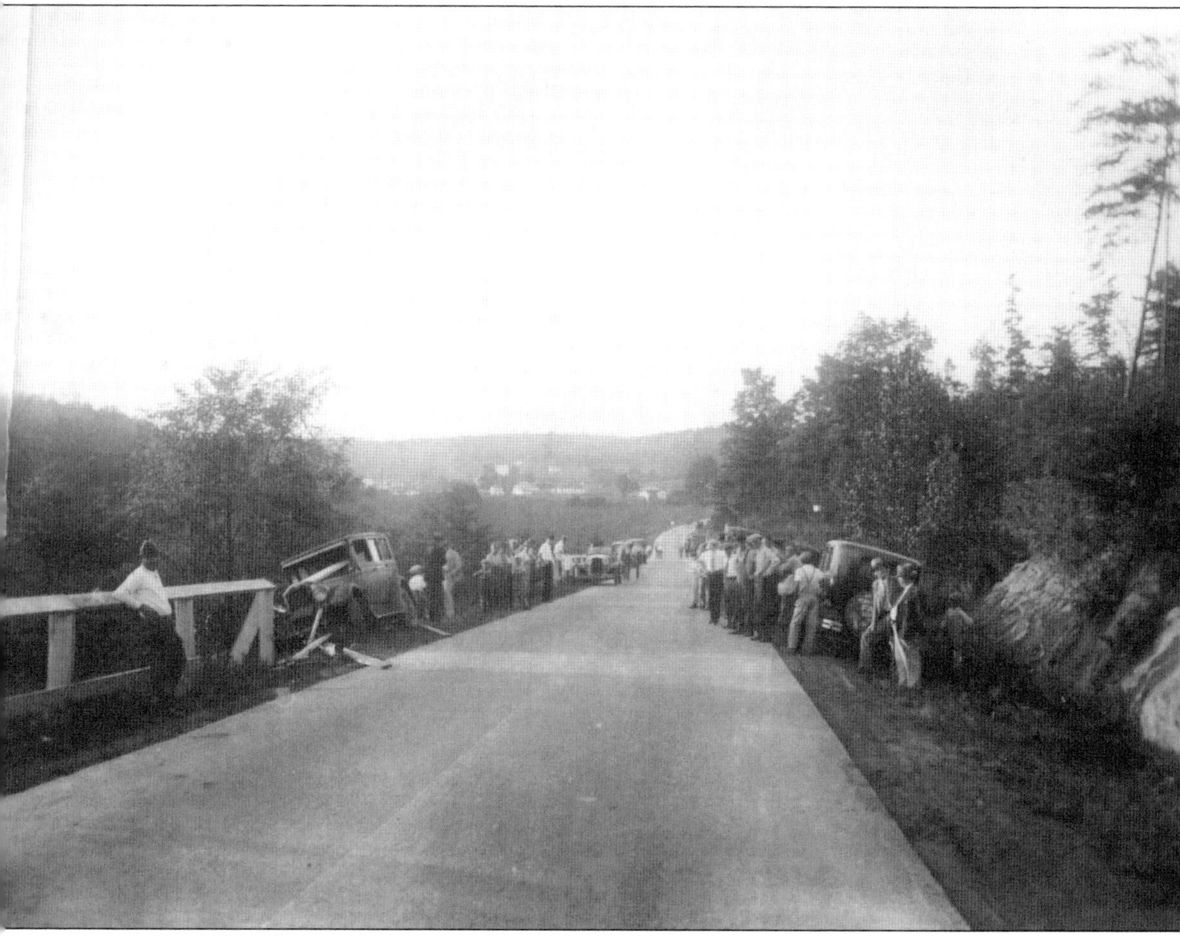

J. B. Stegall and others are pictured at a wreck near Koehler on the road to Martinsville in the 1920s. Built due to the construction of Marshall Field Company's plant along the Smith River, one of the first paved roads in the county was between Fieldale and Martinsville. (Courtesy of Teddy Compton.)

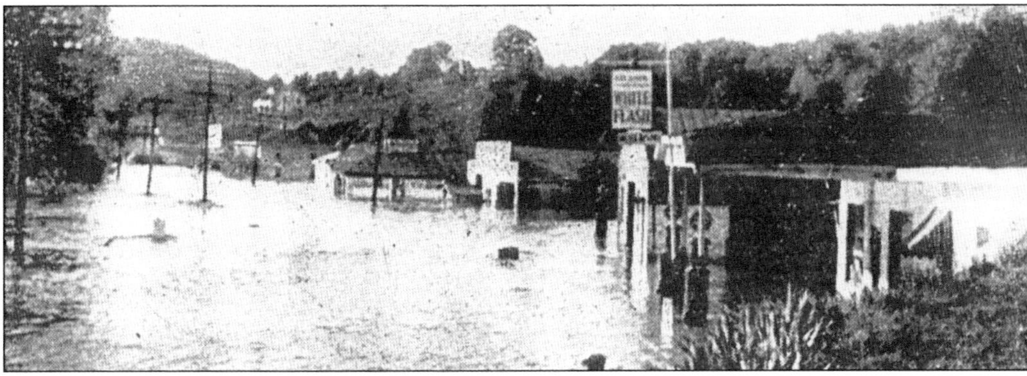

The 1937 flood of the Smith River hit Koehler, Virginia, as it did many Henry County communities. Above is the street of the community under water. Below, the Lester Building is surrounded by water during the flood. The Lester family operated a tobacco and lumber businesses in the county. This building of George Tilden "Cap'n Till" Lester used sand from the river to create blocks beginning in 1933. Today the vacant factory is used by the Jaycees each Halloween as a "Haunted Castle." Lester also built the "Wedding Cake" house on Starling Avenue in Martinsville and made the reservoir for his sawmill into a community swimming pool on Liberty Heights. (Courtesy of Teddy Compton.)

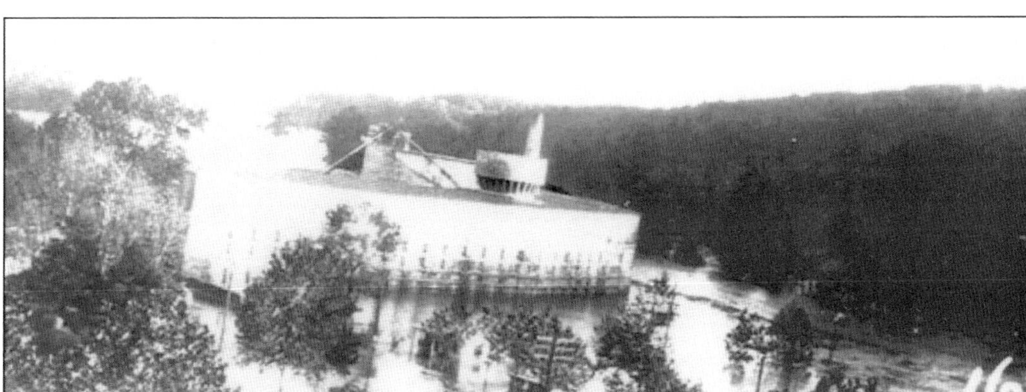

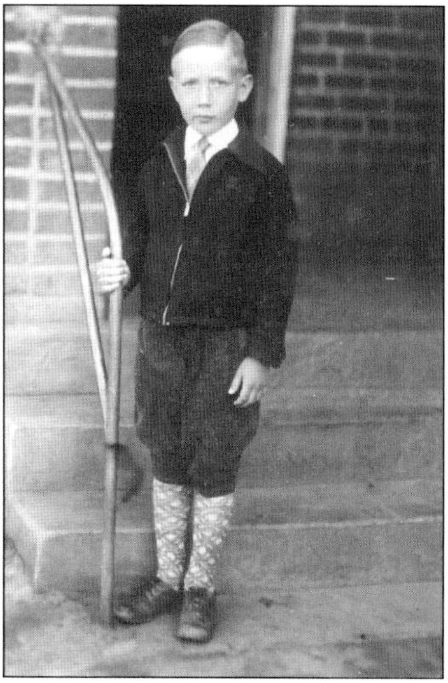

Elbert Conner Turner, born on April 15, 1930, is shown in Stanleytown on the steps of the Patrick Henry Elementary School, which he attended. Turner worked at Stanley Furniture Company until retiring in 1994. He married Avis Carter in 1957 and had two children, Mark and Aleta. The school became the Stanleytown Recreation Center, where Turner was a Boy Scout leader, and was later a car dealership. The Stanley family of Stanleytown and Stanley Furniture produced Gov. Thomas Stanley, who built Stoneleigh from 1929 until 1931; his home is now on the National Register of Historic Places. Stanley married into the Bassett family and got his start in the furniture business through those connections. (Courtesy of Avis Turner.)

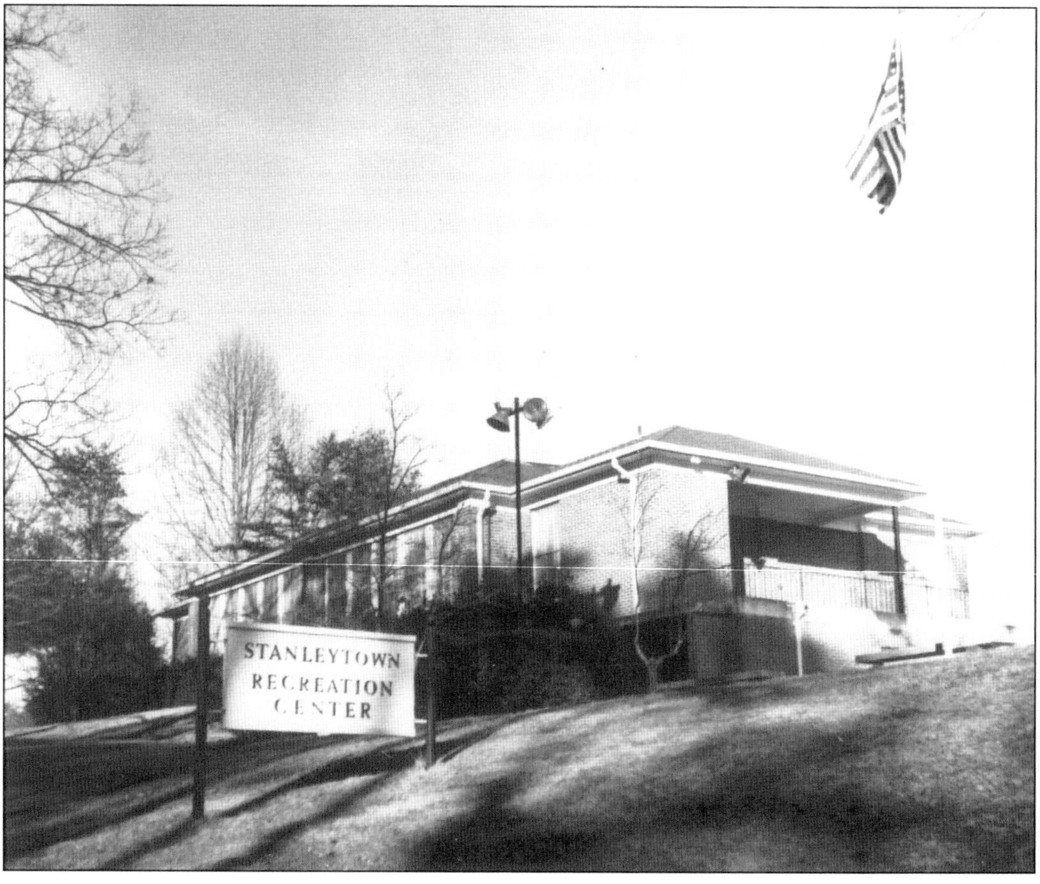

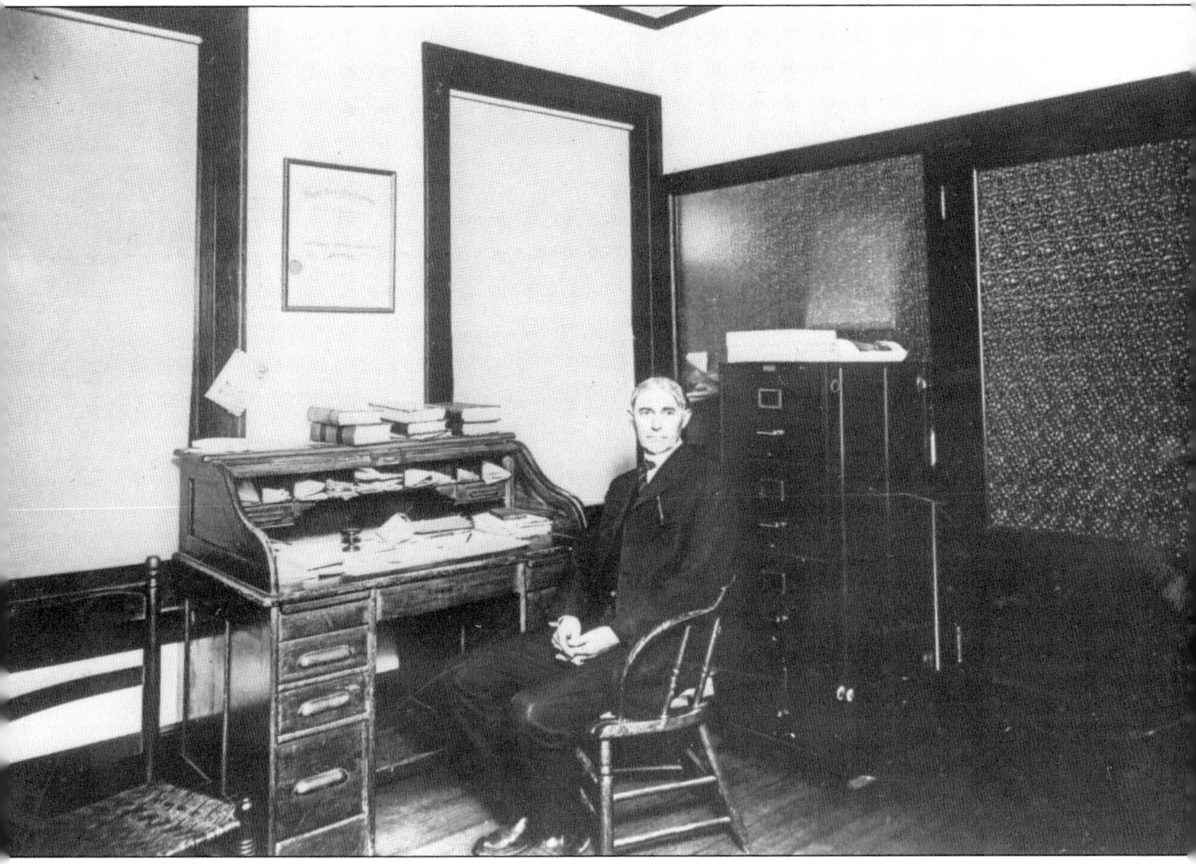

Joseph Reuben Taylor received his law degree from Wake Forest and practiced law in Martinsville for 45 years. He was appointed commonwealth's attorney of the city and county to fill an unexpired term of two years, and the people elected him to four successive four-year terms before he retired in 1928. He died on August 16, 1941, of a heart attack while sitting on his front porch on Brown Street at the age of 74. (Courtesy of the Bassett Historical Center.)

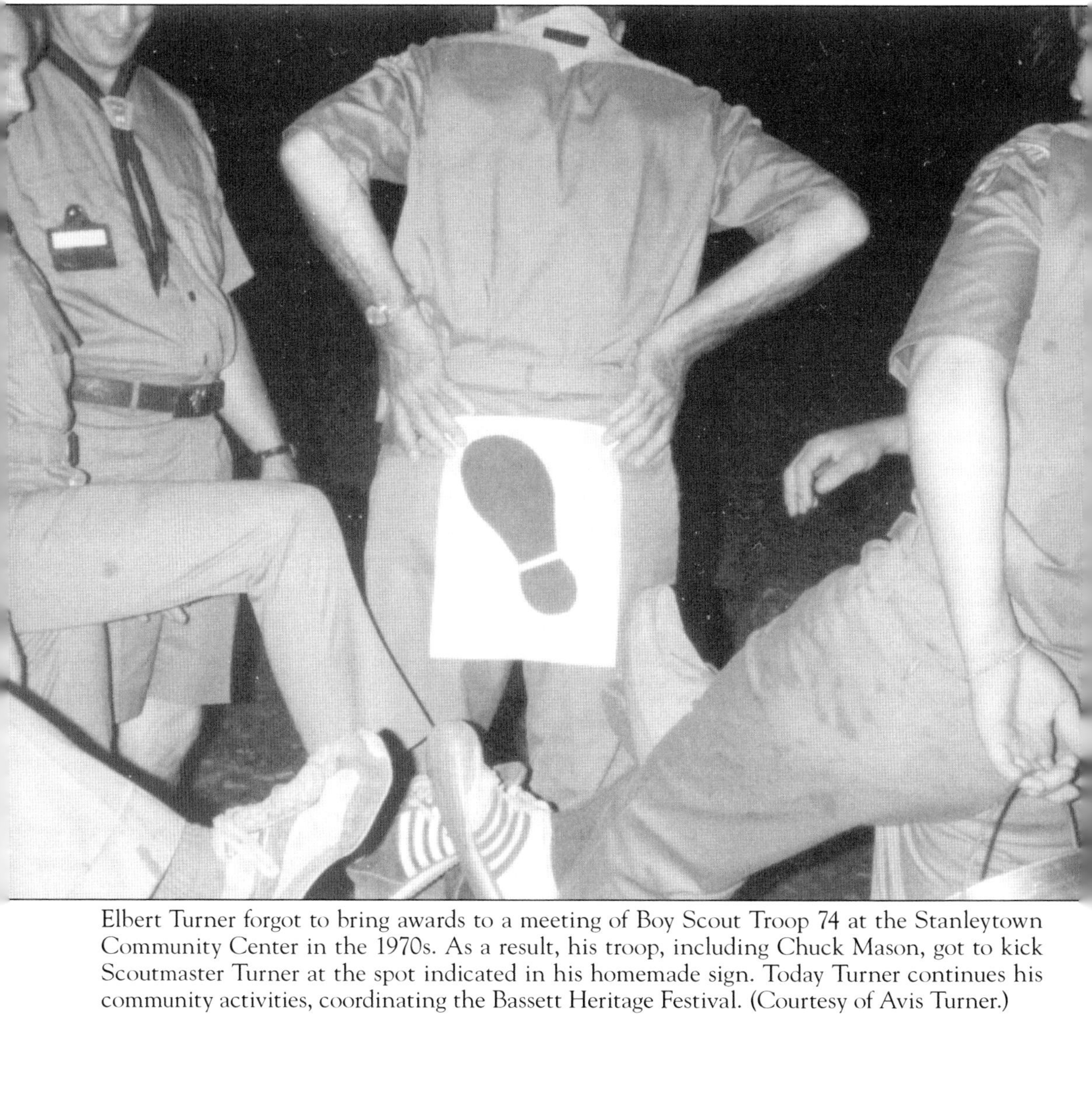

Elbert Turner forgot to bring awards to a meeting of Boy Scout Troop 74 at the Stanleytown Community Center in the 1970s. As a result, his troop, including Chuck Mason, got to kick Scoutmaster Turner at the spot indicated in his homemade sign. Today Turner continues his community activities, coordinating the Bassett Heritage Festival. (Courtesy of Avis Turner.)

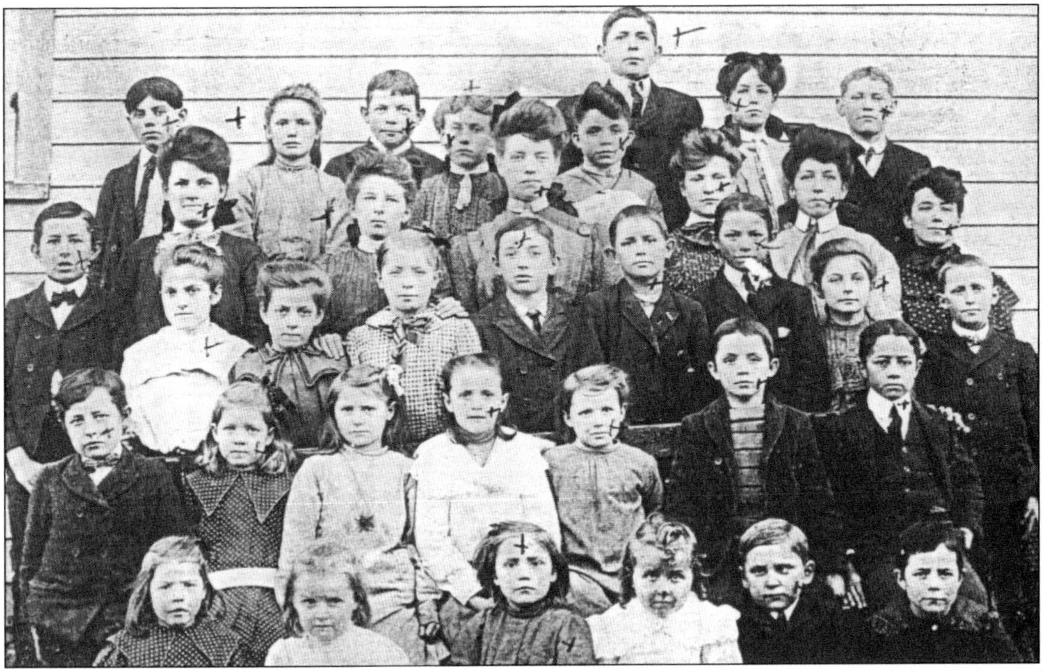

Emma Davis Helms, the daughter of Emma Lee Davis and Peter Henry Davis and the widow of M. Edward Helms (second row, third from left), is among the students at Reed Creek Elementary School. The Reed Creek District, including the Davis land, encompassed much of the Reed Creek area where the school was located, from the cloverleaf on Highway 220 at Bassett Forks going north toward Oak Level. (Courtesy of Rachel Koontz.)

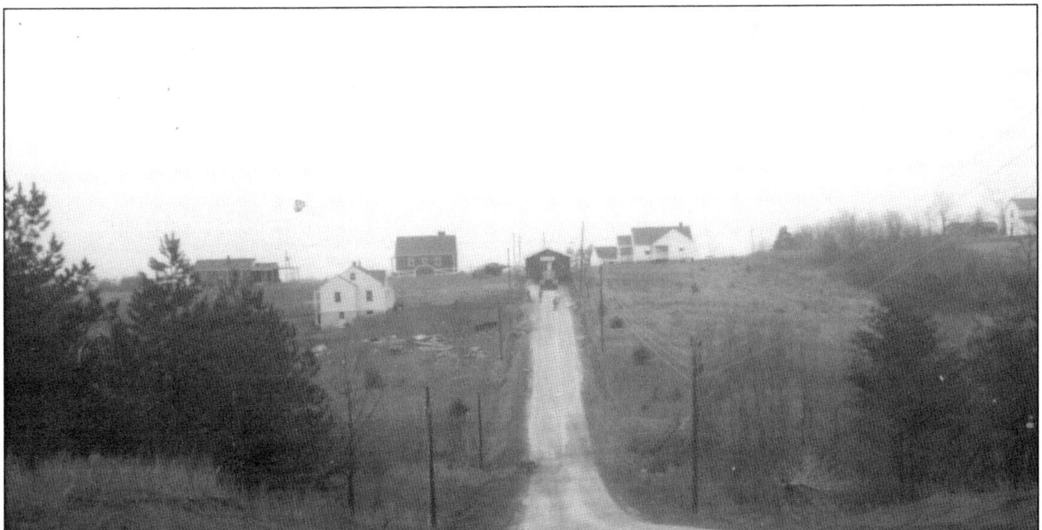

Rich Acres Christian Church began on September 9, 1953, with 10 original members. The first preacher was Allen Nance, who first held service in a tent on Joseph Martin Highway on a lot donated by Horsepasture Christian Church and Mr. and Mrs. Tom Ford. In 1955, the congregation of Rich Acres moved their entire church, as shown in this image of the church coming down the road. (Courtesy of Julia Terry.)

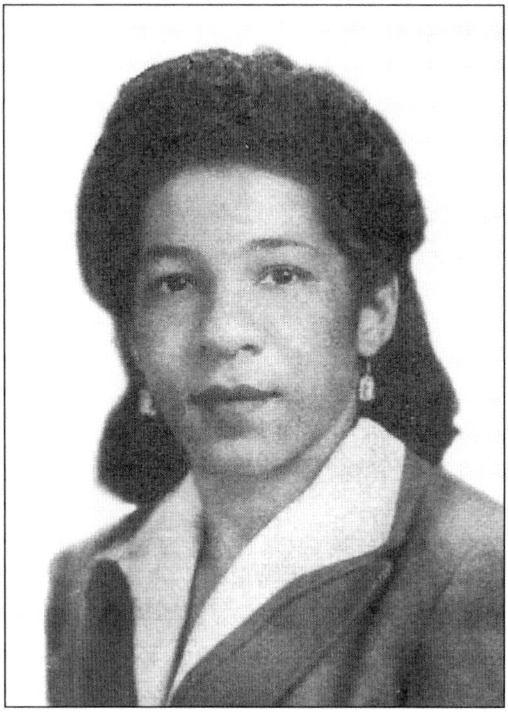

One of the prominent African American families in Henry County is the Millners. Thelma Maud Millner (1918–1973), from Irisburg in Henry County, moved to Fairmont, West Virginia, to attend high school while staying with her uncle, Jessie Lampkin. She married Clyde Stanley Williams Sr., the son of Daniel B. and Lettie Florence Edwards Williams. (Courtesy of Beverly Millner.)

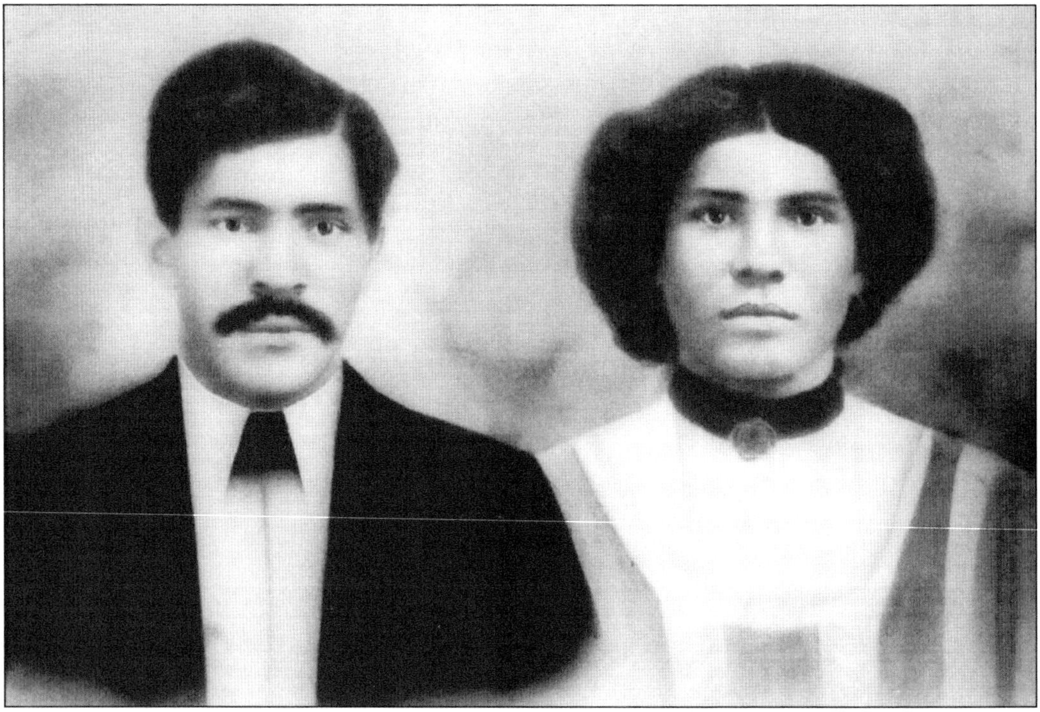

William Millner, the son of Henry R. and Katie Hodge Millner, married Georgia Anna Lampkin, the daughter of John D. Chetham and Maria Susan Lampkin. Their son Beverly R. Millner, quoted at the beginning of this book, wrote *Something to Build On*, a history of the African American families of Henry County. (Courtesy of Beverly Millner.)

Joseph Clifton Martin of Drewry Mason High School played for the Cubs and White Sox from 1959 until 1972 and with the New York Mets in 1969. During the 10th inning in game four of the 1969 World Series, Martin became part of baseball history. With the score 1-1, Martin pinch-hit for Tom Seaver. He bunted and was hit while running to first, allowing the winning run to score. Although he was inside the baseline, the umpire did not call him out for interference. Now a running lane extends down the baseline from the mid-point to the bag on all major-league fields. A player in this lane can be hit and not called out for interference. (Courtesy of the Bassett Historical Center.)

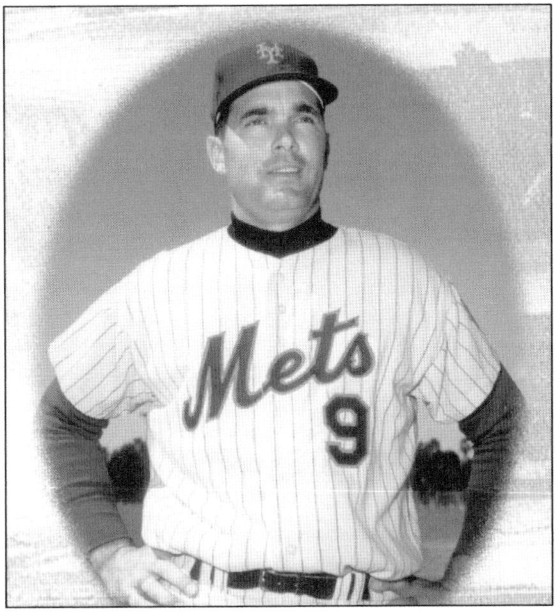

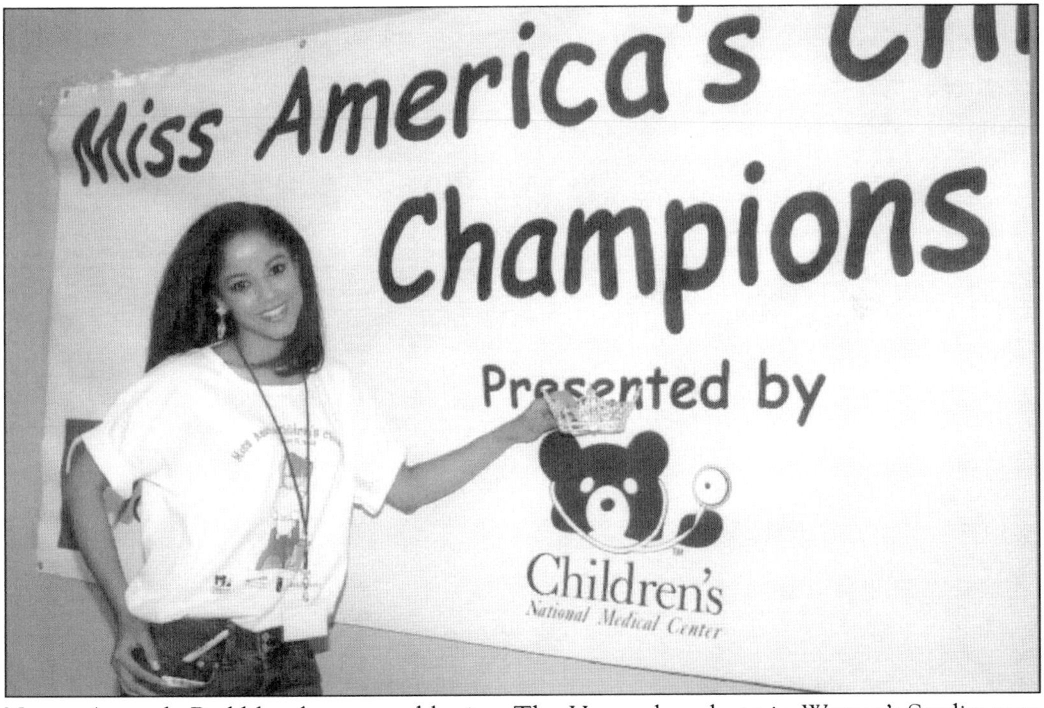

Nancy Amanda Redd has beauty and brains. The Harvard graduate in Women's Studies won $250,000 on *Who Wants to Be a Millionaire* in 2002 and donated part of her winnings to the 4-H Club. Redd was in the top 10 in the "Lifestyle and Fitness in Swimwear" competition in the 2004 Miss America Scholarship Pageant after winning the Miss Virginia Pageant from Martinsville and Henry County. She wrote *Body Drama: Real Girls, Real Bodies, Real Issues, Real Answers* in 2007. That same year, she married her college sweetheart, actor Rupak Ginn. Other Henry County Miss Virginias are Becky Lou Richardson (1956), Barbara Gutherie (1958), Vicki Pulliam (1981), and Gail Doyle (Junior Miss Virginia, 1970). (Courtesy of the Bassett Historical Center.)

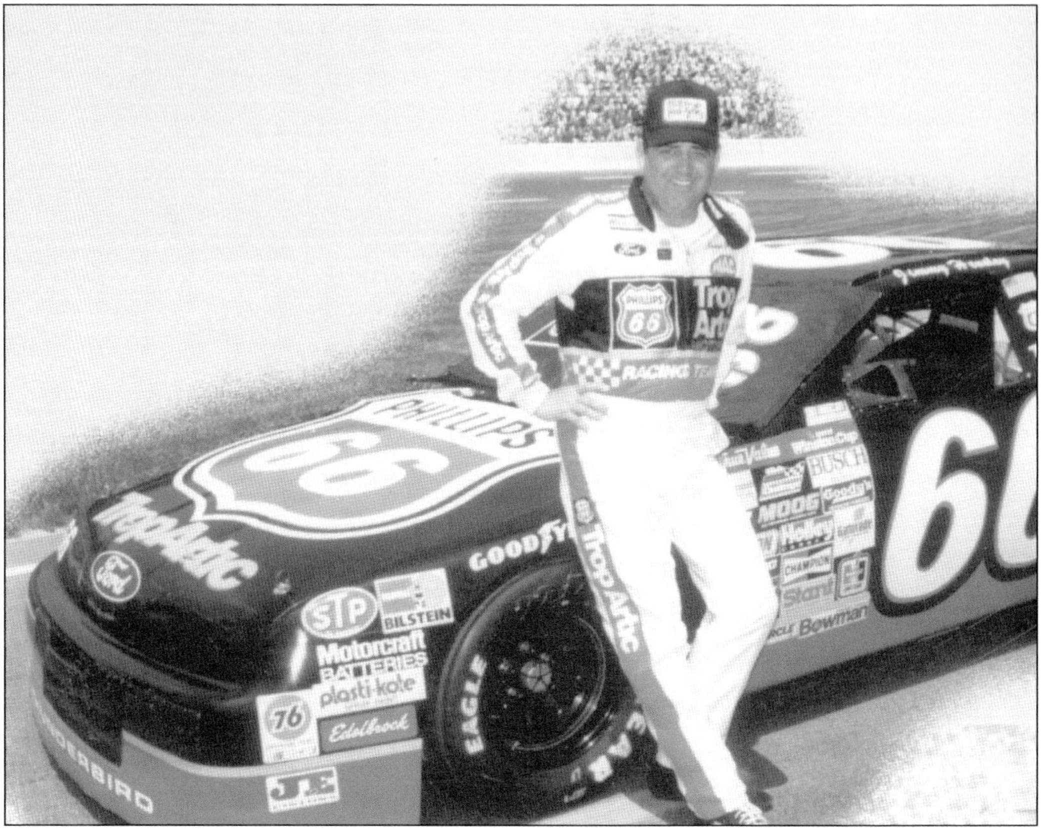

Drewry Mason High School graduate Jimmy Hensley began driving in 1972 at the Martinsville Speedway. He was the 1992 Winston Cup Rookie of the Year and two-time Grand National Most Popular Driver in NASCAR. He raced the Winston Cup, Busch, and Craftsman Truck Series, winning over 200 features in his racing career. (Courtesy of the Bassett Historical Center.)

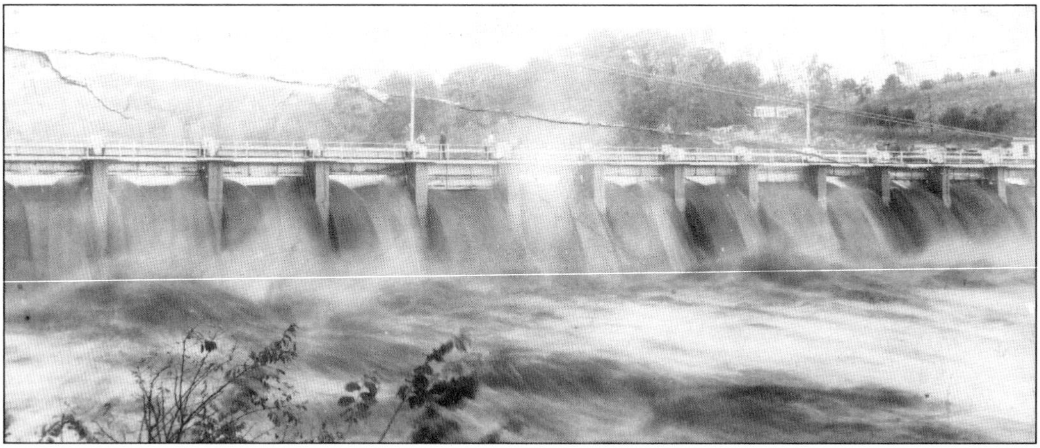

Cars are not the only thing that moves fast in Henry County, as this water rushing over the Martinsville Reservoir Dam south of town from a postcard shows. Built in 1932, the 175-acre lake from the waters of Beaver Creek is located on land once owned by the Hairstons. Fishing and bird watching are just some of the recreational opportunities it provides. (Courtesy of Juanita Wells.)

This 1886 image is from the H. C. Lester Tobacco Company in Figgsboro. Before cigarettes, plug chewing tobacco was popular. John Turner established a factory and hired young Lester, who later bought the company and produced "Lester's Fig." The Lester Tobacco Factory was three stories with a basement icehouse. Tobacco dominated the local economy for two centuries, with families such as the Gravelys and Hairstons growing the crop. R. J. Reynolds tried to buy the brand name and the process, but the Lesters did not sell. Later George Tilden Lester developed a mass-production cutting and pressing machine that gave the plugs uniform size and weight. The Lesters operated sawmills and a block company in other parts of Henry County and the Liberty Heights Swimming Pool. (Courtesy of Sam Eanes.)

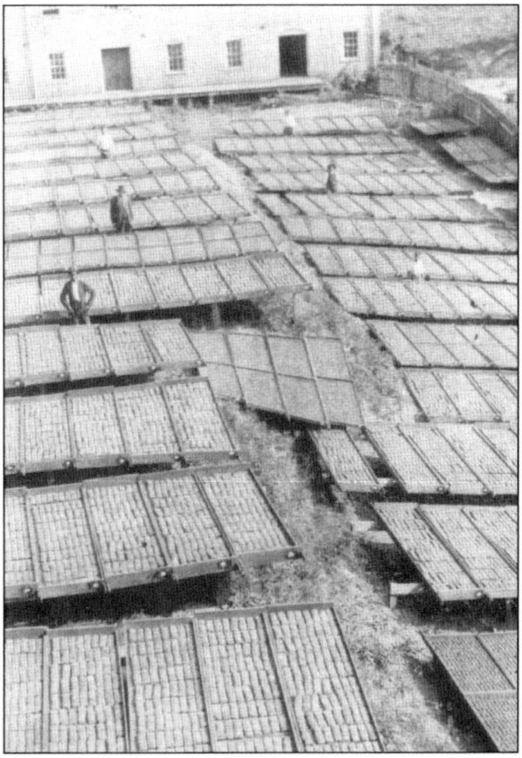

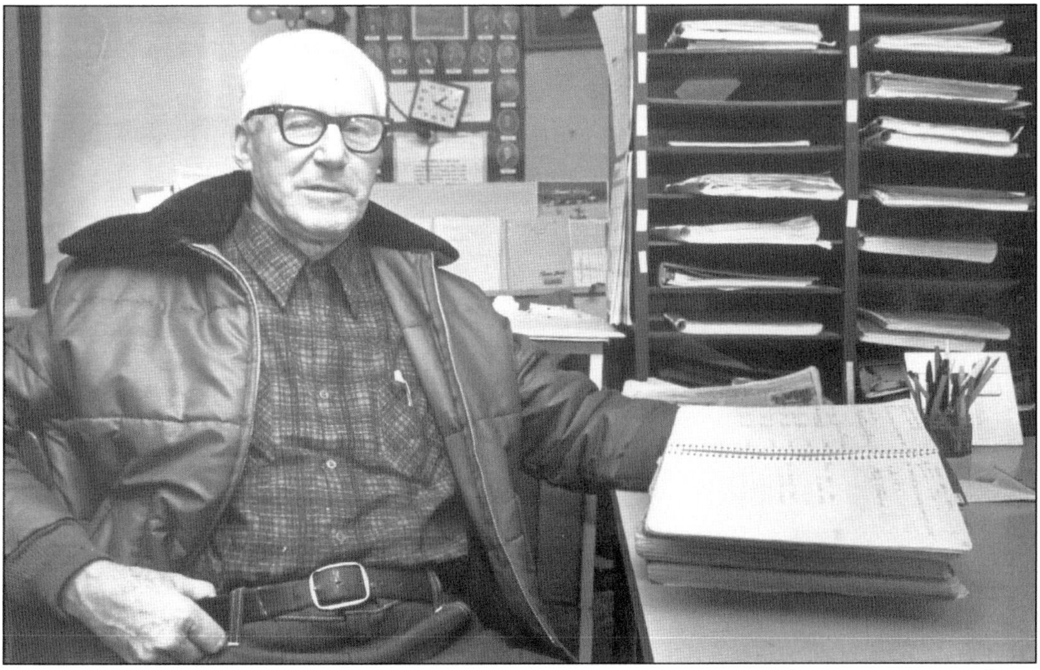

Ophus Eugene Pilson, an educator from Patrick County, came to live in Ridgeway, amassing a huge collection of historical and genealogical information before his death in 1999. His collection was so large that he purchased the house next door to keep it. Today the Bassett Historical Center contains his collection in a dedicated room. (Courtesy of the Bassett Historical Center.)

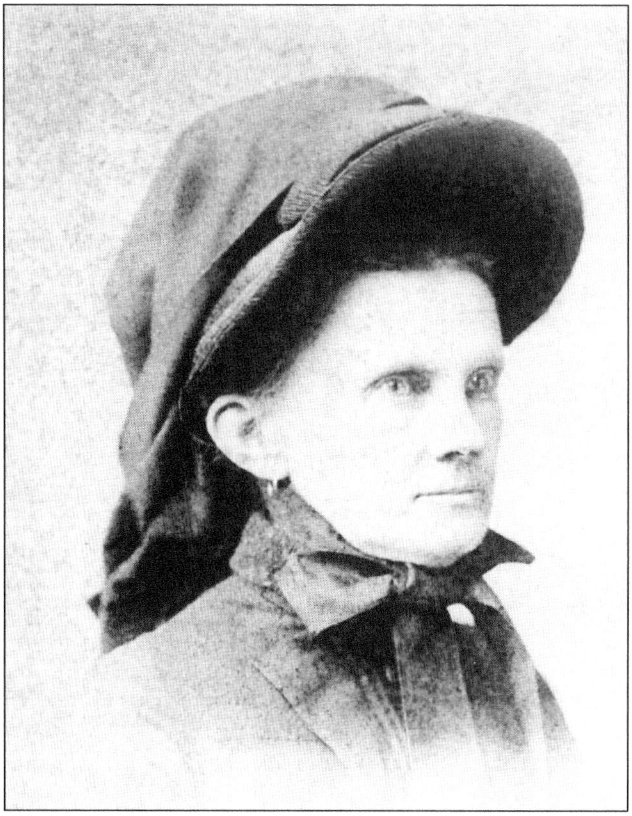

Elizabeth "Bettie" Perkins Hairston, the daughter of Marshall Hairston, grew up at Beaver Creek Plantation north of Martinsville. Her family dominated Henry County agriculture and politics in the 19th century. Her grandfather, George, gave 50 acres for the first Henry County Courthouse. George was one of the largest landowners and slaveholders in Virginia. The original Beaver Creek was the second Hairston home in Henry County (Marrowbone was first). Built in 1776 by George Hairston on a king's grant of 30,000 acres, the family rebuilt the house in 1837 after a fire. Later in the 1800s, they added two wings to the home. Other owners added a third wing with a sun porch. Dr. J. Michael Bestler practiced plastic surgery in this home in the 20th century. (Above, courtesy of the Bassett Historical Center; below, courtesy of Douglas Stegall.)

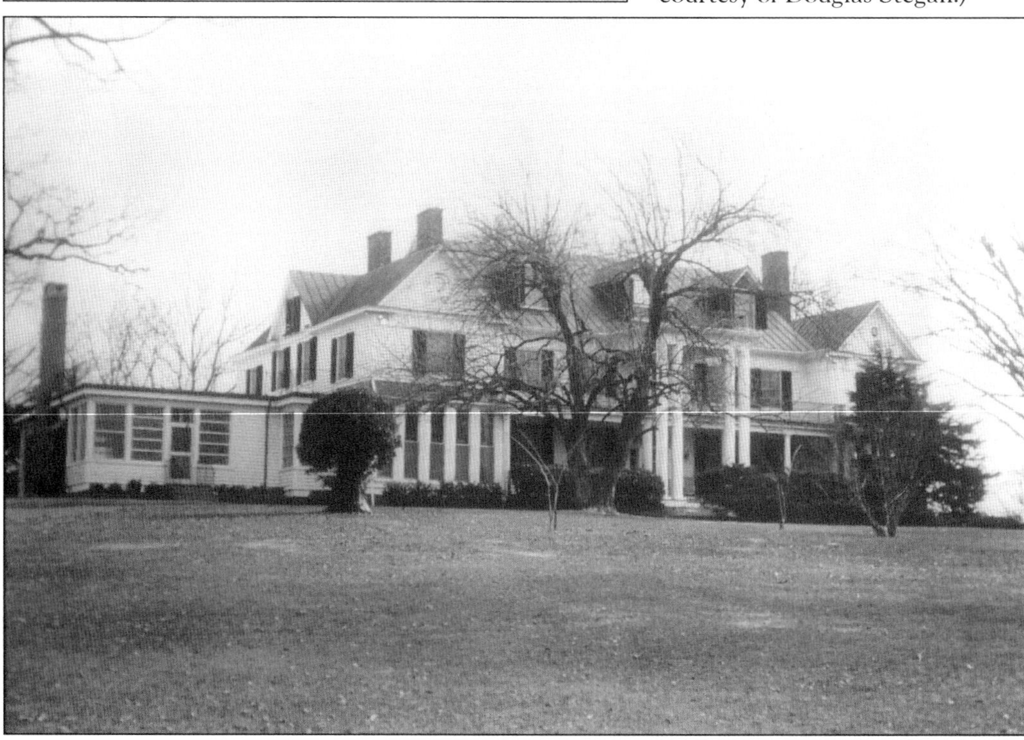

One of those who walked among the 30-foot-high boxwoods of Beaver Creek Plantation was James Ewell Brown "Jeb" Stuart, shown in this 1850 photograph as his cousin Elizabeth Perkins "Bettie" Hairston knew him. Stuart graduated from the U.S. Military Academy at West Point and went on to a career in the U.S. Army. In the Civil War, he was a cavalry commander under Robert E. Lee. (Courtesy of Tom Perry.)

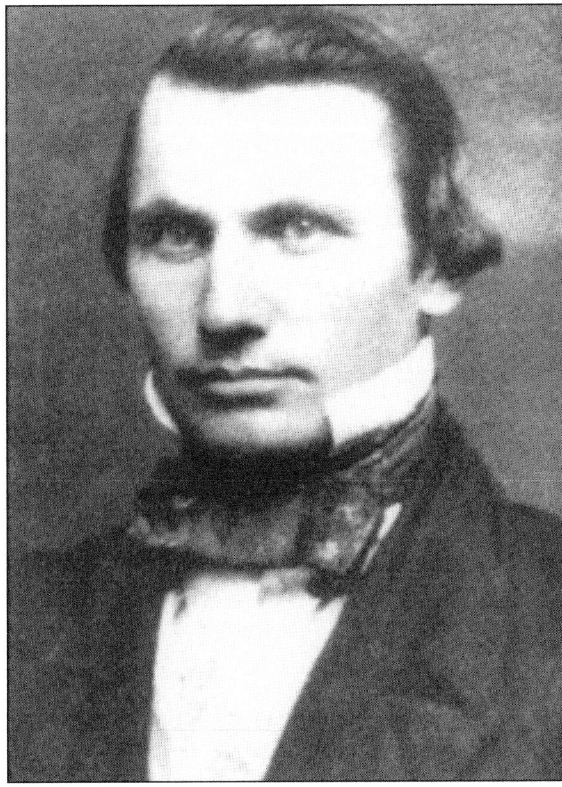

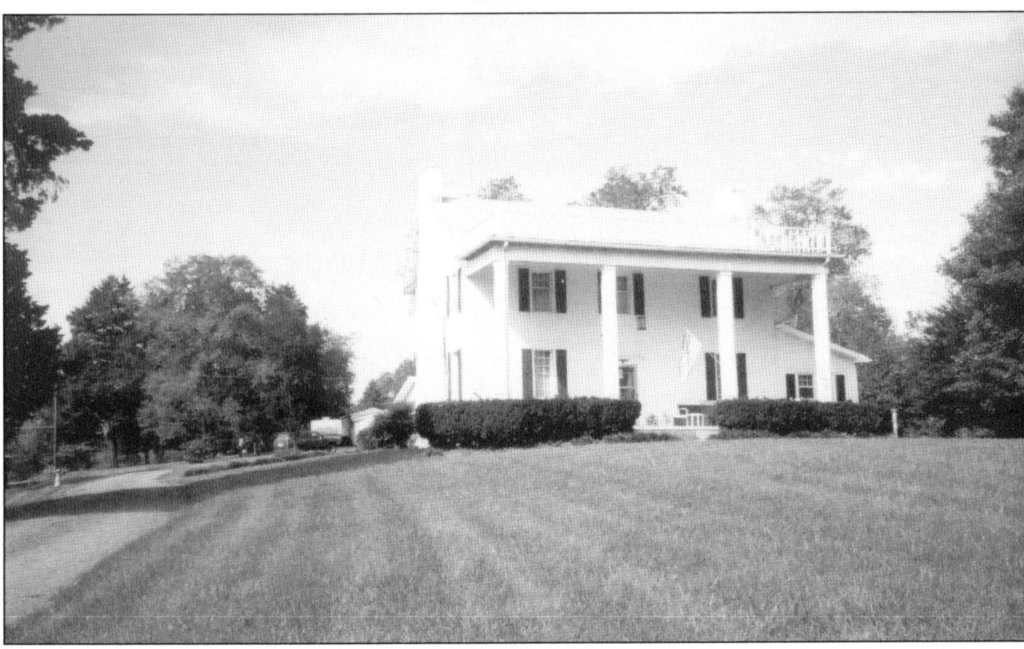

Locust Grove, built in 1858 by William and Elizabeth Anglin on 419 acres along the north bank of the Mayo River, was sold to George K. DeShazo on February 22, 1859. One of the many prominent tobacco farms in Henry County owned by the Martins, Redds, Gravelys, and the Hairstons, it represents a time long gone. (Courtesy of Jane Eggleston.)

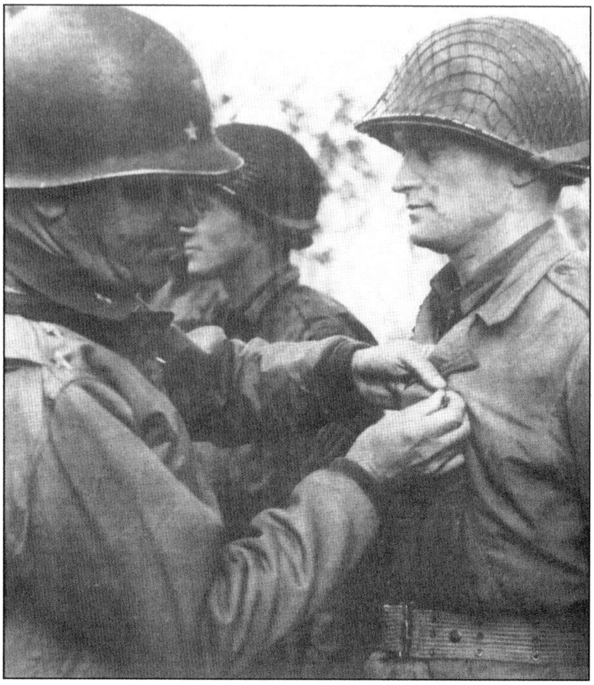

Gen. Omar Bradley pins a Distinguish Service Cross on S.Sgt. Paul R. Shorter in 1944 for Shorter's "extraordinary heroism." Shorter served in Africa, French Morocco, Sicily, Tunisia, and Normandy. He received the Silver Star, Bronze Star, Purple Heart, and Good Conduct Medal and retired in 1965 after 23 years in the U.S. Army, including 14 in Europe and the Far East. Wounded in the foot by shrapnel on D-Day, he led his men through a minefield under fire to destroy machine gun and sniper nests. He organized patrols and led five separate assaults himself. He received the Silver Star for holding out until he ran out of ammunition, saving the lives of many men before he was captured. He was a German prisoner for 10 days before the British liberated him. (Courtesy of the Bassett Historical Center.)

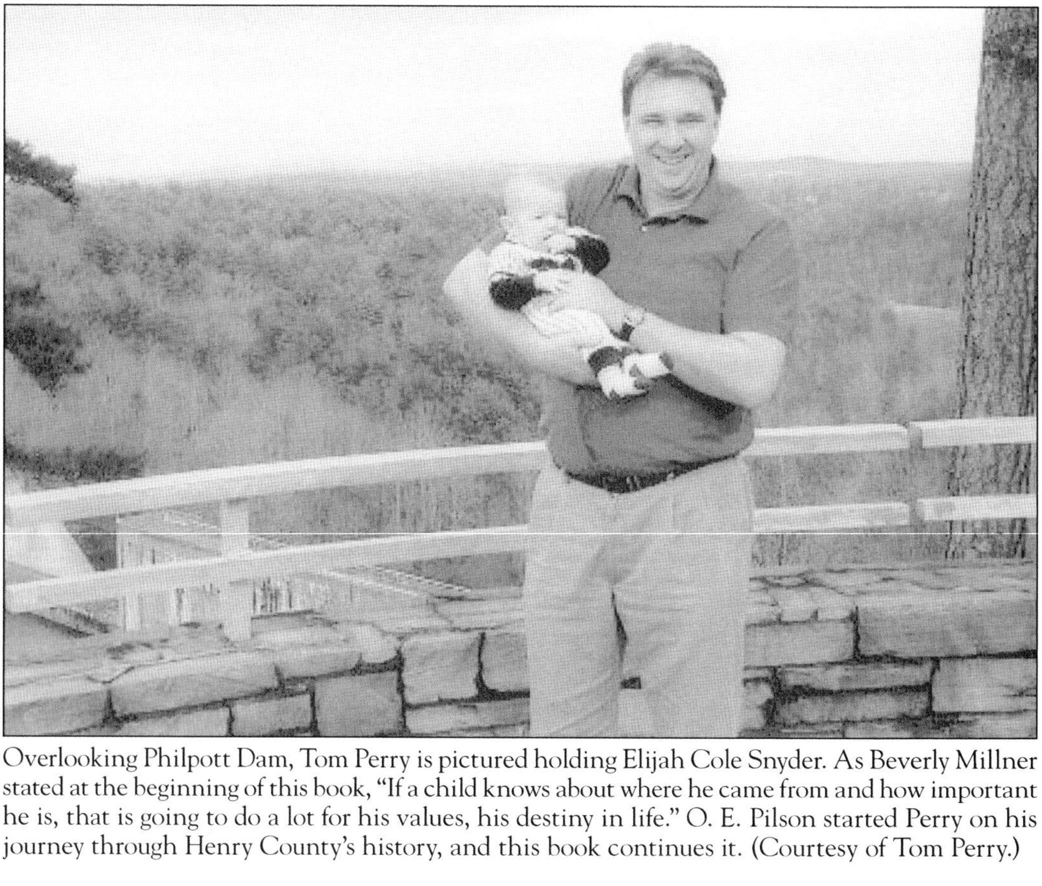

Overlooking Philpott Dam, Tom Perry is pictured holding Elijah Cole Snyder. As Beverly Millner stated at the beginning of this book, "If a child knows about where he came from and how important he is, that is going to do a lot for his values, his destiny in life." O. E. Pilson started Perry on his journey through Henry County's history, and this book continues it. (Courtesy of Tom Perry.)

THE BEST LITTLE LIBRARY IN VIRGINIA

From the Domesday Book of William the Conqueror written in 1085 England to the latest research on the Goblintown Grist Mill in Patrick County, there is only one regional resource that holds both, and that is the Bassett Historical Center of the Blue Ridge Regional Library, the best local history library in Virginia.

For years, the historical center was located in the back room of the regular library in the present building, but in 1998, the library moved across Highway 57 to a new facility, leaving the entire building on the banks of the Smith River to history and genealogy. Today the back room overlooking the river contains military and Native American materials. If one wants to find an ancestor in the Civil War, there is no better room to begin that search. All of the Virginia and North Carolina regimental series, along with the entire index of Confederate soldiers, are present, with many books and supplementary publications. One can work with large-screen computers as George Stoneman and Jubal Early peer down from pictures above. If one sits in the right place, one can look upon Sauratown Woman or a glance at the shelves to my favorite item, a brick from J. E. B. Stuart's birthplace, which I preserved.

People make a visit to the library worthwhile. The staff of the Blue Ridge Regional Library's Bassett Historical Center will come through for visitors too. Over the years, in researching J. E. B. Stuart, I have traveled from West Point to Kansas and to many libraries. Many years ago, while reading *The Hairstons, An American Family in Black and White*, I came across a section on finding obscure material at the library. Intrigued, I began to visit the library, and I never cease to return to the banks of the Smith River, even though it is a drive of over 50 miles, because it is my library home. This book is my way of giving back to the library and the staff, as proceeds will go towards the expansion of the library. I encourage anyone with photographs to share their images for future publications to help the library. Anne Copeland summed up what any historical library should do: "The amount of material we are able to share with the public only came about because so many people were willing to share with us."

—Thomas D. Perry